Improving Personality

Means, Measures and Methods

R.C. Bhatia
M.A. (Economics), M.Com., Ph.D.
Associate Professor (Retd.)
Department of Commerce
Shyam Lal College (Evening)
University of Delhi

ATLANTIC
PUBLISHERS & DISTRIBUTORS (P) LTD

Published by
ATLANTIC
PUBLISHERS & DISTRIBUTORS (P) LTD
7/22, Ansari Road, Darya Ganj, New Delhi-110002
Phones : +91-11-40775252, 23273880, 23275880, 23280451
Fax : +91-11-23285873
Web : www.atlanticbooks.com
E-mail : orders@atlanticbooks.com

Branch Office
5, Nallathambi Street, Wallajah Road, Chennai-600002
Phones : +91-44-64611085, 32413319
E-mail : chennai@atlanticbooks.com

Printed in India at Nice Printing Press, A-33/3A, Site-IV, Industrial Area, Sahibabad, Ghaziabad, U.P.

Preface

The demand for professionally qualified managers in various fields is increasing day-by-day in India and abroad because of rapid industrialization and growing number of business and other organizations. To achieve professional competence, managers—both present and prospective—are required to be fully equipped with personality development which includes means, measures and methods.

Innovations and technological developments have brought the most sophisticated products in the market. As a result of this, business establishments have become complex and require new managerial skills. The success of a business enterprise depends on the efficiency and personality of its personnel.

Recognizing the importance of managerial professionals, universities in India and abroad have prescribed personality development as a subject at the undergraduate as well as at the post-graduate level.

This book is an attempt to explain the principles and practices of improving personality, including means, measures and methods in simple language and lucid manner. The book will be very useful for the students pursuing M.Com., MBA, Company Secretary, Hotel Management, Air Hostess and other professional courses. Even a lay person, who is interested in knowing about the fundamentals of personality, will find this book extremely useful.

I am very happy to place this book in the hands of my readers, especially the students. I am confident that they will find the book useful. I request the readers to send me their valuable suggestions and comments for further improvement of the book.

I am very grateful to Professor Sunil K. Choudhary, Department of Political Science, Director, Developing Countries Research Center [dcrc] University of Delhi, Delhi-110007 INDIA for suggesting the title of this book, after a thorough study of the contents of the book.

I am also thankful to Atlantic Publishers & Distributors (P) Ltd. for bringing out this book in a very short span of time.

R.C. Bhatia
Email: mailrcbhatia@gmail.com

185-E, Mayur Vihar-I
Pocket-IV, Delhi-110091
Mobile: 9818632242

Contents

1
Understanding Personality

1.1 THE MEANING OF PERSONALITY

The term "personality" is derived from Latin word persona or Greek word prosopon, which means "mask". Among the Greeks, actors used a mask to hide their identity on stage.

The personality of an individual accompanies him anywhere and everywhere he goes and exhibits itself in whatever he does. Most people mistake physical attributes of an individual as his/her personality. They talk about a marvelous personality when they may just be referring to an individual's stature, fair complexion on chiseled features.

Well, if you thought that personality has anything to do with height, good looks, complexion or the physique of a person, it is the time you re-think what you think you know. Any physical shortcomings can hardly influence your personality. A person of repute is identified because of his personality traits such as superior character and behaviour, and not by other mundane and frivolous considerations.

As per modern management concepts, "personality is the BRAND IMAGE of an individual". It is made up of three broad aspects, namely:

1. Character (few behavioural authors have a different opinion that character has little to do with personality, but in this book we shall consider it as its foundation).

2. Behavioural traits.
3. Attitude.

Personality development is the improvement of behavioural traits such as communication skills, interpersonal relationships, attitude towards life and restoring our ethics. Character is the prerequisite to achieving a better individual personality. There are several behavioural scientists who argue that improving behavioural traits in a short-cut course of fifteen days to development personality can effectively influence other and help win the race. But we must never forget that excellent behavioural traits such as communication skills, interpersonal relationships, higher order of motivational levels and excellent leadership qualities also fail miserably at the time of crisis if not based on solid character foundation.

Behaviour is just the showcase of the larger inventory inside a person, i.e. character. If personality is developed on the solid base of values and ethics, it will last forever. Fake smile and mannerisms are short-lived and do not help in improving one's personality.

1.2 TYPES OF PERSONALITY

Well-known behavioural scientists and psychologists have identified many types of personalities. We shall concentrate on the nine types of personalities. These are perfectionists, helpers, achievers, romantics, observers, questioners, adventurers, asserters, and peacemakers. They have their own unique personality traits that are briefly analysed below.

1. The Perfectionist

Perfectionists are realistic, conscientious and principled. They strive to live up to their high ideals. They can be got along well with if you take your share of the responsibilities so they do not end up with all the work. You need to knowledge their achievements. It is better if you tell a perfectionist that you value his/her advice. Perfectionists also expect others to be fair and considerate, as they are.

(a) A perfectionist would like to be self-disciplined and be able to accomplish a great deal. He would like to work hard to make the world a better place, having high standards and ethics. They are reasonable, responsible and dedicated in everything they do.

(b) They are disappointed with themselves or others if their expectations are not met. They also feel burdened by too much responsibility. In such moments, they can think, "What I do is never good enough." They may be tense, anxious, and take things too seriously.

Example: The great Indian software business leader Narayana Murthy falls in the category of a perfectionist. Another name that fits the bill is pole-vault world record holder Sergey Bubka of Ukraine, who always strove to better his own record.

2. The Helper

Helpers are warm, concerned, nurturing, and sensitive to other people's needs. They can be got along well with if you tell them that you appreciate them. They would expect you to share fun times with them. They would like you to take interest in their problems, though they will probably try to focus on your problems also. They want you to know that they are important and special to you.

(a) A helper likes to be able to relate easily to people and make friends, know what people need and be able to make their lives better. They are generous, caring and warm. They are sensitive to and perceptive about other's feelings. They are fun loving and generally possess a good sense of humour.

(b) A helper faces a problem when he is not able to say no. They have low self-esteem and are drained due to overdoing things for others. They cannot do things they really like to do for themselves for fear of being selfish.

Example: Mother Teresa is one such personality who was sensitive not only to the needs of few people around, but for the millions of poor in the country.

3. The Achiever

Achievers are energetic, optimistic, self-assured and goal-oriented.

(a) An achiever gets along well with his co-workers. He welcomes honest, but not subjective, feedback. He expects you to keep his environment harmonious and peaceful. You cannot burden him with negative emotions. He likes being optimistic, friendly and upbeat and likes to provide well for his family. He is happy if he stays informed, knowing what's going on.

(b) Achievers face problems when they have to put up with inefficiency and incompetence. They are gripped with the fear of failure or of not being seen as successful. They keep on struggling to fight for their success.

Example: Sachin Tendulkar, the greatest batsman, and Kapil Dev, the greatest all-rounder, fall in the category of achievers, always full of energy to achieve something big.

4. The Romantic

Romantic has sensitive feeling and is warm and perspective.

(a) A romantic would like to get plenty of compliments. They mean a lot to them. He expects you to be a supportive friend or partner. If you care for him, you respect him for this special gifts of intuition and vision. He would like to establish warm connections with people, admire what is noble, truthful, and beautiful in life; he would like to be creative, intuitive, and have a sense of humour. He is unique and is seen as unique by others.

(b) A romantic faces a problem when he is experiencing dark moods of emptiness and despair, feeling of self-hatred and shame; believing he does not deserve to be loved, feeling hurt or attacked when someone misunderstands him, fearing being abandoned, longing for what he does not have.

Example: The great Indian painter M.F. Hussain falls in the type of romantic personality. He has a sensitive heart and romantic personality for his creativity.

5. The Observer

Observers have a need for knowledge and are introverted, curious, analytical and insightful.

(a) An observer likes to be independent, not clingy. He prefers to speak in a straightforward and brief manner. He desires and needs time alone to process his feelings and thoughts and may doubt your sincerity if you intensely welcome him. He dislikes intrusions on his privacy. He remains calm in a crisis.

(b) An observer faces a problem when he/she is not sure of the situation and is unable to understand the relation between cause and effect. He gets disturbed if his integrity is doubled.

Example: The great economist and Nobel laureate Amartya Sen is one such observer personality, who is curvious, analytical and insightful.

6. The Questioner

Questioners are responsible and trustworthy. They value loyalty to family, friends, groups and causes. Their personalities range broadly, from reserved and timid to outspoken.

(a) A questioner likes to be direct and clear. He likes others to listen to him carefully. You are required to reassure him that 'everything is right between us' and not judge him for his anxiety. He is committed and faithful to family and friends, responsible and hardworking, compassionate towards others, direct and assertive.

(b) A questioner faces a problem when under constant push and pull, involved in trying to make up his/her mind. He fears failure, having little confidence in his own ability. He tends to be too critical of himself when he was not lived up to his own expectations.

Example: The outspoken Bollywood actress and former Rajya Sabha member, Shabana Azmi, may fall in the category of a questioner. She can raise relevant questions in all platforms.

7. The Adventurer

Adventurers are energetic, lively and optimistic and seek to contribute to the world in their own ways.

(a) An adventurer likes to get companionship, affection and freedom. He likes engaging you in stimulating conversation and laughter, and expects you to appreciate his grand visions and listen to his stories. He is optimistic and does not let life's troubles get his down. He is spontaneous and free-spirited.

(b) An adventurer faces a problem when he does not have enough time to do all the things he wants to and is unable to complete the things he starts.

Example: The energetic NRI businessman, Vijay Mallaya, may be categorized in the adventurer type for trying something new that was not done by any Indian earlier.

8. The Asserter

Asserters are direct, self-reliant, self-confident, and protective.

(a) Asserter likes to stand up for you and is confident, strong and direct. He is vulnerable and shares his feeling and at the same time acknowledges your tender, vulnerable side. He likes to get space to be alone. He is curious to hear about his own contributions, but do not flatter him. He likes being independent and self-reliant, able to take charge and meet challenges head on. He is courageous, straightforward, honest, supporting, empowering and protective of those close to him.

(b) An asserter faces a problem when he is being restless and impatient with other incompetence, receiving no appreciation for good work done for others.

Example: The former Chief Election Commissioner, T.N. Seshan, the straightforward bold officer, is the best Indian example of an asserter.

9. The Peacemaker

Peacemakers are receptive, good-natured and supportive. They seek union with other and the world around them.

(a) A peacemaker does not like expectations or pressure. If you want him to do something, how you ask is important. He likes to listen and be of service, but do not take advantage of this. He is very easy to deal with if given time to finish things and make decisions. He likes good discussion but not a confrontation. He is very caring and concerned about others. He is a good mediator and facilitator; has heightened awareness of sensations, aesthetics, is non-judgmental and accepting.

(b) A peacemaker faces problems when he is being judged or is misunderstood as indecisive. He is sensitive to criticism, taking every raised eyebrow and twitch of the mouth personally. He may be confused about what he really wants and worry too much about what others will think of him.

Example: The former Indian Prime Minister Atal Bihari Vajpayee was a peacemaker type of personality, who is receptive and can run a government supported by different groups in the Parliament.

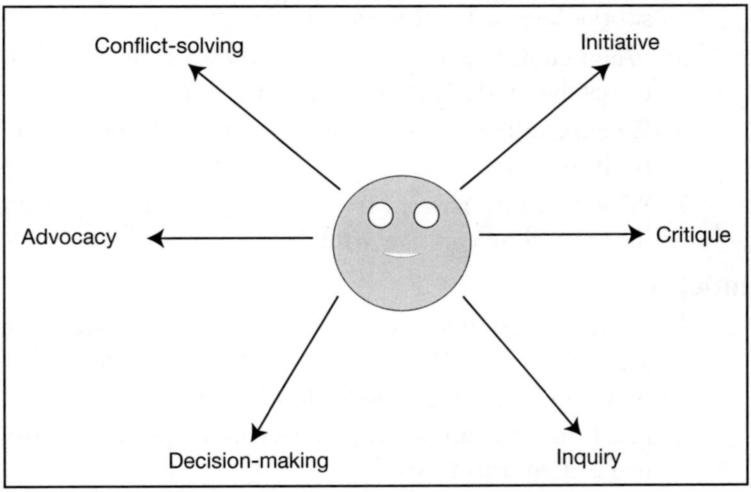

Fig. 1.1: Evaluation sheet of your style

There is another classification of personality types. The style or the behavioural personality traits are made up of a few important elements. The elements of a personality are conflict solving, initiative, inquiry, advocacy, decision-making and critique. All these six elements can give different shapes to personalities. We can explore how these six elements can determine the type of personality you have. To get this query solved you may attempt to undertake the following exercise:

The elements of a personality are briefly described in the following sections. Rank the sentence from 7 down to 1 where 7 represents the sentence within each element that you feel typifies your own personality the most.

Conflict Solving

1. I maintain a neutral stance or try to stay out of conflict altogether.
2. When conflict arises, I shift and turn in an effort to get around it; I avoid getting caught head on.
3. When conflict arises, I acknowledge it but re-emphasis the importance of what I purpose to do to bring others around to my point of view.
4. I avoid generating conflict, but when it appears I try to soothe feeling to keep people together.
5. When conflict arises, I seek out reasons for it in order to resolve underlying causes of tensions.
6. When conflict arises, I try to cut it off or win my position.
7. When conflict arises, I try to find a reasonable position that everyone can live with.

Initiative

1. I initiate actions that are in my own best interest by seeking a trade-off with other. I help them get something that will help me get something I want.
2. I seek to maintain a steady peace and confine my effort to be tried and true.
3. I put out enough to get by, generally in response to requests from others.
4. I exert vigorous effort and others enthusiastically join in.
5. I expect other to follow my lead and extend positive appreciation to those who support my efforts.
6. I drive others and myself.
7. I initiate whatever actions might help and support the efforts of others.

Inquiry

1. I dig out areas of vital private concern to me in an inquisitive but non-threatening way.
2. I expect others to keep me informed and I show appreciation when they do; I look with disfavour upon those who fail to keep me up-to-date.
3. I search for and seek to verify information. I also invite and listen to ideas and attitudes different than my own.
4. I continuously treat the soundness of my own thinking by comparing it with the thinking of others.
5. I stay on top of information to be sure that I am in control and double-check everything I hear to be sure that others are not making mistakes.
6. I search for information that suggests all is well, for the sake of harmony, I am not inclined to challenge what others say.
7. I solicit information in order to see where others stand on an issue; this lets me know whether my thinking is on track.

Advocacy

1. I keep my own counsel but respond to questions when asked. I rarely reveal my convictions because then I do not have to stand behind them.
2. I tell others what they want or expect to hear.
3. I express my convictions in a tentative way and try to meet others halfway.
4. I feel it is important to express my concerns and convictions in order that others know what I am thinking. I respond to ideas sounder than my own by changing my mind.
5. I stand up for my conviction because I know I am right. If others oppose me, I try to prove them wrong.
6. I embrace the ideas of others even though I may have private reservations. I feel it's better to be supportive than right.

7. Although I seldom back off my own conviction, I do permit others to express their ideas so I can understand where they are coming from and help them see the error of their thinking.

Decision-making

1. I search for decisions that maintain good relations and encourage other to make the decisions for me when possible.
2. Although I see the final say in decisions, I still listen to what others have to say. In this way they get the benefit of my thinking, by maintaining their loyalty.
3. I let others make decisions or else leave it to fate.
4. I lobby my points of view to others in order to 'sell' my position; or may use persuasion or indirect threats to ensure that my wishes are carried out.
5. I search for workable decisions that others find acceptable.
6. I place high value on arriving at sound decisions; seek input from others and work for understanding and agreement.
7. I place high value on making my own decisions and am rarely influenced by what others have to say.

Critique

1. I pinpoint weaknesses or failure to measure up; in the event of a mistake, I assess blame.
2. I give encouragement and offer praise when something positive happens but avoid saying anything negative.
3. When I give feedback to others, I expect them to appreciate it because it is for their own good.
4. I avoid giving feedback and rarely critique the work of others or myself.
5. I use critique to motivate and inspire others to further the action that is in my best interest; I tend to discount negative aspects of performance as this lowers the level of enthusiasm.

6. I give informal or indirect feedback to keep others moving forward at an acceptable pace; if I have to say something negative, I make sure I have something positive to say as well.
7. I encourage two-way feedback to strengthen operations. I place high value on critique and it is evidenced in everything I do.

1.3 PERSONALITY DEVELOPMENT—WHAT ARE THE RIGHT MOVES?

The world is getting tougher and with globalization becoming a reality, executives need to be smaller and polished enough to take up responsibilities with confidence and self-awareness. The personality factor has proved to be the key to modern corporate and business success. The most important prerequisite for such success is personality with a capital P. It is true that not everyone is born with presence and style. "Personality re-engineering" can do the needful. Personality re-engineering helps groom the new generation executives and provides a finishing touch along with mannerisms, etiquette, diction and stress management. These days most institutes as well as corporate houses are emphasizing personality development courses in their curriculum. The course on personality development can help a person in the following ways:

1. To learn the business etiquette of exchanging cards, wishing on first meeting, bowing when visiting Japan, and the like.
2. Voice modulation, diction, communication skills, phone etiquette, hygiene, empowerment skills, time management and positive thinking.
3. To cultivate a friendly, interactive manner are essentials like giving a speech, voice development and modulation of voice.
4. Personality development can help teach a marketing executive the art of convincing clients with charm and well-presented arguments.

5. Personal projection is done with personality. All other things remaining equal, personal projection is what makes or breaks a commercial relationship.
6. Every person can realize his full potential. The personality development course helps in enhancing the sense of confidence and self-worth.

The veteran personality trainer, Sabira Merchant puts it in her own words, "there is a demand for professionals who are perfect and polished, so more and more people in business circles want to be better".

1.4 COMPONENTS OF PERSONALITY

Different people have different opinions about what makes a man's personality complete. There are several behavioural scientists who have the viewpoint that character does not form a part of personality, but Steven Covey, one of the all-time great authors and motivators, says that the best of behavioural traits fail if they are not based on the solid foundation of character.

1.5 THREE ELEMENTS OF SUCCESS

The Indian management guru, Arindam Choudhuri, has come up with the concept of three basic elements for accomplishing any task effectively. He terms it as ASK (Attitude, Knowledge and Skill). These three elements are essential in the right proportions to achieve the desired success.

Let us take an example. An athlete who wants to win a gold medal in the Olympics must be skillful in the first instance. He must sharpen his skills with regular and rigorous practice. But practice alone cannot make him suitable for becoming a champion at that level. He must acquire the knowledge of intricate in details. Apart from this, he must also possess the latest techniques in the track and field arena. He must analyse the weakness and strength of all his opponents. He can win this race if he starts thinking that he is representing a country that has never been able to prove its mettle at that level. If he is to become a champion, his attitude must also be that of a champion. He must see it as the opportunity to grab the attention of people and achieve his target. Thus, a right proportion of these three elements are essential for achieving targets.

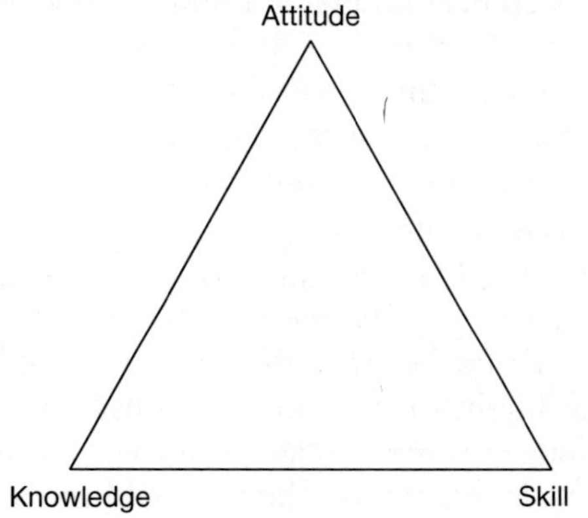

1.6 PERSONALITY THEORIES

Many personality theories, not only from the field of psychology but even from other fields dealing with human behaviour also, have carried on researches to find answers to the questions: What is personality? The various theorists, however, could not give the answers on which consensus could be reached; rather these have resulted into a number of theories of personality. Just as everyone has his own definition of personality, practically, everyone has his own theory of personality. Thus, grouping the various theories and labelling the various categories becomes a difficult task. Each theorist cannot really be grouped with another, even though he may have operated from similar positions. However, the most logical grouping of personality theories seems to be into psychoanalytic, socio-psychological, trait and self-theories.

1.6.1 Psychoanalytic Theory

Psychoanalytic theory is based on the notion that man is motivated more by unseen forces than he is controlled by conscious and rational thought. Although Sigmund Freud is most closely related with this theory, others, such as Carl Jung, Alfred Aster, Karen Horney and Eric Eromm, who all differ from Freud, made additional contribution. Clinical techniques were used primarily to develop psychoanalytic theory; Freud noted that hid patients behaviour could not always be consciously explained. This clinical finding led him to conclude that major motivating force in man was unconscious framework. This framework contains three aspects, though interrelated, yet often conflicting. These are id, ego, and super ego. They are so interrelated that they can only be artificially separated for individual study and analysis.

1. The id: The id is the source of psychic energy and seeks immediate gratification for biological or instinctual needs. Freud believed that instinct could be classified under life-instincts and death-instincts. Life-instincts are hunger, thirst and sex; the energy involved in their activity is the libido. The id would proceed unchecked to satisfy, motives, particularly the sexual relations and pleasures. As an individual matures, he learns to control the id, but even then, it remains a driving force throughout life and an important source of thinking and behaving.
2. The ego: The ego is the conscious and logical part of the human personality and is associated with the reality principal. While id represents the unconscious part, ego is conscious, thus, ego keeps the id in check through the realities of the external environment through intellect and reason. Out of the functioning of the id and ego, many conflicting situations arise because it wants immediate pleasure, while ego dictates denial or postponement to a more appropriate time and place, in order to resolve the conflict, the ego gets support from the super ago.
3. The super ego: The super ego represents social and personal norms and serves as an ethical constraint on behaviour, it can best be described as the conscience. The super ego provides norms to ego to determine what is wrong or right. However, a person is not aware of the working of the super ego and conscience is developed by absorption of cultural values and norms of society.

The psychoanalytic theory by Freud is based on a theoretical conception, rather than a measurable item, for scientific verification. The theory does not give a total picture of behaviour emerging from the personality. That is why this theory is not very relevant from behavioural science point of view. However, this theory gives an important insight into personality structure and the idea of unconscious motivation which can be used by behavioural scientists.

1.6.2 Socio-psychological Theory

Socio-psychological personality theory recognizes the interdependence of the individual and society. The individual strives to meet the needs of the society, while society helps the individual to attain his goal. Out of this interaction, the personality of an individual is determined. Thus, the theory is not exclusively sociological but rather a combination of two. The names associated with this theory are Adler, Homey, Fromm and Sullivan.

Socio-psychological theory differs from psychoanalytic in two respects, first, the social variables and not the biological instincts, are the important determinants in shaping personality, second behavioural motivation is conscious; man knows his needs and wants, and his behaviour is directed to meet these needs.

The theorists accept that socio-psychological factor determine personality; however, there is no general agreement as to the relative importance of social variable. For example, from emphasized the importance of social context, while Sullivan and Homey stressed interpersonal behaviour, and Adler employed different variables. Horney's model suggests that human behaviour results from three predominant interpersonal orientations: complaint, aggressive and detached. Complaint people are dependent on other people and mice towards others. Aggressive people are motivated by the need for power and move against others. Detached people are self-sufficient and move away from others. Socio-psychological theory offers to a very great extent, the answer to the problems of emergence of personality, particularly in terms of the influence of social factors in shaping personality. The managers, in the organizations can take clue from this theory shaping the behaviour as determined by personality.

1.6.3 Trait Theory

Trait theory presents a quantitative approach to the study of personality. This theory postulates that an individual's personality is composed of definite pre-dispositional attributes called traits. A trait may be defined as any feature which is distinguishable. Relatively enduring way in which one individual differs from another. Thus, traits can be considered as individual variables. There are basically three assumptions in this theory:

1. Traits are common to many individuals and vary in absolute amounts between individuals.
2. Traits are relatively stable and exert fairly universal effects on behaviour regardless of the environmental situation. Thus, a consistent functioning of personality variables is predictive to a wide variety of behaviour.
3. Traits can be inferred from the measurement of behavioural indicators.

Two most widely trait theories come from the work of Allport and Cattell. Allport bases his theory on the distinction between common traits and personal dispositions. Common traits are used to compare people. He has identified six categories of values: religious, social, economic, political, aesthetic and theoretical for comparative purpose. Besides the common traits, there are personal dispositions which are completely unique. These are cardinal (most pervasive), central (unique and limited in number) or secondary (peripheral). This uniqueness emphasizes the psychology of the individual that Allport has developed.

Cattell has developed a similar set of traits through the construction of tests and the determination of factors or trait families which may emerge from these psychological measures. However, he has taken a different approach from Allport. He has identified two categories of traits: surface traits and source traits. He determined thirty-five surface traits by finding cluster of traits that are correlated. For example, wise-foolish, affectionate-cold, sociable-seclusive, honest-dishonest, and so on. Such traits lie on the surface of the personality and are largely determined by the underlying source traits. He identified twelve source of traits. Examples of such traits are affectothymia (good nature and trust-fulness) versus sizothymia (critical and suspicious); ego strength (maturity and realism) versus emotionality and neuroticism (immaturity and evasiveness); dominance versus submissiveness; sergency (cheerfulness and energy) versus desurgency (depressed and subdued feelings).

Trait theory gives recognition to the continuity of personality. This theory is based on personality research, and in this research, typical study attempted to find a relationship between set of personality variables and assorted behaviour. This contributes personality tests to the behavioural science. However, this theory a very descriptive rather than analytical and is a long way from comprehensive theory of personality.

1.6.4 Self-theory

The psychoanalytic, socio-psychological and trait theories of personally represent the organismic approaches to explain the complex human personality. Self-theory, also termed as organismic or field theory, emphasizes the totality and interrelatedness of all behaviour. This approach treats the organismic as a whole to a greater degree than id any of the other theoretical formulations.

Though there are many contributors, notably Maslow, Herzberg, Lewin, etc., the most important contribution comes from Carl Rogers. His self-theory of personality is very relevant in organizational behaviour. He defines the self-concept as organized consistent, conceptual, Gestalt composed of perceptions of the "I" or "me" and the perceptions of the relationship of the "I" or "me" to others and to various aspects of life, together with the values attached to these perceptions. There are four factors in self-concept.

1. **Self-image:** The self-image is the way one sees oneself. Every person has certain beliefs about who or what he is; taken together, these beliefs are a person's self-image

or identity. Erikson has defined identity as a "life-long development largely unconscious to the individual and his society". Its roots go back all the way to the first self-recognition: in the baby's earliest exchange of smiles, there is something of a self-realisation coupled with a mutual recognition.

2. **Ideal-self:** The ideal-self denotes the way one would like to be. The ideal-self differs from self-image in the fact that the self-image indicates the reality of a person as perceived by him, while ideal-self indicates the ideal position as perceived by him. Thus, there may be a gap between these two characteristics. The ideal-self is important in stimulus selectivity because a person will select those stimuli for processing which fit in with the characteristics of his ideal-self.
3. **Looking Glass-self:** Looking glass-self is the perception of a person about how others are perceiving his qualities and characteristic. This is the perception of others' perception, that is, the way one thinks people perceive about him and not the way people actually see him. The looking glass-self is predominantly a social product which emerges from face to face interaction with others from the very beginning of the life. This interaction is directed towards cues about how others see him as an individual. Thus, beliefs about self are in large measure a reflection of others' perception about the person.
4. **Real-self:** The real-self is what one really is. The first three aspects of self-concept are the functions of individual perception and they may be same as real-self or different from it. An individual's self-image is confirmed when other persons' responses to him indicate their beliefs about who and what he corresponds with, in the face of feedback from the environment, the person re-evaluates himself and readjusts his self-image to be more consistent with the cues he was receiving. Thus, there is a mutual recognition of his real-self, and the validity of his self-image is confirmed.

A person's self-concept gives him a sense of meaningfulness and consistency. Gellerman observes that "the average individual is not particularly well acquainted with himself, so to speak, but he remains quite faithful to his not-so-accurate image of himself and thereby acquires some consistency". In analyzing organizational behaviour, the self-concept plays a very significant role. A person perceives a situation depending upon his self-concept which has a direct influence on his behaviour. This implies that person with a different self-concept needs different types of managerial practices.

1.7 PERSONALITY TEST

There are several tests to judge the mental aptitude, motivation level, attitude, interpersonal skills and communication skills of a person. Many companies, prior to recruitment, conduct these tests as they find the formal way of face-to-face interviews not good enough to judge the personality of an individual. These personality tests are done in a controlled environment. The following personality tests can identify an individual's:

1. Value system,
2. Emotional reaction to a critical situation,
3. Moods and characteristic behaviour traits,
4. Maturity in handling a crisis,
5. Ability to adjust himself to the stress of day-to-day executive lifestyle,
6. Self-confidence, personal ambition, emotional control and sociability, etc.

To assess some of the behavioural traits such as impulsiveness, emotional reaction, tear, patience, distrust, optimism, initiative and leadership capability, the companies generally conduct these tests. This can be used for the selection of the right candidate who can handle difficult situations with ease.

For Example: A company is recruiting a construction supervisor for a project of a fly-over construction in Kolkata. The person has to control a group of fifty skilled and unskilled personnel and look after a host of construction materials and T&Ps (tools and plants). In a normal situation, a person who will be selected for the post of construction supervisor will have to apply very little technical knowledge that he has learnt in college, but with the suitable personality traits to match the job requirement.

There are three types of personality tests which are conducted by several companies. We may like to know what they are intended for and how they are conducted.

Objective Tests: These tests are conducted to assess the level of irrational tendencies in a person that arise in a not so conducive working environment. A person may not always get a working environment where all his subordinates are co-operative of his endeavor. These tests indicate the self-confident of the person and also help in assessing the domination and submission of the person.

Projective Tests: These are some of the tests in which a person is required to interpret the situation or react to a stimulus. The response of the person is required to interpret the situation or react to a stimulus. The response of the person to these stimuli will indicate the person's motives, values and his personality in total. When we are required to react to such a situation, we always try to interpret it in a way we deem is right as per our own value. The results will be biased if the person conducting the test has indicated his own view.

Situational Tests: These assess a person's capability of handling stress. These tests are conducted in a room with no identified leader to guide it to structured discussions. The discussion is allowed to take its own course and people are allowed to come out freely and openly to express themselves. People generally behave spontaneously in such an environment.

1.8 STAGES OF PERSONALITY DEVELOPMENT

Human personality development is a continuous process. It starts since the child is in fetal stage. After birth, the child develops and learns and this process continues throughout his life. Therefore, personality development can be seen through different stages of age of an individual. At each stage, a person develops different aspects of personality. These stages have been described differently by different aspects of personality. These stages have been described differently by different personality theorists. These descriptions may be classified into:

1. Freudian stages.
2. Neo-Freudian Stage: Erikson's Psychological stages.

1.8.1 Freudian Stages

Although the stages of personality development may be found in the writings of ancient Greek, it was Freud who first formulated a meaningful stage theory of personality. According to Freud, personality develops as a result of interaction of four main sources of stress. These are physical growth process, frustration, conflicts, and threats. These sources affect differently at each stage of the life of a person and these stages can be classified into five categories: oral stage, anal stage, phallic stage, latency stage, and genital stage. Freud believes that these stages are the main driving forces of personality development. Let us see how it happens.

1. Oral Stage: Oral stage covers the period from birth to 18 months of age. This period may be divided into two stages—oral sucking and oral biting. Oral sucking period is from birth to eight months in which a child satisfies his sexual instinct by sucking from mouth, lips, and tongue. The child in this condition is totally in id's effect and driven by pleasure principal. If he is not breast fed properly, he satisfies himself by sucking his thumb or finger. After around eight months, the mother starts weaning. However, if the weaning is abruptly stopped, it creates disturbances in personality development. Oral biting starts at the age of eight months and lasts up to 18 months. This stage consists of the earlier characteristics, and other specialities of personality also develop. The child enjoys in biting, sucking and feels pleasures in this stage. Ego starts separating from id. The child resents if he is denied breast feeding which again creates problems of personality development.

2. Anal Stage: This stage is from 18 months to three years. The child satisfies his sexual instinct by releasing urine and faeces. He expresses his anger by urinating or defecating at wrong places, ego is developed at this stage and the child understands that he is from a particular sex. At the later period of this stage, he understands the social value of toilet control. However, if proper attention is not paid to the child, he experiences stresses which affect his personality.

3. Phallic Stage: This stage extends from three to seven years. At this stage, the child learns to discriminate genitals. He seems this difference in his brothers and sisters or others children. The sexual instinct is satisfied by touching the sex organs. At this stage, the child is prone to develop many types of complexes—doedipus complex, electra complex, castration complex, penis envy, etc.

4. Latency Stage: This stage is from seven to 12 years. At this stage, the child's sexual instincts are usually at sleep because of social fear, his outwardly interests grow: he enjoys playing and talking with his friends. He does not like the love shown by his parents but the masturbation learnt at the phallic stage persists.

5. Genital Stage: This stage is from 12 to 20 years. The boys and girls see their genitals—as their sex organs grow. Phallic stage is again aroused. The children at this stage, start telling false stories, day-dreaming, and may involve in homosexuality. It is observed that when boys and girls are alone, they feel depressed and defeated and to satisfy themselves, they masturbate.

Freudian stage theory of personality development is based on the satisfaction of sexual instincts at the stage of childhood, and the conclusions have been drawn from behaviour of children in the family. However, most of the modern psychologists do not agree with Freudian stage theory, though agree that Freud has provided some very basic insight for understanding the developing of personality. Their disagreement revolves around the terms used for describing various stages like oral for dependent, and for compulsive, or genital for mature, and so on.

1.8.2 Neo-Freudian Stages: Erikson's Psychological Stages

Modern psychologists do not agree on the over-emphasis of sexual instincts as determinants of personality development as identified by Freud. Prominent among these psychologists are

Jung, Adler, Homey, Fromm, and Erikson. They have emphasized the role of environmental variables in the development of personality. Out of these, Erikson's psychological stages of personality development provide more valuable insights for understanding the development of personality.

1.8.2.1 Erikson's Psychological Stages

While formulating his stage theory of personality, Erikson has felt that relatively more attention should be given to the social rather than the sexual adaptations of the individuals. Based on this theme, he has identified eight psychological stages of personality development, each stage covers a particular span of a person's life and in each stage, a particular type of crisis is experienced as shown in Table 1.1.

Table 1.1: Erikson's Psychological Stages

Stages of Development	Age	Crisis
Oral sensory stage	0.1	Trust versus mistrust
Mascular and anal stages	1-2	Autonomy versus doubt
Locomotor genital stage	3-5	Initiative versus guilt
Latency stage	6-puberty	Identity versus inferiority
Puberty adulthood	12-19	Identity versus confusion
Early adulthood	Early 20's	Intimacy versus isolation
Young and middle adulthood	Late 20's	Generativity versus stagnation
Mature adulthood	30's	Integrity versus despair

Erikson has asserted that a psychological crisis occurs within each of the stages and that in order to have a normal fulfilling personality, each crisis should be optimally resolved. However, these eight stages are not totally separable, and the crisis at a particular stage is not fully resolved. A belief description of different stages of personality development is presented below:

1. **Oral Sensory Stage:** This is the stage of infancy and the child tries to resolve the crisis of trust versus mistrust. The infant who is cared well develops trust in people while the infant who is not cared well develops mistrust. This stage makes a serious impact on a child

that influences his behaviour for the remaining life. The child will resolve the crisis and develop his personality based on the way he live in the family. In this context, following generalizations have been made:

If a child lives with criticism, he learns to condemn.

If a child lives with ridicule, he learns to shy.

If a child lives with shame, he learns to feel guilty.

If a child lives with tolerance, he learns to be patient.

If a child lives with encouragement, he learns to be confident.

If a child lives with praise, he learns to appreciate.

If a child lives with fairness, he learns to be just.

If a child lives with security, he learns to have faith.

If a child lives with approval, he learns to like himself.

2. **Mascular and Anal Stage:** This is the early childhood stage of the life in which the child develops the sense of autonomy if his behaviour is approved by the parents and other people. If the child faces disapproval by the elders, he develops a sense of doubt and shame.
3. **Locomotor Genital Stage:** This is the play stage of the life and the child tries to resolve the crisis of initiative versus guilt. He tries to discover how much he can do. If the child is encourages to experiment and to achieve reasonable goals, he develops the sense of initiative. If the child is blocked and made to feel incapable, he develops a sense of guilt and lack of self-confidence.
4. **Latency Stage:** This is the school-going stage of the life and the child tries to develop many new skills and social abilities. If the child experiences progress at a rate compatible with his abilities, he develops a sense of enterprise. In the reverse case, he develops a sense of inferiority.
5. **Puberty Adulthood/Adolescence:** This is the teenage stage of the life and the adolescent person tries to gain a sense of identity; a sense of feeling about himself

and tries to establish himself as socially different from his parents. The autonomy, initiative and enterprise development at the earlier stages of the life are very important in helping the teenager to resolve the crisis of identity versus confusion and to prepare himself for the adulthood.

6. **Early Adulthood:** This is the stage of early 20s of the life in which the person tries to resolve the crisis of intimacy versus isolation. The sense of identity development during the teenage stage; help the early adult to develop deep and lasting relationship.
7. **Young and Middle Adulthood:** This is the late 20s stage of the life in which the person tries to resolve the crisis of generativity versus stagnation or self-absorption. Generative persons attach more importance to the society as compare to themselves.

   Productivity at the work and societal advancement become more important for them. They try to become innovative and creative. Self-observed person do not develop an ability to look beyond themselves. They remain preoccupied with their own development and do not show concern for future generations.
8. **Mature Adulthood:** This is the 30s stage of the life in which the person faces the crisis of integrity versus despair. At this stage, the person gets maturity, wisdom, and perspective that can guide the younger generations.

According to Erikson, probably the most widely known crisis is the identity experience of adolescents and the optimum outcome of this teenage crisis is the re-integration of past goals with present goals, from organizational behaviour point of view, most relevant stage is that of the young and middle adulthood as the crisis that the person faces at this stage is one of generativity versus stagnation. The best outcome for personality fulfillment would be an attitude of production and concern with the world and future generation. Thus, young and middle-aged adults who solve their psychological crises by being productive will develop the healthiest personalities.

1.9 IMMATURITY-MATURITY CONTINUUM

Argyris, an organizational behaviour theorist, has made a significant departure from the strict stage, approach of personality development and has identified specific dimensions of the human personality as it develops. He has proposed that personality, rather than going through precise stages, progresses along a continuum of immaturity as an infant to maturity as an adult. People can have their degree of development plotted according to the seven dimensions shown in Table 1.2.

Table 1.2: Immaturity-maturity continuum

Immaturity characteristics	Maturity characteristics
Passivity	Activity
Dependence	Independence
Capable of behaving in a few ways	Capable of behaving in many ways
Shallow interest	Deep interest
Short-term perspective	Long-term perspective
Subordinate position	Superordinate position
Lack of self-awareness	Self-awareness and control

According to Argyris, seven changes should take place in the personality of individuals if they are to develop as mature people. These changes are as follows:

1. Individual moves from a state of passivity as a child to one of his increased activity is characteristically in the hand of his environment: his life is a series of events occurring without his choice. On the other hand, an adult knows how to control the environment and can control the occurrence of events.
2. He develops from a state of dependence as a child to a state of relative independence as an adult. This proves occurs unevenly making some people very independent and leaving others quite nestled close to protective people.
3. Individual, as a child, behaves in only a few ways but, as adult, he is capable of behaving in many ways, the

adult is both less predictable and more adaptable than the child.

4. Individual has erratic, casual and shallow interests as child, but develops deeper and stronger interests as adult. Gradually, he acquires a fairly well-defined set of interests, some of which can absorb him for hours and offer him great deal of satisfaction.
5. Individual, as a child, is almost exclusively concerned with the present; his time perspective is very short, as a mature, his time perspective increases to include the past and the future, his behaviour is influenced by past events also. He is also very much concerned with what may or may not happen in future.
6. Individual, as a child, is subordinate to everyone. As an adult, he moves to equal to superior position to others. Though he might be working as superior or subordinate depending upon the situation, he does not think himself as being inherently to be a follower.
7. Individual, as a child, does not have a habitual set of attitudes about himself and indeed does not have much of a self to have attitudes about. As adult, he thinks about himself and is aware of the kind of person he is. He has an ego and may go to some extent to protect it.

Implications: These changes are only general tendencies, but they give some light to the matter of maturity. The tendency is to move towards the maturity end of the continuum with age, though norms of the individual's culture and personality inhibit and limit, maximum expression and growth of the adult. Argyris himself accepts that very few persons develop to full maturity. The views that immaturity tends to exist in individuals not because of their nature of laziness, but because of organizational setting and management practices. When individual joins an organizations, they are given very little opportunity to control the environment; they are encouraged to be passive, dependent, and subordinate, and hence they behave immaturely. He feels that keeping people immature is built into the very nature of formal organization which is based on four principles of classical approach management: task specialization, chain of command, unity of direction and span of management, coupled with organization structure, directive, leadership and management controls, such as budgets, time and motion study, and standard operation procedures restrict the initiative and creativity of the individuals. Argyris has suggested that a healthy organization is one which is realistic about both itself and its situation, flexible, and able to summon its best resource of any organization, there should be a proper integration between organizational and individual goals. Therefore, what is best for an individual is also best for an organization and vice versa. He proposes a programme of gradually phasing from existing pyramidal organization structure to humanistic system; from existing management system to the more flexible and participative management. Such situations provide individuals the opportunity to grow mature and keep them satisfy more than just physiological and safety needs, which, in turn, motivate them and allow them to use more of their potential in accomplishing organizational goals.

1.10 DETERMINANTS OF PERSONALITY

As pointed out earlier, personality represents a process of change and it relates to the psychological growth and development of individuals. While it may be possible to detect underlying personality characteristics, these characteristics may be useful only at that point of time and only for a limited member of situations therefore it becomes important to know the factors that cause a given personality to change or develop. Managers can deal more effectively, then, if they understand how an individual's personality develops. There are various determinants of personality and these have been categorized in different ways. McClelland has categorized these factors into four fundamental theories: traits (acquired propensity to respond), schema (beliefs, frame of reference, major orientations, ideas, and values), motives (inner drives) and self-schema (observation of one's own behaviour). Similarly, Scott and Mitchell have classified various determinants into heredity, groups. And cultural factors, both physiological and psychological which play an important role in human personality. These factors are interrelated and interdependent. However, for the purpose of analysis, these can be classified into four broad categories:

1. Biological factors,
2. Family and social factors,
3. Cultural factors, and
4. Situational factors.

The impact of these factors on the personality may be seen in Fig. 1.3:

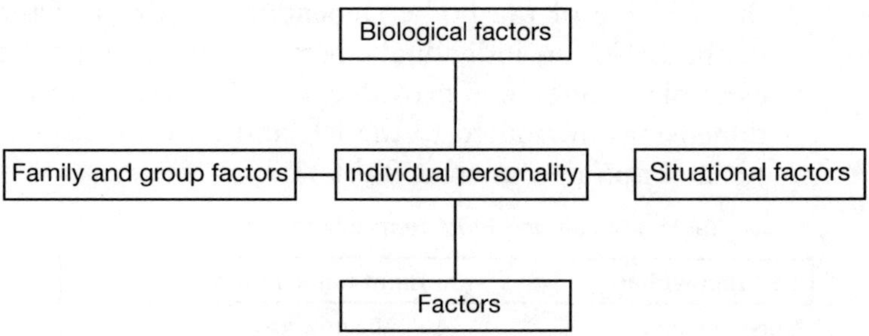

Fig. 1.3: Immaturity-maturity continuum

Out of the various factors of personality determinants, only biological factor have one-sided impact, while other factors have interactive impact as the individual himself can also have some impact on these factors.

1.10.1 Biological Factors

The general characteristics of human biological system influence the way in which human being tends to sense external even data, interpret and respond to them. The study of the biological contribution to personality can be divided into three major categories—heredity, brain and physical features.

1. **Heredity:** Heredity is the transmission of the qualities from ancestor to descendant through a mechanism lying primarily in the chromosomes of the germ cells. Heredity predisposes to certain physical mental, and emotional states, it has been established through research on animals that, physical and psychological characteristics can be transmitted through heredity.

However, such a conclusive proof is not available for human beings, though psychologists and geneticists have drawn the conclusion that heredity plays an important role in personality.

2. **Brain:** The second biological factor is brain which is supposed to play role in shaping personality. Though not conclusive as yet, physiologists and psychologists have studied the structure of human brain and have divided it into two parts: left hemisphere which lies in the right side of the body and right hemisphere which lies in the left side of the body. Depending on the structure of the brain, an individual's personality develops. For example, trotter has provided the characteristics and dimensions attributed to the left and right hemisphere of the brain as shown in Table 1.3.

Table 1.3: Left and Right Hemisphere of the Brain

Left hemisphere	**Right hemisphere**
Speech/verbal	Spatial/musical
Logical, mathematical	Holistic
Linear, detailed	Aristic, symbolic
Sequential	Simultaneous
Controlled	Emotional
Intellectual	Intuitive, creative
Dominant	Minor (quiet)
Wordly	Spiritual
Active	Receptive
Analytic	Synthetic, gestalt-oriented
Reading, writing, naming	Facial recognition
Sequential ordering	Simultaneous comprehension
Perception of significant order	Perception of abstract patterns
Complex motor sequences	Recognition of complex figures

3. **Physical Features:** The third biological factor determining personality formation is physical characteristics and rate of maturation. An individual's external appearance, which is biologically determined, is an important

ingredient of personality. In a narrow sense, personality is referred to physical features of a person. However, it is not true if we take a comprehensive view of the personality. A person's physical features have some influence on his personality because he will influence others and, in turn, will affect his self-concept. Mussen observes that "a child's physical characteristics may be related to his approach to the social environment, to the expectations (exigencies) of other, and to their reaction to him." These, in turn, many have impact in personality because persons of varying maturity are exposed to different physical and social situations and activities differently.

1.10.2 Family and Social Factors

The developments of the individual proceed under the influence of many socializing forces and agencies from nuclear family to more distant or global grouping. Family and social groups have most significant impact on personality development. These groups have their impact through socialization and identification processes.

Socialization is a process by which an individual infant acquires, from the enormously wide range of behavioural potentialities that are open to him at birth, those behaviour patterns that are customary and acceptable according to the standards of his family and social groups. Socialization process starts with initial contact between mother and her new infant. Later on, other members of the family and social group influence the socialization process.

Identification process occurs when a person tries to identify himself with some person whom he feels his family. Generally, a child in the family tries to behave like his father or mother. The identification process can be examined from three different perspective. First, identification can be viewed as the similarity of behaviour (including feeling and attitudes) between child and model. Second, identification can be looked as the child's motives or desires to be like the model. Third, it can be viewed as the process through which the child actually takes on the attributes of the model.

Socialisation and identification process is influenced by home environment, family members, and social groups.

1. **Home Environment:** Total home environment is a critical factor in personality development. For example, children, with markedly institutional upbringing or children in a cold, unstimulating home have a much greater potential to be emotionally maladjusted than children raised by parents in a warm, loving, and stimulating environment. The key variable is not the parents *per se* but rather the type of environment that is generated for the child.
2. **Family Members:** Parents and other family members have strong influence on the personality, i.e., child. Parents have more effect on the personality development as compared to other members of the family. The study by Newcomb showed the high correlation between attitudes of parents and children with a further consistency in patterns. The relationship between parents and children was higher than that between the children and their teachers. Besides parents, siblings (brother and sisters) also contribute to personality.
3. **Social Group:** Besides a person's home environment and family members, there are other influences arising from the social placement of the family as the person is exposed to agencies outside the home, particularly the school, friendship, and other work groups. Similarly, socio-economic factors also affect personality development.

1.10.3 Cultural Factors

Culture is the underlying determinant of human decision-making. It determines attitudes towards independence, aggression, competition, and cooperation. Each culture expects and trains its members to behave in the ways that are acceptable to the group. To a marked degree, the child's cultural group defines the range of experiences and situations he is likely to encounter and the values and personality characteristics that will be reinforced and hence learned, despite the importance of cultural contribution to the personalities, a linear relationship cannot be established between personality and a given culture. One problem stems from the existence of numerous subcultures within a given culture. Thus, workers are not influenced by the same culture as managers are.

1.10.4 Situational Factors

Apart from the biological, sociological, and cultural factors, situational factors also determine personality development. The Stimulus, Organism (a person) Behaviour and Consequence (S.O.B.C.) model of human behaviour considers the situations under which the behaviour is occurring. Milgram's research study suggests that very powerful role the situation may play in human personality. On the basis of his research study, he states that a situation exerts an important pressure on the individual. It exercises constraints or provide push. In certain circumstances, it is not so much the kind of person a man is, as the kind of situation in which he is placed, that determines his actions. For example, a worker whose personality history suggests that he had need for power and achievement, may become frustrated and react aparthetically and aggressively if he is put in a bureaucratized work situation.

1.11 UNDERSTANDING (SELF AND OTHERS)

For building up better personality I suggest following ten things:

It is needless to state that the list is of an indicative nature. It is not exhaustive. You can add many to them.

1. Do Your Home Work: If you have completed your formal education and joined any organization like a bank, or insurance company, hospital, etc. please bear in mind that your working hours are not restricted from 10.00 a.m. to 5.00 p.m., do not rest content with that.

Even in your spare time, outside your office, in your home, in your leisure hours and read them repeatedly. Educational expenses are our best investments. Think about many EXTRAS that you can put in your assignment. More knowledge about your work will instill confidence and cheerfulness in your mind. You are sure to attract favourable attention of your early career.

Micheal Korda is a motivational author, who enjoys a high status at current times. He is the chief editor of famous American publishing company—Simon Schuster Inc. He has successfully applied this principal from his early age—about acquiring sound control on his assignment. This quality has lent praiseworthy depth in his books, like power, success and queenie (girl name).

He says: "Burning the midnight oil is Oakey at 20s even at 30s but nobody should have to lose sleep learning something new at 40-plus. So when you are young, do your homework in your workplace, in your hobby areas (place) strive to achieve excellence in them."

2. Develop Your Own Style: Before you cross the age mark of 25-30 years, learn to find out: What you are comfortable with? How you wish to dress? What type of food habits you want to develop? Which books you desire to read? What are your broad objectives in reading them? Will you be reading just 'to kill time'—just to get short-term pleasure or you will read to increase your frontiers of knowledge?, etc. Will you not strive your best to become a strong—very strong young man—or woman? What are your major aims in life and how you are going to fulfill them?

I will remind you of a basic point—how to be a winner and how to think like a winner—that don't—don't be a carbon copy of any successful man or woman. Remember the instance of our greatest show-man Raj Kapoor. He started from the humble position of a 'clapper boy' assisting Kedar Sharma and climbed to the mighty heights in the areas of acting, producing, directing great Indian movies. He originally derived inspiration from great Charlie Chaplin, but he did not remain content to become and remain a carbon copy only. He studied our Indian life and changed his style accordingly. He hated violence—so even at the time when pictures full of violence were being produced, he gave the message of love and peace through his films.

He strived to understand life from the angles of a common man—and he captured his feelings on the screen from that level.

Raj Kapoor is living on and on, not only in our own country but also in other countries of the world because he was original. He had the courage to follow his conviction firmly.

Take the instance of *Mera Nam Joker*, his message was very clear. Each one of us has our own private sorrows—Each one of us has our some personal problem or the other; but we must not give expression to them in our public life. We must laugh, laugh and make other happy. He sustained heavy monetary and other losses in that 'great picture' of his—which he bore it bravely. Learn from his great life and career are to be original. Dare to do something new. Do not walk on the trodden paths. Build up new lanes and by lane and by lanes. Have no false modesty about your efforts. Dream-dream-dream in big ways. Work honestly and ask your reasonable price. Do not be apologetic on the front.

Once you have decided that some things are not good for you, like non-veg food, drinks or watching late adult movies on TVs, say 'No' to such things. Stick to your viewpoints.

For a postal stamp it is said, "it remains stuck to the envelop till it reaches its destination". Be like a postal stamp, to your own styles, to your own aims, to your viewpoints very fast.

3. Develop Positive Emotions: Ask pointed question about other people's response, behaviour and attitudes towards you. Who responds to you in a loving manner. To whom you own the greatest sense of gratitude? Are you reciprocating their love and are in the best ways?

Your best relations will assume fine shape with your parents, with your brothers and sisters, your co-workers, your friends, your teachers in the first run. If you are married, you will give best out of you to your life partner—husband or wife. Are you doing best for them? Are you neglecting them in any manner? If so make suitable changes to give them your best.

If you are working on a full-time job, a major portion of your 'working hours' are spent with your co-workers. They are more than your relatives. What are you doing for them? Are you taking deep interest in their lives or in their problems? Are you helping them in their difficult times?

Your positive emotions of love, friendliness and sacrifice can be made to have deeper expression in these circles. Avoid hating anyone. Try to be friendly to all. If all people do that—our human society will become more rich, more happy and more prosperous.

When you are working for others, when you are living for others, when you are full of positive thoughts, emotions and actions, chances of your becoming unhappy or depressed are very much reduced.

At such times you are full of 'Divine Energies' flowing into your life and you shall be able to face any difficulties or problems with tremendous powers. Sense of fulfillment, prosperity, plenty, peace, etc., are closely connected with healthy personality development. Make your spirit strong. Try to find out various ways and means to do that.

Be blind to the faults of others. Do your best to find out good points—plus points—of others. Encourage them to develop them. Direct your emotions and efforts for those creative works. You will destroy your enemies and convert them into your friends.

4. Know Your Weaknesses: Accept your weaknesses and then proceed ahead to keep them in background. Say your body is not strong but your mind is very active and highly developed for creative works. In that case you may not accept the job where more physical energy is required. It would not be advisable for you to take up the jobs, where much travels would be required. In modern days people who travel for 20-21 days a month need strong physique. In such cases you may take up desk work, where more mental faculties will have to be used. Many people do not like routine works—they wish to take up creative work where they would be able to express their talents effectively. Such was the case with famous English author George Bernard Shaw. He once declared: I am going to live only one life in this world and that I am not going to waste in office drudgery. He gave up a clerical job of the post office and determined to write at least 10 good pages a day. He had great trust in his bright future. Even when he passed age mark of

40 years his life—his mother worked hard and supported him. Then he came up—up and up. So understand your weaknesses and try to select the works which are not against your skills—mental, physical and emotional.

5. Find Out Your Strengths: When you are drawing up your personal balance sheet, strive to find out your plus points. You can be helped in this search by your intimate friends, parents, teachers and other members of the family. Build up your personality and life works on those strong points.

6. Start Building Up Savings: In our country because of multiplicity of reasons a great majority of people are not in a position to secure jobs of their likings. They are called upon to make sacrifices, and take up jobs which are not suitable to them.

Such people can start building your savings for future change-over. When such people have reached the age mark of 50 years and have built up enough savings, they can quit their jobs and can start activities which are very near and dear to their hearts.

The management people say this as quit money, once you have enough money resources at your command and if you are not properly respected—you can take "exit" gracefully. So, each one of us build up savings, slowly and steadily.

About this need someone said: nothing is so depressing as absolute dependency—the knowledge that you cannot afford to quit your job or take a risk in changing careers—that you are stuck...put enough money away so that you have a 'Safety Net'. You may never use it, but sometimes the only appropriate response to a situation is—'Gentlemen, I Quit' and you will hate yourself, if you are not in a position to say it.

7. Establish a Network of People: Develop friends, well-wishers, supporters from your young age only. Help people in this circle of yours, when they need your help, do best for them. So when you need their help and assistance they will extend them to you cheerfully. Find out the needs of people. Fill their needs. Make others happy, cheerful and enthusiastic.

Help noble projects. Go to the hospital, orphanages, schools and other service organizations where you can extend your helping hand, listen to the problems of organizations where you can extend your helping hand. Listen to the problems of other people. Listen them with love.

Help them with love. Give the best you have and best will come back to you, by God's grace.

A network is not something you can establish overnight—it takes long years of nurturing. In business, as in politics, you need a lot of people, spread out in right places on whom you can depend on—and they in turn can depend on you. Cultivate maximum number of contacts. Countless contacts established by you, cultivated by you, will add much to your total personality.

8. Learn to Delegate: Delegation is half of success. If you cannot do that—you will find yourself fatally handicapped. Be an expert in your field. Decide what you can entrust to other profitably. Select right people. Test them well in your own way and then trust them absolutely.

9. Keep Silence: Learn when to keep your mouth shut. Many careers are destroyed—Many promotions are lost—Many friendships are broken—Many married lives are wrecked by careless talk than by anything else. So keep your mouth shut on critical times—and in trying situations.

Learn to keep quiet and look wise. Do not gossip and do not talk about your plans. A reputation for keeping secrets far outweighs the easy popularity, that spreading gossip may win you. The further and higher up you go in your life and career, the more true this is. In higher places—Secrecy is golden.

10. Be Loyal: If you have not established a reputation for solid, 100 percent loyalty from your age, you will be haunted by this defect, for the best of your life. A reputation for disloyalty is bound to make you unwelcome anywhere in human life.

You make your way to the top not by back-stabbing but by establishing your early unshakable reputation, straightforward person. You will get find rewards in long-long years to come.

The other famous motivator and behavioural scientists, Shiv Khera, has propagated the theory of four D's for success. He says that determination, direction, dedication and desire are the four main factors for anyone to succeed. In spite of better intelligence and potential the real winner will be the one who has an abundance of the four D's mentioned above.

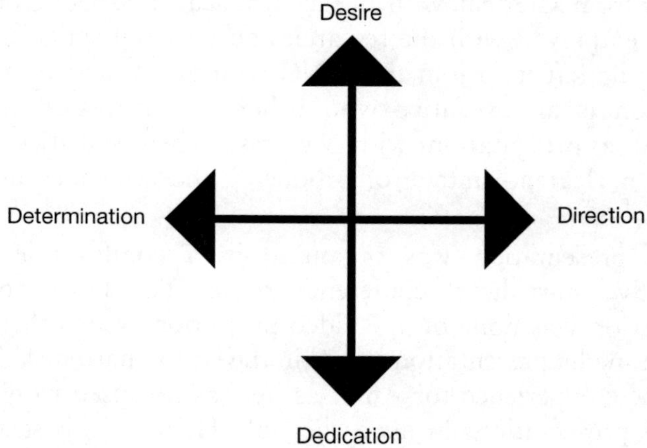

Fig. 1.4: Theory of four D's determination, direction, dedication and desire

The person who wants to improve his personality has to have desire and determination; he has to identify the direction for his goals to achieve it. Once all the above three steps are taken he has to dedicate himself—to the task of achieving his goals.

We need to develop personality traits that are very unique. Blindly following someone else who is successful will never take you to the direction which is right for you.

> "If I am not myself, who will be? to be nobody else but yourself—in a world which is doing its best, right and day, to make you everybody else—means to fight the hardest battle any human being can fight, and never stop fighting."
>
> —E.E. Cummings, American, Author

> "Every man is unique and he has his peculiar ambition."
>
> —Abraham Lincoln

CASE STUDY

Ankit Kapur, 32 is the country manager of a multi-national cosmetic company. The company is planning to launch a new range of products in India. The Asia Pacific Director Robertson is currently in India to review the prospect of producing the cosmetic in the Indian factory at Nasik. Ankit is a chemical engineer from Mumbai, with an excellent academic background. He was employed with the research and development wing of HLL till he left it to join the MNC with an attractive salary. Robertson is an executive who believes in statistics. Ankit prepared a presentation with well-researched statistics that showed a clear advantage of producing the cosmetics in the Indian factory.

The presentation was organized in a comfortable and serene five start hotel conference room. The Power point presentation was done on the video projection system through the multimedia presentation stored in the laptop hard disk. This was a new experience for Ankit as he was not used to giving business presentations in his earlier job. He asked his second-in-command, Ravi, to be present in the conference room with all the necessary details. The hesitation and lack of experience in giving a presentation was more than evident when he began. Ankit was not following the sequence and kept on shifting from one point to another without any clue. Within a few minutes Robertson was thoroughly confused. He was not sure of the project. He left India saying that initially he was convinced that the Indian project was a feasible one, but Ankit's presentation showed more of the negative side rather than the advantages. The decision was kept on hold.

Ankit too was not happy with his communication skills. He joined a professional training course to improve his skills in presentation. In two months he was very confident and wanted to repair the damages done in the last presentation. In Paris, when he finished the presentation in front of the entire company board, the board was more than convinced that the project was not only feasible but highly profitable too. The difference in these two months was not because of any change in government policy in India or the investment strategy of the MNC, but the change in Ankit's presentation style.

Questions

1. Can the presentation style change the fate of an investment?
2. Was Ankit's presentation full of data and statistics a right decision?
3. What is Personality? Discuss its three important aspects.
4. Discuss Trait Theory of Personality.
5. Personality development is a continuous process. Discuss?
6. What are the key determinants of personality? Elaborate.
7. Explain the different stages of personality.
8. Explain the different tests to judge the mental aptitude motivational level, attitude interpersonal skill and communication skill of a person.
9. As per behavioural scientist and psychologist there are nine type of personalities. Illustrate them.
10. What is the difference between Freudian stages and Neo-Freudian stages?
11. Explain the theory of four D's for success.

2

Interpersonal Relationships

2.1 INTRODUCTION

It is proven fact that the effectiveness of a person is highly dependent on his capability to deal with people. Many people with high intellect and competence fail to succeed in the race of life. In real life your success also depends on other external factors. The factor vital for any person to succeed is the relationship with people. There are a few things in our life that we all like to change, but we cannot do much as the result is dependent on others. The relationship between you and other members in the group you belong to or with some other group

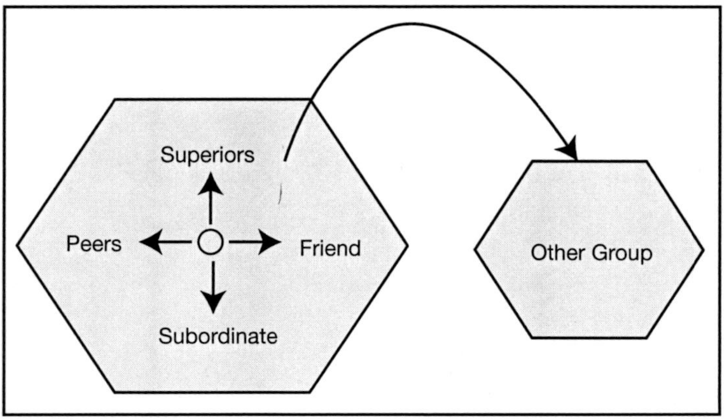

Fig. 2.1: Interpersonal Relationship Hierarchy

is called interpersonal relationship. There are several members in the group—some may be your peers and friends, others your superiors in the company or in the institution you are, and subordinates who report to you. Therefore, the art is to have an excellent relationship within the group, not only with your superiors, but also with your colleagues and subordinates. Interpersonal skills are not restricted to a small group. They are equally applicable for effective relationships between different groups. The basic relationship can be depicted in a very simple picture like the one shown above.

2.2 DETERMINANTS OF INTERPERSONAL RELATIONSHIP

There are several determinants that are important to decide what our behaviour towards other people is. There are several behavioural scientists who have devised models to understand why a person behaves in a unique way with someone. We need to see what the determinants of interpersonal relationships are. They may be listed as under:

1. **Self-Analysis:** Human beings are different from all other living beings because they can think and analyse their behaviour. Self-analysis is the strongest of all the determinants that can help a person to improve any relationship to a great extent.
2. **Misperception:** Most of the strain in a relationship is due to a mental box, a frame of mind we are in. The mental frame does not allow us to make our unbiased perception about the other person. The misperception can spoil the relationship.

   Example: When a teacher calls a parent to the school, in anticipation that it must be for addressing a complaint of their son, the parents starts, with a defensive mode. The relationship between the teacher and the parents is determined by such a mental frame.
3. **Selective Interactions:** The relationship between individuals in a group can have an adverse effect if the interaction is limited to a subgroup. People always

tend to form a sub-set in the larger set of people. Such selective interaction does affect the relationship in the group.

Example: If a person is attending an official party in a metropolitan city, he may like to find someone from his state talking in the same language and liking the same food, but that can destroy the change of a good relationship with other persons in the group.

4. **Selective Evaluation of other People:** We may evaluate some persons on a biased scale, thereby not developing good relationships. Similarly, people whom we want to boost are evaluated on a higher scale.

   Example: The relationship is badly damaged if some rumours or someone else's briefing affects the evaluation of the other person. When a new student joins a class, he meets other in the class with the background of what his roommate has told him about everyone else. He sees the relationship through the eyes of his roommate.

5. **Selective Evaluation of Self:** We must assess correctly where we stand. If we portray ourselves as what we are not, there is little chance that the relationship will be honest and based on a solid foundation.

   Example: The chief of a company feels too important and thinks of himself as more than a normal human being because of his position in the office. He will behave with others in office as if he is the master and other are there to follow him. Even when he is not in the office he has similar feelings and expects the same treatment he gets in office.

2.3 INTERPERSONAL COMMUNICATION: THEORIES AND CONCEPTS

There are four basic theories that can explain the behaviour of a person to others when he is dealing with them. These are:

1. Social Penetration Theory
2. Self-Disclosure

3. Uncertainty Reduction Theory
4. Relational Dialectics Theory

2.3.1 Social Penetration Theory (SPT)

SPT is a theory about the development of 'relational closeness'. Social penetration can help as far as a relationship is concerned. The key points in SPT are that relational closeness can progress from superficial to intimate and that closeness develops through self-disclosure. Closeness varies with factors such as rewards/benefits, costs, vulnerability, satisfaction, stability and security.

2.3.2 Self-Disclosure

> Please listen carefully and try to hear what I am not saying....
> What I'd like to be able to say....
> What for survival I need to say....
> But what I can't say.—Unknown

In this theory, importance is given to the fact that if you disclose yourself, there shall be a better relationship. Self-disclosure is sharing with someone information that helps him or her in understanding you. Self-disclosure is most revealing when the sharing is the present and least revealing when the sharing is about the past. —D. Johnson, Self-Disclosure Characteristics.

Self-Disclosure Definitions

S. Jourard defines self-disclosure as making ourselves 'transparent' to others through our communication, i.e., when we tell other things about ourselves which help them to see our uniqueness as a human being.

Pearce and Sharp make an interesting distinction among three related terms: self-disclosure, confession and revelation.

Self-disclosure—voluntary communication of information about one's self to another.

Confession—forced or coerced communication of information about one's self to another.

Revelation—unintentional or inadvertent communication of information about one's self to another.

2.3.3 Uncertainty Reduction Theory (URT)

In this theory of relationship, it is presumed that 'the beginning of personal relationships is fraught with uncertainties' and that people want to reduce uncertainty in relational through knowledge and understanding. To know others we can do it actively, passively or interactively.

2.3.4 Relational Dialectics Theory (RDT)

As per Baxter. No relationship can exist by definition unless the parties sacrifice some individual autonomy. However, too much connection paradoxically destroys the relationship because individuals' identities become lost. In RDT, Baxter and Montgomery claim that people want a certain amount of mystery and spontaneity in relationships to 'spice things up'. Without variety, the relationship will become dull and too predictable and, therefore, 'emotionally dead'. The key points in this theory are that relationship reflect tensions (conflicts), contradictions, that are played out in communication interaction (dialectical tensions).

2.4 JOHARI WINDOW

This is a conceptual way of studying interpersonal awareness. The name Johari is a combination of the names of two behavioural scientists (Jo + Hari) namely Joseph Luft and Harry Lagham who developed this model. This is a conceptual model to tell how people expose themselves to other people and how receptive they are to the suggestions and feedback from others. There is a window that is divided into four compartments and have four different perspectives, namely:

(a) **Arena:** The compartment, in which a person knows the self as well as others. This has openness of mind as far as relationship is concerned.

(b) **Blind-Spot:** It is the area that others know, but the person concerned is not aware of. It may create awkward situations.

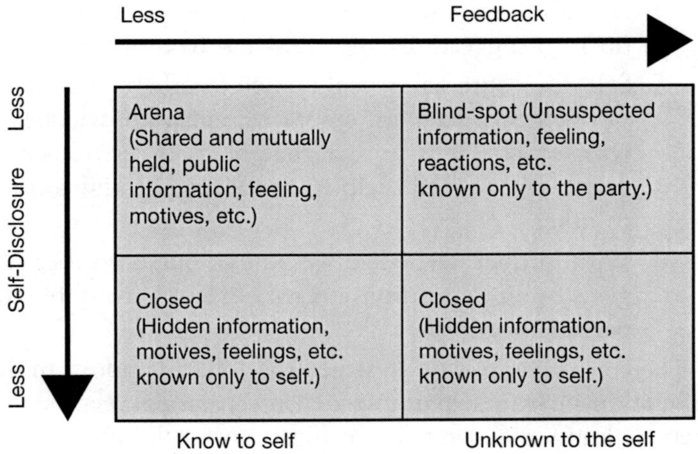

(c) **Closed Area:** It is the compartment in the model where a person is sure of himself, but he does not allow others to know it. He does not allow others to share the information and feelings.

(d) **Dark Area:** It is the compartment that is neither known to the other person nor to the person in question. This compartment has tremendous scope for improvement.

1. From these we can see that a relationship is mutually useful and trustful if there is a big Arena (I know you, you know me). In this compartment the accurate perceptual judgement will help to develop more realistic mutual expectations. This mutual and satisfying relationship is the basis of a long-lasting relationship.
2. The expansion of arena will automatically reduce the compartments of closed area (I know, but you do not know). In this closed area, the person generally hides the information from others and denies things one knows or feels.
3. Blind sports (I do not know, but you know) will push a person in a relationship where he would like to protect himself from all the ignorance and self-protection mechanism will come into play.

4. Arena or open arena can be increased of when we are open to suggestions and feedback from other people.
5. Self-disclosure will reveal oneself to others. It is sharing of one's own feelings, emotions, facts, knowledge, etc. with others. It is an act that helps a relationship to grow. The act will help to show respect and intimacy to other.
6. With proper feedback we know ourselves better. It gives us an opportunity to see ourselves from the other person's viewpoint.

There are several ways in which the Johari window analysis of a relationship can help us improve interpersonal relationships. When we know that the relationship is not well, but we cannot do much to know what is wrong, we may do something as under:

1. **Solicit Feedback:** One should feel no shame in asking for feedback from the other side.
2. **Institute Self-Disclosure:** You can take initiative in telling how you feel about things in question.
3. **Do not Defend:** Be ready to listen to negative feedback too. There is no point in defending when you want feedback from others.
4. **Define the Mutual Expectations:** We must analyse the basis of a relationship and the expectation from such a relationship.
5. **Communicate Your Concern:** Based on the feedback it is advisable to convey your concern for a better relationship.

2.5 TA (TRANSACTIONS ANALYSIS)

Oxford Dictionary defines transaction as 'a piece of business that is done between people'. In a behavioural science, it is the exchange of communication, both verbal and non-verbal, between two or more individual. Transaction analysis is the scientific way of studying the state of mind of the persons when he sends or receives the communication.

Transactional Analysis (TA) is psychoanalysis of personality that was developed by psychologists with strong humanist leanings, amongst whom the best known is probably Eric Berne, author of Games people play and what do you say after you say hello? Transactional analysis generally seems to be glossed over in psychology textbooks, both as a form of therapy and as a personality theory. However, people I know, who have tried TA as therapy, have often found that it seems to work. My students also often find that TA offers plausible explanations of interpersonal communication, especially of communication breakdowns and find it particularly useful in analyzing interactions involved in the development of their practical work. Around the late 1950's, Eric Berne began to develop his theories of Transactional Analysis. He said that verbal communication, particularly face-to-face, is at when two people encounter each other; one of them speaks to the other. This he called the transaction stimulus. The reaction from the other person he called the transaction response.

The person sending the stimulus is called the agent. The person who responds is called the respondent. Transactional analysis becomes the method of examining the transaction wherein "I do something to you, and you do something back".

Berne also says that each person is made up of three alter ego statics: parent, adult and child.

In a 'transaction' (an interaction with one or more people), one of the other of these ego states will predominate us as well as other people in the transaction. Particular communicative behaviours are associated with each of these ego states, but it is important to understand that they are not necessarily associated with chronological stages of psychological development. An adult can exhibit child-like communicative behaviour and a child can exhibit adult-like behaviour. The complete personality diagram of any human being encompasses everything he may feel, think, say or do.

2.6 COMPONENTS OF EGO STATES

If we examine peoples' personality more closely, we do not discover more ego states, but we may discover components of those ego states. Berne accepts that the parental ego state proves to be composed of two states, one deriving from the mother and the other from the father. Father, within the child ego state we will find parent, adult and child states. It is important to realize that, although we will be looking at each of these ego states in turn, there is no implication that we would use only one in a transaction. It is quite likely that we will move from one to the other, since we all have these three ego states as part of our personality.

Transactional Analysis is one of the most commonly studied theories of modern psychology. The transaction between two groups is always a necessity. Whether a person is in business, a parent, a social worker or runs a fast food stall, Eric Berne's very interesting theory will enrich ones dealings with people and understanding of oneself. Throughout history and from all standpoints—philosophy, medical science, religion—people have believed that each man and woman has a multiple nature.

2.7 TRANSACTIONAL ANALYSIS: THE THEORETICAL BACKGROUND

In the early twentieth century, Sigmund Freud first established that the human psyche is multi-faceted and that each of us has warring factions in our subconscious. Many theories have come up in the last century. New theories are continuously being put forward, all concentrating on the essential conviction that each one of us has unique parts of our personality which surface and affect our behaviour according to different circumstances.

In 1951, Dr. Wilder Penfield began a series of scientific experiments. He concluded that the human brain acts like a tape recorder and whilst we may 'forget' experiences, the brain still gets them recorded, along with events the brain also records the associated feeling, and both feelings and events study locked together.

It is possible for a person to exist in two states simultaneously (because persons replying hidden events and feelings could talk about them objectively at the same time). Hidden experiences when replying are vivid, and affect how we feel at the time of replying. There is a certain connection between mind and body i.e., the link between the biological and the psychological, e.g., a psychological fear of a spider and a biological feeling of nausea.

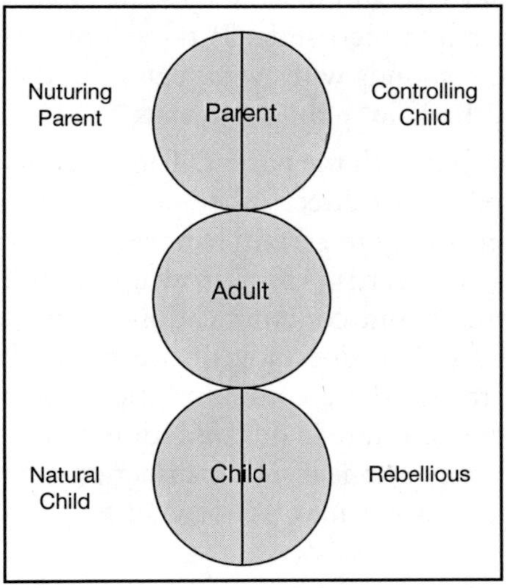

2.8 PARENT

This is our voice of authority, absorbed conditioning, learning and attitude from when we are young. We are conditioned by our parents, teachers, elders, next door neighbours, aunts and uncles. Our parent ego state is made up of a huge number of hidden and overt recorded playbacks typically embodied by phrases and attitudes starting with 'how to', 'under no circumstances', 'always', 'never forget', 'don't lie, cheat, steal', etc. Our parent ego is formed by external events and influences as we grow through early childhood. We can change it, but doing so is not easy. These are the physical expressions of parent ego state—angry or impatient body language and expressions, finger pointing, patronizing gestures. The verbal communication will include—'always', 'never', 'once and for all', judgemental words, critical words, patronizing language.

Parent Characteristics

The first ego state is the parent ego state in which the person who is communicating is passing on the instruction just as a father who tells his children to do and not to do something.

The parent ego state is the mode of communication when the sender is communicating with a command and instruction. A person when saying, 'you must keep your table near and clean' is talking in a parent ego state. If the person who is receiving the instruction responds with 'what can I do, the office sweeper is always late,' he is in a child ego state.

We are familiar with the parent. The parent is a status figure who has the power to direct other persons' lives by means of demanding conformity to certain behavioural norms, reinforced with sanctions or rewards. As we grow up, we learn our parents' behaviour patterns and communication styles, and then apply them to ourselves. This does not, of course, imply that we have to be parents to use these communication styles. A child may adopt the parent ego state in a transaction with its toys or other people, a man may adopt it in a transaction with his girlfriend and, naturally, a parent may adopt it in a transaction with his own child.

The Nurturing Parent and Controlling Parent

Berne distinguishes between the nurturing (or natural) parent and the controlling parent. Essentially, the nurturing parent's characteristics are quite positive, but can be overbearing and limiting. The Nurturing Parent is concerned with his child's welfare. So he rewards, protects and cares for the child and tries to pass on good moral standards—'always be on time', 'save your money', 'work hard' are some of the typical examples given by Berne. The Nurturing parent can help the child feel okay about his relationships, but can also be overprotective, smothering the child's development.

The controlling parent is a different type of parent, who wants to command, instruct and pass judgements. This parent is strict and judgements before the behaviour, and sees to it that the child should succeed on the parent's terms.

Communications Behaviour

The nurturing parent is likely to use comforting phrases, such as 'don't worry, it will be okay' or 'let me see if I can help you with that,' as well as offering frequent praise. The controlling parent will offer quite a number of orders, which, if necessary will be justified by appeal to some kind of moral criteria or principles of behaviour which appear to have some kind of absolute value. This verbal behaviour will of course be paralleled by appropriate non-verbal behaviour: encouraging gestures, indulgent smiles in the case of the nurturing parent, hostile glares and fixed stares in the case of the controlling parent.

Example: Bosses are generally a typical example of parent ego state. At times he may assure that a hard working executive is 'a highly valued member of the team'. But when the same boss is confronted with the open hostility of the worker's union, he may tell them they would not receive a pay-rise again. He may invite an unhappy worker as union representative, who has refused to accept the worker for spoiling the working environment of the office. He can use abusive words to bully some unfortunate individual. Bosses generally are in a parent state, whether nurturing or controlling.

2.9 CHILD

Our internal reactions and feelings to external events form the 'child'. This is the seeing, hearing, feeling, and emotional body of data within each of us. When anger or despair dominate reason, the child is in control. Like our parent we can change it, but it is not easy. These are the physical expressions of child ego state—sad expressions, despair, temper tantrums, whining voice, rolling eyes, shrugging shoulders, teasing, delight, laughter, speaking behind hand, raising hand to speak, squirming and giggling. The verbal expressions are baby talk—'I wish', 'I don't care', 'oh no', 'not again, things never go right for me', 'worst day of my life', 'bigger', 'biggest', 'best', and many superlatives to impress.

2.10 ADULT

'Adult' is the most sensible ego state. It is the ability to think and determine action for ourselves based on received data. The adult in us begins to form at around ten months old, and is the means by which we keep our parent and child under control. These are the physical expressions of adult ego state—attentive, interested, straightforward, tilted head, non-threatening and non-threatened. The verbal expressions of adult ego state are: 'why', 'what', 'how', 'who', 'where', 'when', 'how much', 'in what way', comparative expressions, reasoned statements, true, 'probably', 'possibly', 'I think', 'I realise', 'I see', 'I believe', 'in my opinion'.

2.11 EFFECTIVENESS OF TRANSACTION

There are several modes of transaction, but the best is one that is complementary. If the two transacting persons are complementing the ego state, the communication will progress in the right direction otherwise it will end in a statement. There is no general rule as to the effectiveness of any ego state in any given situation. Some people get results by being dictatorial (parent to child), or by throwing temper tantrums (child to parent), but for a balanced approach to life, Adult to Adult is generally recommended.

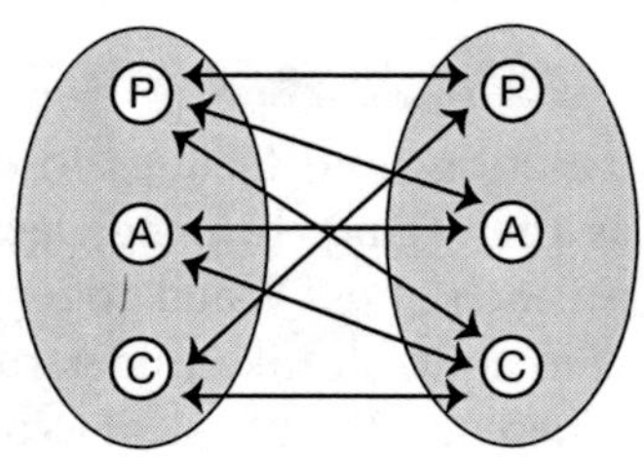

Fig. 2.2: Transaction between two groups of persons

Transactional Analysis is effectively a language within a language of true meaning, feeling and motive. It can help you in every situation, firstly through being able to understand more clearly what is going on, and secondly, by virtue of this knowledge, we give ourselves choices of what ego states to adopt, which signals to send, and where to send them, that enables us to make the most of all our communications and therefore create, develop and maintain better relationships.

The most sensible and nice way of communication is when there is communication between two persons in the adult ego state. The communication between two groups of persons in a business meeting is a communication between two adult ego states.

Fig. 2.2 shows a transaction between two groups of persons. It depicts different modes of transaction (exchange) between the sender and receiver.

1. If the transaction is between P and P that is between two persons only trying to command and dominate, then there shall in all possibility be a communication full of harsh talk and chances of confrontation are very high. Examples of such communication are the debates in a court-room where both lawyers are arguing to score points over the other. In our day-to-day life such a transaction is not a welcome state.
2. The transaction between P and A is a very common in office environment where there is one boss and few subordinate, the boss will pass on the instructions to the subordinates, who in turn will follow that.
3. The transaction between A and A is a very sensible way of communicating. Both the groups are receptive to each other and talk logically. Such transaction can result in an effective and fruitful communication. Example of such communication can be between two diplomats negotiating an international issue of common concern.
4. The other transaction, which is very ineffective and one we need to avoid, is the transaction between C and C ego states. In such a transaction, the response as well as the original communication is irresponsible. The person who is sending such communication is communication between two drunk persons in a bar. They start a conversation with, 'this world is very funny and all the persons in the city are jokers'. At this the response from the other person is 'God is not kind to human being and has created this city to make fun of his own creation'.

The other kind of transaction is between P to C, a person is instructing but the person receiving it does not take it in the right spirit. A boss comes and says, 'we must adhere to the deadlines'. Hearing this the subordinate says, 'sir, you always pressurize us with impractical deadlines'.

If we are to change our parent or child we must do so through our adult. In other words: P is our 'taught' concept of life, A is our 'thought' concept of life, C is our 'felt' concept of life.

When we communicate we are doing so form one of our own alter ego states, parent, adult or child. Our feelings at the time determine which one we use, and at any time something can trigger a shift from one state to another. When we respond, we are also doing this from one of the three states, and it is in the analysis of these stimuli and responses that the essence of transactional analysis lies.

At the core of Berne's theory is the role that effective transactions (i.e. successful communication) must be complementary. They must go back from the receiving ego state to the sending ego state. For example, if the stimulus is parent to child, the response must be child to parent, if the transaction is 'crossed', there will be a problem between sender and receiver. If a crossed transaction occurs, there is ineffective communication. Worse still, either or both parties will be upset. For the relationship to continue smoothly agent or the respondent must rescue the situation with a complementary transaction. In serious breakdowns, there is no chance of immediately resuming a discussion about the original subject matter. Attention is focused on the relationship. The discussion can only continue constructively when and if the relationship is mended.

When we are trying to identify ego states, words are only part of the story. To analyse a transaction you need to see and feel what is being said as well.

1. 7 per cent of meaning is in the words spoken.
2. 38 per cent of meaning is paralinguistic (the way that the words are said).
3. 55 per cent is in the facial expression.

2.12 SHARPEN YOUR INTERPERSONAL SKILLS

It may be very easy to mould your action because it is very much in your control, but a person who can have positive influence on others is the one having interpersonal relationship skills. There are few basic methods of influencing others.

We all are a subset of the larger set in society, which has several individuals with different tastes, likes and their own identity. We all want to have a positive influence on other people in our personal and professional lives. We do this with the motive of forming new business ties, keeping customers, maintaining friendships, changing behaviour, improving marriage and family relationships. But it is certainly essential for all of us to maintain and nourish this important relationship.

There are some easy ways we can do it. We may like to influence the lives of other people and do it powerfully and ethically. If we categorise, we may arrive at three basic categorises of influence:

1. **Model by Example (Others see):** We are highly influenced by the public faces in society. The cinema artist and sports personality has always been a role model for the younger generation. This is how a leader should influence the others.
2. **Build Caring Relationships (Others feel):** This is an emotional bonding and the person is highly influenced by what he feels. This is very useful for persons who are sensitive to their emotional needs.
3. **Mentor by Instruction (Other hear):** Many a time we may not see a person, but still the person can have a positive influence on us by hearing from some other source.

The following methods of influence fall under the above mentioned three categories:

2.12.1 Never Talk Negative and Unkind Words

We do talk negative and harsh when we are frustrated, tired and fed up with our own problems. We must refrain from saying unkind or negative words, particularly when we are provoked or fatigued. In these circumstances, not to say unkind or critical things is a supreme form of self-mastery. Courage is quality at its highest testing point. If we have no model of restraint to follow, we will take out our frustration on our fellow workers. We may need to find new models, new examples to follow, and learn to win our battles privately, to get out motives straight, to gain perspective and control, and to back away from impulsively speaking or striking out.

2.12.2 Do not Allow Personal Ego to Dictate Relationships

We may not be happy with the performance of an individual but that should not affect the relationship. We must distinguish between the person and the behaviour or performance. While we may disapprove of bad behaviour and poor performance, we first need to communicate and help build a sense of intrinsic worth and self-esteem totally apart from comparisons and judgements. Doing this will powerfully inspire superior effort. The power to distinguish between person and performance and to communicate intrinsic worth flows naturally out of our own sense of intrinsic worth.

2.12.3 Exercise Patience with Others

In times of stress, our impatience surfaces. We may say things we do not really mean or instead to say. Or we may become sullen, communicating through emotion and attitude, rather than words, eloquent massages of criticism, judgement and rejection. We then harvest hurt feelings and strained relationships. Patience is the practical expression of faith, hope, wisdom and love. It is a very active emotion. It is not indifference, sullen endurance or resignation, patience is emotional diligence. We nurture any relationship with great care and if we do not have patience we have lose the same.

2.12.4 Never Advertise the Good You Do to Others

We should perform anonymous service. If we are doing some good for others anonymously, our sense of intrinsic worth and self-respect increase. We must do it without expectation of publicity or reward. Selfless service has always been one of the most powerful methods of influence.

2.12.5 Promises Made to Others are to be Kept

We must know that when we say something it is like a contract we have with the person. It is generally a termination in relationship if we have not kept it. If you cannot keep it do not commit it. By making and keeping our promises, we win friends. It is good to make promises (resolutions, commitments, oaths and covenants), but never make a promise you will not keep.

2.12.6 Focus on the Circle of Influence

There are some things which are well within our control and there are a few not in our control. We need to increase our area of influence by focusing on the requirement of others. As we focus on doing something positive about the things we can control, we expand our circle of influence.

Changing our habits of doing and thinking solves direct control problems. Indirect control problems require us to change our methods of influence. For instance, we complain from time to time, 'if only the boss could understand my problem'. But few of us take the time to prepare the kind of presentation that the boss would listen to and respect, in his language, with his problems in kind. With no control problems, we can control our reaction to them, deciding with. With no control problems, we can control our reaction to them, deciding within ourselves how anything or anybody will affect us. As William James said: "We can change our circumstances by a mere change of our attitude."

2.13 THE IMPORTANCE OF CARING IN A RELATIONSHIP

Faith is the foundation of a relationship. We must treat all people around as faithful and never doubt their intentions. There are chances that ninety-five per cent of the people around us are faithful and only a very few of them are unfaithful. Just think, should the five per cent of unfaithful persons guide your behaviour towards the ninety-five per cent faithful? we must assume that good faith produces good fruit. If we think that others want and mean to do their best, as they say it, we can expect and bring out the best in them. Our efforts to classify, categorise, judge and measure, often emerge from our own insecurities and frustrations in dealing with complex, changing realities, each person has many dimensions and different potential, some evident, most dormant, and they tend to respond to how we treat them and what we believe about them. Some may let us down or take advantage of our trust, considering us naive or gullible, but most will come through, simply because we believe in them. Whenever we assume good faith, born of good motives and inner security, we appeal to the good in others.

Goethe said: "Treat a man as he is, and he will remain as he is. Treat a man as he can and should be, and he will become as he can and should be."

Example: There were only a few cricketers in the world who were engaged in match fixing, but when the allegations started coming it was free for all. The doubts in the mind were enough to spoil the gentlemen image of the popular game of cricket.

Try to understand others first. We have our own preconceived notions about most things. We behave according to these notions. Seek first to understand, then to be understood. When we are communicating with another, we need to give full attention, to be completely present. Then we need to empathise and walk in his moccasins (shoes) for a while. This takes a courage and patience. But until people feel that you understand them, they will not be open to your influence.

Example: Anil went to a public bank to get a demand draft for his son in some other city. He got it after three hours, and was furious with the service. He used foul language at the front desk official for not putting a 'only A/C payee' stamp on it. The person was facing a similar hostile long queue since morning as it was a pay day for a local factory. The other help desk personnel was on sudden casual leave and it was a tough day for the bank personnel. Unwanted fight could have easily been avoided had Anil understood the agony of the bank employee.

Encourage openness, honest, expressions. We expect others to be transparent, honest and faithful. These qualities can help a relationship be strong and everlasting. Too often we punish honest, open expressions or questions. We upbraid, judge, belittle, and embarrass people. Others learn to cover up, to protect themselves, and not to ask. The greatest single barrier to rich, honest communication is the tendency to criticize and judge. We are required to give an understanding response. By using the understanding response (reflecting feeling), three good things happen:

1. You gain increased understanding and clarity of feelings and problems,
2. You gain new courage and growth, and
3. You build real confidence in the relationship.

This response has its greatest value when a person wants to talk about a situation laden with emotions and feelings. But note that this response is more of an attitude than a technique. It will fail if you are trying to manipulate another. It will work if you deeply want to understand.

Example: The principal of Jadavpur University called all the second year mechanical students for banking second half class to see a football match between the favourite teams in Kolkata. The class representative Sunil was honest enough to tell the principal the truth, and they apologized for their behaviour but the principal fined all the students. Was the open expression is well rewarded?

Try to repair a relationship, apologise. Try and show genuine effort to repair a strained relationship. If you are offended, take the initiative. If someone offends you unknowingly and continues to do so, take the initiative to clear it up. Consider two tragic consequences of not taking the initiative: first, the offended one often broods about the offence until the situation is blown out of proportion; and second, we then behave defensively to avoid being hurt further. When taking the initiative, do it in good spirit, not in a spirit of vindication and anger. Also, describe your feelings when and how you were offended rather than judging or labeling the other person. This preserves the dignity and self-respect of the other, who then can respond and learn without feeling threatened. All that is needed from your side is to admit your mistake, apologise and ask for forgiveness.

Example: Many marital relationship get strained to the extent of divorce because both partners do not want to repair the hurt feeling. If you said something in a fit of anger, come forward and sincerely apologise. Soothing the hurt feeling can reduce tension between enemy countries; it can certainly help the fighting couple build an amicable relationship.

There is no use of arguments. Generally we want to defend our ego by arguing for the sake of argument Dale Carnegic has very correctly said that in an argument you are a loser if you win the argument, as you have lost a good friend, and if you lose the argument you are a loser anyway. We must never argue for anything, a polite way of expressing your feelings is more than sufficient than trying to win an argument. Covey has said, 'let argument fly out open windows'. Give no answer to contentious arguments or irresponsible accusations. Let such things 'fly out open windows' until they spend themselves. If you try to answer or reason, you only serve to gratify and ignite pent-up hostility and anger. When you go quietly about your business, the other person has to struggle with the nature consequences of irresponsible expression. Do not be drawn into any poisonous, contentions orbit, or you will find yourself bitten and afflicted similarly.

Do not expect the other person to change. By no means can we change any person as we want him or her to be. God has made us with some unique qualities. If we want a person to change as we think it will be good for our relationship, we are doing a business exchange rather than relationship building. Such a conditional relationship will never last long. Covey said, accept the person and the situation. The first step in changing or improving another is to accept him as he is. Nothing reinforces defensive behaviour more than judgement, comparison or rejection. A feeling of acceptance and worth frees a person from the need to defend and help release the natural growth tendency to improve. Acceptance is not condoning a weakness or agreeing with an opinion. Rather, it is affirming the intrinsic worth of another by acknowledging that he does feel or think a particular way.

2.14 THE RULES FOR PASSING INSTRUCTIONS

1. **Before you start speaking, words and actions must be well prepared.** What we say, may be less important than how we say it. Before we speak anything harsh we must rethink. When a child returns from school full of its own needs, stop and get control on what you need to say to him. Choose pleasantness and cheerfulness. We need to give full attention to his needs. Doing something good for others, even in your family, can change the environment of the whole house. Choosing to be your best self will arrest fatigue and renew your best resolves.

   Example: Rudra came back from school with his results for class ten. His father has always expected him to score more than 80 per cent in his exams. The results were not to the expectations of his father. Rudra was upset and hesitant to tell his father that he could score only 68 per cent as his marks in literature were not good. But he scored 98 per cent in his science subjects. At the dinner table Rudra's father was critical of his performance. He called him worthless and never thought to say a few encouraging words for his good performance in the science subjects.

2. **We must try to resolve the differences.** If we are powerful, generally we try to sort out the differences by saying harsh words and trying to dominate that other person. Bulldozing others with rude words in the most common way to settle a difference. But if you are weak you will try to avoid the unpleasant situation. Covey said, "many people either fight or flight when they disagree. Fighting takes many forms, running from violence and open expressions of anger and hate to subtle sarcasm, sharp answers, clever comeback, belittling humour, judgements and reactions."

Example: In a worker's union meeting the issue of a proposed strike by the union to put forward the demands of the workers was being discussed. Mohan, a new employee did not want to participate in the strike. He was avoiding the situation and did not attend the meeting. On the strike day he tried to attend the factory. The union leaders did not take it lightly and threatened him with dire consequences. Mohan did not say anything, but he had an urge for revenge to his insult. All this could have been avoided had he gone to the leaders with a proposal and his problems of participating in the strike.

3. **Do not protect people for their actions.** Every person likes to see what he has done. It gives him or her sense of some achievement even it is not to his choice. If you want a dignified relationship, it is unkind to shield people from the consequences of their behaviour. In doing so, we teach them that they are inadequate and weak. This is generally to show that we love and care for them, but in fact it will give them a sense of unfulfilled desire to face the result of their action. A mother is very caring for her child and would like to protect her baby from all the bad things in this would. But have you ever thought that not allowing her to face the pain of falling on the ground may defer her learning process. In the process she is also doing, more harm than, good.

   Example: At a family gathering an uncle who has just returned from London, asked his nephew Rohit about his performance in the school final exam. As soon as the question was put up and even before Rohit could frame an answer, Rohit's mother replied that he got star marks in all the papers and he could still have done better had he gone for his coaching to a better institute. The fact was that Rohit could get marks just sufficient for first class. Rohit was not ashamed of his performance but his mother's blatant lie belittled his achievement and he was feeling ashamed of what he could have achieved.

4. **Be there at the crossroads.** None of us want the people we care most about, to make decisions that have important long-range consequences on the basis of short-range emotional perspectives and moods, personal insecurity and self-doubt. How can we influence them? First, think before you act. Do not be controlled by your own short-range emotional moods and by doing something that injures whatever relationship and influence you have. Second, understand that people tend to act in terms of how they feel instead of what they know. Motivation is more a function of the heart than the head. When we sense that our language of reason and logic is not communicating with their language of sentiment and emotion, we should try to understand their language as we would a foreign tongue, without condemning or rejecting them. This effort communicates respect and acceptance, lowers defenses, diminishes the need to fight, and restores the desire to do what is right.
5. **Speak the languages of logic and emotion.** The language of logic and the language of emotion are as different as English and French. When we realize that we do not have a common language, we need to communicate in one of the four other ways:
   (a) Give time, for when we cheerfully give time, we transfer its worth to another;
   (b) Be patient, as patience also communicates worth and says, I'll go at your speed; I'm happy to wait for you; you're worth it;
   (c) Seek to understand, because an honest effort to understand eliminates the need to fight and to defend; and
   (d) Openly express your feelings and be congruent with your non-verbal expressions.
6. **Delegate effectively.** Effective delegation takes emotional courage as we allow, to one degree or

another, others to make mistakes on our time, money and good name. This courage consists of patience, self-control, faith in the potential of other, and respect four individual differences. Effective delegation must be two-way: responsibility is given, responsibility is received. There are three phases. First in the initial agreement. People have a clear understanding of what is expected and what the resources, authority, latitude and guidelines are. Second, sustaining the delegates. The supervisor becomes a source of help, the advocate, and not the feared adversary. He provides resources, removes obstacles, sustain actions and decision, gives vision, provides training, and shares feedback. Third, is the accountability process. It is largely one of self-evaluation, since delegates are supervised by results and actual performance.

7. **Involve people in meaningful projects.** Meaningful projects have a healing influence on people. However, what is meaningful to a manager may be meaningless to a subordinate. Projects take on meaning when people are involved in the planning and thinking processes. We all need to be engaged in a good cause. Without such projects, life loses its meaning; in fact, the life span is short for people who retire, looking for a tensionless state. Life is sustained by tension between where we are now and where we want to be.
8. **We reap what we sow.** If we make people understand that as nature will give them what they sow, in our life we will get the rewards of what action we have taken to give shape to our future. We must train all the people the law of harvest. We teach the 'agricultural principles' of preparing the soil, seeding, cultivating, watering, weeding, and harvesting. We focus on natural processes. We align the system, especially compensation, to reflect and reinforce this idea.
9. **Let natural consequences teach responsible behaviour.** One of the kindest things we can do is to let the natural or logical consequences teach responsible behaviour.

They may like it or not, but popularity is a fickle standard by which can measure character development. We care enough for their growth and security and suffer for their displeasure.

10. **The relationship fails because** overcoming the generally committed mistakes is essential for any relationship to grow. In our attempts to influence others, we commonly make mistakes.

Blunder 1: Understand Before Advise: We generally rush to advise and instruct others for what we feel is right. The advice will have an impact only if there is some sort of confidence and proper understanding. In issuing such advice we first need to establish an understand relationship. Unless we understand the unique situation and feeling of the other person, we will not know how to advise or counsel him. The cure is very simple and it is to show empathy (not sympathy). We need to understand, than to be understood.

Blunder 2: Do not Expect Others to Change: The relationship cannot last long if it is based on conditions and if we expect others to change for us. Attempt to build/rebuild relationship without changing conduct or attitude. As Emerson so aptly put it, "what you are shouts so loudly in my ears I can't hear what you say". Cure: show consistency and sincerity.

Blunder 3: Assume that Good Example and Relationship is Sufficient: We assume that a good example and a good relationship are sufficient, that we do not need to explicitly teach people. Just as vision without love contains no motivation, so also love without vision contains no goals, no guidelines, no standards, and no lifting power. Cure: teach and talk about vision, mission, roles, goals, guidelines and standards.

Questions

1. What do you mean interpersonal relationship?
2. Explain the determinants of interpersonal relationship.
3. Explain interpersonal communication, theories and concepts of the behaviour of a person to others.

4. Explain the different ways in which the Johari Window Analysis of a relationship can help us to improve interpersonal relationship.
5. Explain the definition of Transactional Analysis.
6. Explain components of ego states.
7. Write a short note on communication behaviour.
8. What are interpersonal skills?
9. Explain the importance of caring in a relationship.

3
Positive Attitude Towards Life

3.1 INTRODUCTION

Attitude is defined as "the way a person feels, thinks and behaves towards a particular issue." In the modern management theory behavioural scientists have defined it as the 'mental-box', which helps to show a person a particular situation in a specific frame of mind.

Example: A thirsty person visit your house and you offer him a glass half-filled with water. If he has a positive attitude he will see the glass as half-filled, but if he is a person with a negative attitude, he will see it as half empty.

Can you answer a very simple question that why only a few people out of millions succeed? The answer is simple—the winner is one who has a positive attitude, self-belief and the determination to succeed. If you priorityse, the single most important factor which is the cause of success and failure is your attitude towards what you are doing.

"You may be disappointed if you fail, but you are doomed if you don't try."

—*Beverly Hills*, American Star

Let us think in this way. The most competent striker of soccer, Ronaldo, is at the goalmouth of the opponent team. Has tackled several of the defenders and has only the goalkeeper to beat. What is that which may convert his effort to either a goal or a miss? If he is positive in attitude and is confident in his effort he will hit the ball at the right spot. Your behaviour reflects how you think, if you have a positive attitude you will think positive and the small and petty issues will not perturb you in attaining your goals.

"Do what you can, with what you have, where you are."

—*Theodore Roosevelt*

"If you don't like something, change it.

If you can't change it, change your attitude. Don't complain."

"Genius is one percent inspiration and ninety-nine per cent perspiration."

—*Thomas Alva Edison*

Man is very similar to a complete computer system and all the organs are like the different hardware which when assembled properly will account for the total system. The system can work to the desired effect only if we have a coordinated approach. The work and social environment has a great role to play in the way we think and perform.

A positive attitude and will to concentrate on the work can help you achieve great heights.

"When pain ends, gain ends too."

—*Robert Browning*

The positive thinker does not see setbacks as stumbling blocks, rather as stepping-stones. The art of dealing with a fall is not to think how much it hurts but to know the reason for the fall and how to avoid it in the next attempt.

The next question that people ask is whether people are born with a positive attitude or is it developed over time? If we develop it, what are the factors which account for positive attitude? The attitude of a person generally takes shape in the formative stages of life. The way we see the environment around us—our family, school, society, media television, political, religious and cultural backgrounds of the country, all have its share of impact during the formation stage. Can we not justify the hardworking and sincere attitude of the Japanese as a work culture consequent to their destruction in the Second World War?

If the environment of the person is so important to develop the attitude, let us review the environment we are in. It is very difficult to think positive in an environment of negative people and culture. In a destructive, barbaric and inhuman Taliban regime, can you expect someone to think positive in advancing the nation towards growth and prosperity? We must plan to leave such a negative environment for the sake of preserving and shaping positive thoughts.

"One machine can do the work of 50 ordinary men. No machine can do the work of the motivated extraordinary man."

—An unknown wise man

What are the personality traits of people with positive attitude, and how to recognize people with positive attitude? It is very easy; they are humble, caring, confident and patient, they are raring to perform, the expectation level of such people is very high, a person of such traits is welcome in all situations, conditions and environment. He changes the scenario wherever he goes and in the grimmest of the situation he can laugh, as he knows the tragedy has already occurred and the future is always better, there are several great advantage of becoming a positive thinker, it enhances productivity, it encourages teamwork, the working environment improves, it helps in improving quality of work as well as relationship, the positive attitude also helps to reduce tension, stress, fosters trust and finally the positive thinker is a pleasing personality. Negative thoughts in our mind give rise to animosity, if healthy, bitterness and resentment. The negative spoils not only himself but also the entire environment. In the life of a negative thinker, all important relationship are at stake.

If we know that negative attitude is so bad for all of us then why are we not changing our attitude! The answer is very simple. We as a part of nature always try to resist change. Any change, whether it is good or bad, is not acceptable to us. The first thing we try is to return to our natural state, of which we are habituated.

"No one can persuade another to change, each of us guards a gate of change that can only be opened from the inside. We can't open the gate of other person either by argument or by emotional appeal."

—*Marilyn Ferguson*

The persons who are negative thinkers always try to find fault with others and the system. These critics are always there to see the negative side of the story. When the health is food they would like to find out what will happen if they become sick, when they are well-off they would try to visualize themselves as if they do not have anything. They are sadists and spend their whole life complaining and screaming at others.

I remember one incident in one office when one of our senior executives Mr. Ramanathan bought a car of the latest model from the market. The looks were great and so were its features. Mr. Ramanathan invited all of us for a ride. The car had extraordinary pic-up and speed. After a fantastic drive we returned to our office. Finally, Mr. Ramanathan asked my friend Mr. Bose how he found the car. We knew that Bose was a great critic who could hardly find anything praiseworthy. He said the car could hardly cross the speed limit of 160 Kmph. We were bemused, for we all know roads in Kolkata can hardly afford a speed of 50 Kmph.

The person who has a positive attitude will remain a positive thinker even if he is protesting against something. It is a state of mind. It will reflect in all his actions. A person cannot be a positive thinker on a few issues and behave negatively on others.

3.2 KILL NEGATIVE THOUGHTS

In every person's life there are periods when negative thoughts come to mind. The fear of failing and not doing well is one such thought. It is important to overcome these negative thoughts. There are many ways these negative thoughts are away from our minds. The worry-breaking formula can be listed below:

1. Stop worrying wherever you are surrounded by worries, start thinking about something good and positive. Either positive or negative can stay in your mind at one point of time.
2. Never participate in worrying conversations. It will always affect you. Try to avoid such groups, talk positive and take initiative in talking positive. There are people who are always worried and blame the system failures. Have you not heard stories from such negatives talkers that law and order is poor, there is corruption in high places, the education system is pathetic, the government is not giving due attention to health and public welfare. In the morning newspaper they search for stories of gloom anywhere in the world and, enjoy sharing it with the 'gloom club'.
3. Help others to come out of their worry habits. It will give you confidence to think positive.
4. Convince yourself that the whole world will be with you to support you. The belief in god will give you immense strength to realize that when the Energy, which created you, is with you, you are not alone.

3.3 HOW TO THINK POSITIVE

Believe in Yourself: Have faith in your abilities. Without reasonable confidence in your own powers you cannot be successful or happy.

A Peaceful Mind Generates Power: A mind full of peace is what we would all like to attain in our life and this is the basic requirement of a positive and fruitful attitude in our life. The other cryptic phrase to be avoided is, 'an ear full of trouble'. Life will be difficult and full of negative feelings if we allow negative feelings to rule our mind. We must generate the energy we need for performing well to form a successful personality.

Stop Fuming and Fretting: Negative feelings start with anger. We show these feelings with expressions such as fuming and fretting. There are many people who try to gain any opportunity to short at someone who is weak. Shouting and fuming generate negative energy and negative feeling. Practice self-restraint in shouting at someone else's fault. This will be the beginning for you to start thinking positive.

Hope for the Best: We can change our negative attitude towards life if we expect that we have seen the worst days of our life and better days are coming.

Inflow of New Thoughts can Remake You: Change is what makes life charming. The new thoughts can give us fresh energy to our mind to bring positive thoughts for doing something constructive. We must always encourage fresh and new ideas.

Healing Touch of Positive Thinking: It is proved by medical science that a patient who has the negative thoughts takes long time to recover from any critical illness. Positive thoughts also help our glands to secrete antibodies and help us recover soon from ailments. Thus, attitudes can kill you or can give you a life full of joy.

Example: If you recall the accident of the greatest film personality in India, Amitabh Bachchan, who was badly injured on the sets of a film in Bangalore. Nobody, including the doctors, had the faith that he would survive the fatal injuries inside his stomach. But strong will and positive thoughts miraculously cured Amitabh. The strong positive thoughts combined with prayers worked well for him.

Focus on Your Strength: Each and every one of us is born with some unique qualities. Some have memory, others have muscle, some have artistic flavor in whatever they do, some are tall, some are small but swift, some are beautiful and others may be having the best voice. It is we who do not recognize their strengths at an early age and cultivate it to great heights. But such successful people are not many; losers keep on counting their limitations and curse their surroundings. Like a management consultant who undertakes the SWOT (strength, weakness, opportunity and threat) analysis for the company, each one of us at regular intervals of time, should try to find out the weaknesses we have and work in the areas of our strength. If Sachin Tendulkar is the greatest cricketer in the world, the reason is that, in spite of his short height, he could identify at an early age his artistic touch and the power he had in his wrist. He recognized his strength, fine-turned it with hard work and dedication and the result is clear to the world.

We need to see what the great personalities have to say about the traits which can lead you to victory in life. The elements of self-confidence, strong will and determination have always superseded other individual capabilities when it comes to the situation of win or loose in life.

> "If you don't have confidence, you will always find a way not to win."
>
> —*Carl Lewis*, Olympic Track Star

> "I don't know the key to success, but the key to failure is trying to pleasure everyone."
>
> —*Bill Cosby*, American Actor

CASE STUDY I

Anil Ramani, 28, was the son of Atmaram, a school teacher, in a small town near Delhi. He lived there with his wife and four children; he did not get sufficient wages to lead a comfortable life. But he raised his son to be an engineer from IIT, Delhi and also to complete his MBA from FMS, Delhi. The whole family was pinning their hopes on a change in their fortune with Anil's success as a young marketing executive in a MNC film in Gurgaon, the young Anil had a very simple lifestyle, he was always at the receiving end for this simple dressings sense, the young man was a bit shy and not comfortable with his peers from the opposite sex. He was not very comfortable with urban colloquial English though he was very good in the language. His problem was in verbal communication.

In his job he was to report to Mr. Chadha, Regional Manager. A not-so-well qualified person, but Mr. Chadha was a hi-flier as far as verbal communication was concerned. The two persons had totally different ways of looking at things. One was meticulous and systematic whereas the other was an impressive person at first sight. Chadha found him a misfit in the marketing job from day one. It was very difficult for Anil to prove himself in a situation where he was not allowed to work freely. There was a serious misunderstanding between the two. Chadha went to the VP, Marketing, and said he did not want Anil in his team. For Anil the job was important for the survival of his family.

Anil became arrogant and started misbehaving with his subordinates to vent out his frustration. He thought assertiveness could be expressed in anger. Slowly, his peers and subordinates started avoiding him. Now he is a dejected person under tremendous pressure to save his job.

Questions

1. Why do you think Anil failed?
2. Has he applied his relationship with the persons in the group properly?
3. State the reasons why Anil was not performing well.
4. How was the Manager's behaviour affecting the performance level?
5. What steps should Anil take for the transformation?

CASE STUDY II

Michael D'souza was the youngest of four sons and was a mill supervisor in a small suburban town of Mumbai. He did excellently in school level athletics. But his father was always concerned for his performance in academics and was worried that in case he does not perform well in class it will be difficult for him to find a suitable job for his career. One day Michael come overjoyed with the news that he had been selected as a sprint runner to represent the zonal school team. He was expecting his parents also to encourage him with appreciation. But to his surprise his father was not at all happy with the news. He was worried that he would miss many important days of class.

D'souza did not dare to ask his father for the new sprint runner kit, which would cost two thousand rupees. The boy was sad now and was wandering if it was possible for him to attend the training camp. The unkind words from his father caused the low motivation level. But he had his strong determination to excel in this arena and finally achieve something great for his parents.

Without telling his father, he applied for a scholarship with the Tara-Foundation and practiced when he got time. After fifteen days he got a positive response from the academy. He discussed the prospect with his sports teacher and in spite of his father's unwillingness, joined the academy. The academy gave him opportunity to practice and learn the art of winning tough competition. The training by a national coach resulted in positive change in the stamina of young D'souza. He was shaping well for the forthcoming All India University Competition. In the competition D'souza was victorious and clocked a timing which was better than the national record, the record breaking timing drew the attention of the Sport Authority of India. The skill of D'souza got the recognition he wanted most. The Asian Track and Field event in Jakarta saw a new star in Michael.

Questions

1. Was overlooking his studies right on the part of Michael?
2. Was the strength of Michael identified correctly?
3. What contributed to the success of Michael the most, will power or attitude?
4. Was his parents' role in shaping his future right?

4

Motivation and Self-motivation

4.1 INTRODUCTION

The process of inducing and inspiring anyone to perform his or her functions more productively and efficiently is known as motivation. It is a catalyst that enhances the performance of an individual. If a person is motivated he will try to put his best effort and complete the task assigned to him. Whereas, a demotivated person may not be able to perform upto his potential and the job that he could have easily completed in a short span of time will take much longer to finish. In any context money acts as the prime motivating factor. This may be true for a person who does not have sufficient money to meet his basic needs, such as food, clothing and shelter. But once he has all his existential needs fulfilled, he may be motivated by some other factors.

Example: A government employee in a corporation office gets his salary on the very first day. As perks he also gets a comfortable life with job-security, but does he perform his duty when you approach him for a birth certificate. Which he is supposed to issue within a few hours? It takes him months to issue that. The reason is that he is not motivated to perform with speed.

When we ask someone to do a certain job, we must identify his motivating factor. Different persons have different motivational needs. Some are motivated by money, others by emotion, and still others by security and, at the same time, there are those who are motivated by recognition and self-esteem. We may be successful in inspiring someone if we can analyse the personal motivational needs of the person.

A person may not have the same motivational needs throughout his life; they change with the growth of the person, the same person at different stages of life has different needs, for a case study try and recall what was the motivating factor for you, three years, six years and nine years back. You will find that it does not remain the same at different stages of life. Some motivating factors are on high priority throughout the lives of successful people and they act as the driving force.

Amit's case study is shown to help you analyse the motivating factors at different ages in his life. Based on it we know that there are different motivating factors for different stages in our life, at the same time, different people are motivated by different motivating factors.

The great behavioural scientist Maslow has evolved the five stage motivational needs of a person. The lowest needs of a person are the physiological needs. He likes to:

- It is very easy to motivate a one-year-old baby Amit with a lovely toy.
- The five-year-old child Amit can be motivated with a chocolate.
- Twelve-year-old Amit has changed; he has different needs and can be motivated to perform well with a promise of a new cricket bat.
- Fifteen-year-old Amit is more fascinated by a new cycle. He is ready to do anything if he is promised a new cycle.
- Twenty-year-old Amit is keen to get a nice job and a lovely girlfriend to enjoy life.
- He is ready to do anything for his job.
- Thirty-year-old Amit is well employed, earns well and drives a car. His need is to marry a beautiful girl and gaining stability is his priority.

- At fifty Amit has achieved all he wanted and has earned enough. Now he is keen to get respect and recognition in his career. That is what inspires him most.

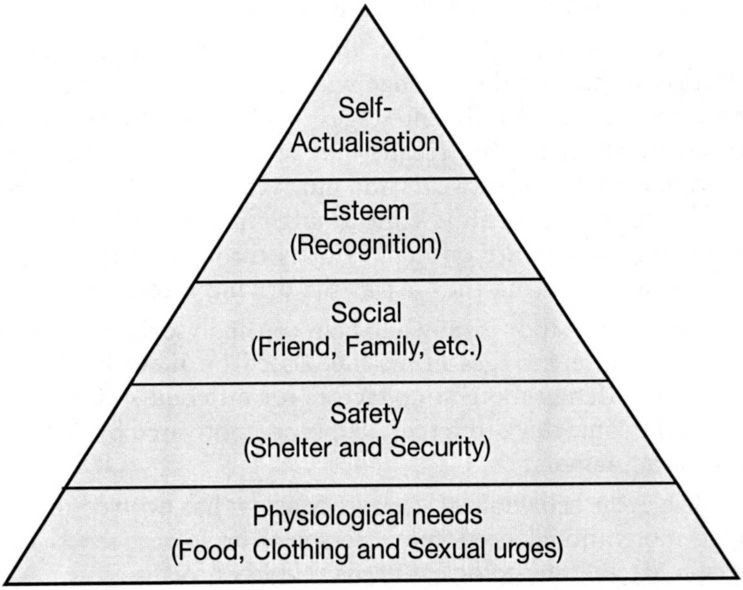

Fig. 4.1: Maslow's Hierarchy of motivational needs

Amit, the father, at his last stage in his life has his son's career highest on this priority list, meet his basic needs such as food, clothing etc. Herzberg, another famous behavioural scientist, further identified these basic needs. He called these basic human needs the hygiene factor, on the layer above the basic needs a person may look for other needs such as friendship and security, as he is confident of getting it, he may not find it motivating enough to perform better. He will look for other motivational needs such as a cordial family, but then he may like to have recognition in the society to which he belongs.

Most people are motivational by external factors and like to achieve greater and greater success with time. But the real achiever is one who inspires himself to achieve the targets that he has set.

4.1.1 Hygiene and Motivators

The great behavioural scientist, Herzberg, has identified the reason for non-performance of highly paid employees of a company. He says that job-satisfaction and motivation are the two dimensions that influence the productivity of an employee. Research shows that in spite of a very good salary, good working conditions, job-security, physical facilities, and good human relationships, the performance of employees is not up to the expected level. Factors such as recognition of work done, status, opportunity for growth, nature of work, responsibility and challenges of work have an integral role to play in motivating factors play an important role in helping people work more and better. There may be various ways of getting better motivation environment in the company, but the dimensions mentioned below help create conditions where the executives and workers can perform better.

1. Ensure that the executive's time and energy are not wasted on petty things.

   Example: In a metropolitan city, government officials are paid a poor salary and are not provided with any accommodation near the office. Conveyance is a problem as most of them travel from far off places. Therefore, their motivation level is low and that is reflected in the service they provide to the people.
2. **Climate of encouraging new ideas and thoughts.** Most Indian companies do not allow any new thoughts or ideas to surface. The ideas of the lower level and younger generation of executives, if given a chance, may prove to be beneficial to the company as well as highly motivating for the young executive. A team may be allowed to work independently till the time the need for the manager's intervention is felt.
3. **Encourage healthy competition and recognize good work.** It is true, companies that give due recognition to its talented executives for their extraordinary efforts do well. In government organizations, where career growth depends on the seniority of a person and the

performance and effort is not taken into consideration, the motivation level of personnel who work hard is not high graded up.

4. Show yourself as an example. If the leader himself is de-motivated he can never expect the team to be motivated. Example: If a general in the army accept defeat, he will present a poor example for other soldiers and the army is bound to lose.
5. Try to create an environment of approach and problem solving. There are many executives who do not want to face any problems, they would like to avoid anything irritating. This creates an atmosphere of mistrust and de-motivation. Whereas, executives who are willing to solve the problems of others as well as their own create an atmosphere where people will take on their responsibility.
6. Provide for the counseling and guidance of the workers under you. If you provide counseling to the workers under you when they need it, the motivation level will go up as the trust and faith on the management will increase with such a gesture. Managers who go out of their way to extend help during distress can get the support of workers when it is needed most.

4.2 OTHER MOTIVATION THEORIES

Vroom's Expectancy Theory: Victory Vroom has propounded the most widely accepted explanation of motivation. His theory is commonly known as the expectancy theory. It argues that the strength of a tendency to act in a specific way depends on the strength of an expectation that the act will be followed by a given outcome and on the attractiveness of that outcome to the individual. To make this simple, expectancy theory states that an employee can be motivated to perform better when there is a belief that better performance will lead to good performance appraisal and that this shall result in realization of personal goals in the form of some reward.

Therefore, an employee's motivation = Valence × Expectancy.

The theory focuses on three things: effects and performance relationship, performance and reward relationship, and rewards and personal goal relationship.

This leads us to the conclusion that

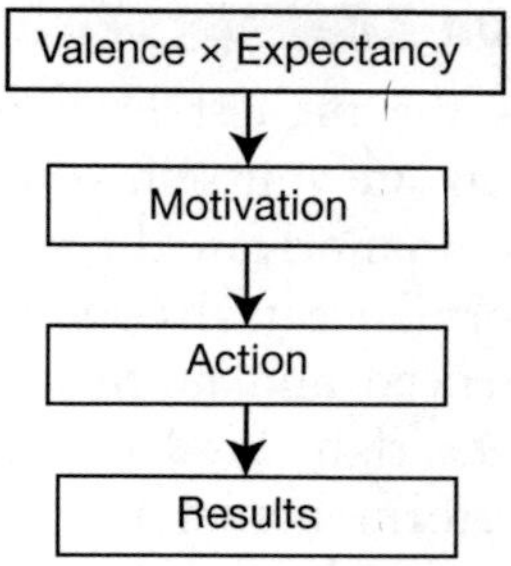

Porter and Lawler Model: Lyman W. Porter and Edward E. Lawler developed a more comprehensive version of motivation based upon the Expectancy theory.

Actual performance in a job is primarily determined by the effort spent. But it is also affected by the person's ability to do the job as also by his perception of what the required task is. So performance is the responsible factor that leads to intrinsic as well as extrinsic rewards. These rewards, along with the equity of the individual, lead to satisfaction. Hence, satisfaction of the individual depends upon the fairness of the reward.

Alderfer ERG Theory: Alderfer has tried to rebuild the hierarchy of needs of Maslow into another model naked ERG, i.e., Existence—Relatedness—Growth. According to him there are three groups of core needs as mentioned above. The existence group is concerned mainly with providing basic material existence. The second group is the individual's need to maintain interpersonal relationships with other members in the group. The final group is the intrinsic desire to grow and develop personality.

Goal Setting Theory of Edwin: Instead of giving vague tasks to people, specific and pronounced objectives help in achieving them faster. As the clarity is high, goal orientation also avoids any misunderstandings in the work of the employees. The goal setting theory states that when the goals to be achieved are set at a higher standard, then in that case employees are motivated to perform better and put in maximum effort. It revolves around the concept of 'self-efficacy', i.e., individual's belief that he or she is capable of performing a hard task.

4.2.1 Self-Motivation

Self-motivation is the highest level of motivation. If you have learnt how to motivate yourself, you need not worry about anything. People who can motivate themselves are rare, but they are always better performance in all conditions and environment. People who are influenced and motivated by external factors may not always get the right kind of environment which can motivate them to perform better. Good remuneration is the motivation for performing better, therefore when this reward is not received the individual gets de-motivated, self-motivated people are, however, not perturbed by short-term gains.

There are a few strokes or kicks a person starts getting once he is self-motivated. He who has already achieved some great feat, will try to perform better and better his own record by an inner stroke or kick that he gets with an improved performance. At the age of 29, when he still has many years of cricketing ahead of him, Sachin Tendulkar has already broken the record of scoring the highest number of one-day centuries. The one thing that will motivate him to perform better is self-motivation or the high that he will feel with every subsequent century that he scores.

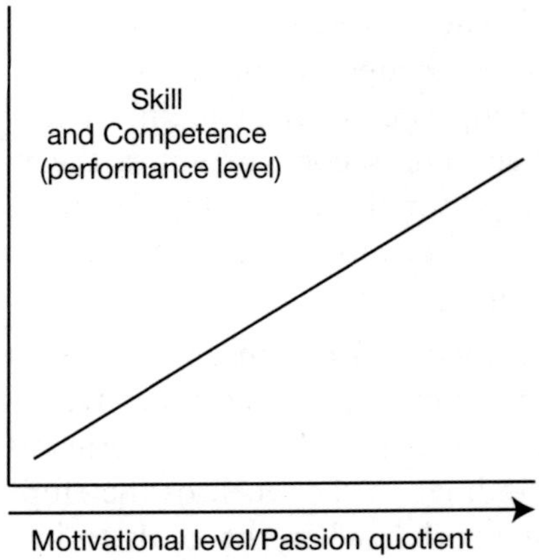

We will do something or the other for our livelihood. The work we do may be to our liking, but many a time it is not. Performance level is highly improved if we get to do the work we like doing and for which we have the necessary skills. The enhancement of performance in such a case can be depicted by the graphical representation below.

From the above diagram we can infer that we need to enhance the self-motivational level and, at the same time, try to identify the work at which we are competent and which is our strong point.

CASE STUDY

Muthu has complicated his graduation with great difficulty. He belongs to a poor family from Coimbatore. He could not continue his PG in Chennai University, as his father wanted him to take up some job or the other. He was trying desperately to find a job for himself. He appeared in several interviews and written tests but success was eluding him. He was willing to do any kind of job for the sake of his family.

His school friend Raghu was working for a textile mill in Coimbatore. He was feeling bad that he good friend Muthu was upset without a job. He suggested Muthu that the should join the mill as a worker. Muthu never wanted to be a worker in the mill but the financial condition of his family was such that he could not refuse the other. He went to the line supervisor of the mill. He was selected and joined his duty the very next day. He was happy to start the job. He was very sincere with his assignment and very soon, by virtue of his intelligence, he became very popular in the mill. The floor manager was highly impressed with his sincerity. One day when the expert mechanic was absent the whole factory came to a standstill due to the failure of a critical machine in the line, the manager himself tried to repair it but with little success. Muthu went to the manager and offered his services to repair the machine. Initially, the manager did not allow Muthu to try his luck but once he discussed the issue with the GM, it was decided that there was no harm in trying. Muthu started to repair the motor in the evening shift and after six hours of hard work put the mill back into operation, it was great news for the management. Muthu instantly became a hero for the workers as well as a blue-eyed boy for the manager.

Muthu was confirmed as a regular worker and was given a cash prize for his performance. Time was running fast but Muthu was not getting the returns for the hard work he used to put in. He was a popular face amongst the workers and his opinion to the workers when there was any dispute with the management on the weekend, when there was some problem in the mill, the manager called Muthu to attend to it. Muthu refused saying that it was not his job.

Next year, the workers union elected Muthu their general secretary. He was not the same young boy from the village anyone. He started discussing all the labour issues competently with the management. Soon the GM recognized Muthu's strength, who is now the spokesperson for Coimbatore Mill Association. Now he is attending meetings with ministers and the District Administration. The following year, a regional party nominated Muthu as the candidate for the General election. He was elected by a large margin and soon was one of the important position in the ruling party.

Questions

1. Was Muthu's decision to join politics right?
2. Were the motivational factors for Muthu, as a young workers, sufficient?
3. What are your suggestions to improve motivation for the mill workers?

5

Leadership Qualities

5.1 INTRODUCTION

Leadership is the quality of a person that helps separate the men from the boys. It can transform an ordinary person into an extraordinary person. Leadership quality is a must for any field of life. Whether it is a battlefield, playground, business establishment or a college students' association. In the history of mankind, there have been few leaders who were gifted with leadership qualities. They were born with it, such as Mahatma Gandhi, JRD Tata, Russi Modi, Nepoleon and Abraham Lincoln. But at the same time there are some leaders who developed these qualities with great efforts. Business leaders such as Darbari Seth, J.J. Irani and Anil Ambani are the people in this category.

We all admire people with great leadership qualities. They command respect from their team members. A good leader needs to be task-oriented, but at the same time he must be a person whom other members of the team can rely upon in the time of crisis. He gives direction, but he always remains a part of the job. Leadership is the process of influencing others to work willingly for a group objective. There may be different style of leadership such as human relationship style, authoritarian, democratic, laissez-faire (no control), employee orientation, consideration and initiated structure styles. It will be too early to say which style is good or bad. Based on the situation, environment and the personality traits of the leader, he can choose the style which suits him best.

There are many leadership theories that were propagated based on some experiment to analyse the leadership style. The first to undertake such studies was Hawthorne of USA in 1932. There are more than ten such theories propagate by famous behavioural scientists. Some of them are:

1. **Hawthorne Studies (1932):** This was the first study conducted to find out how leadership styles have an impact on other people's performance. The studies were conducted in an electrical bulb factory and with the conclusion that a change in the attitude of worker with each other and their feeling of togetherness can help increase productivity. The experiment caused an improvement in the importance of workers thereby increasing production, the study suggest that a good leader does take care of his aspect in his leadership.
2. **McGregor, Theory X and Y (1960):** The theory says that there are two categories of leaders having different viewpoints about their subordinates. One group (say X) who believes that most people dislike work and will try to avoid it as soon as they get a chance. Only a small group of people are responsible and like to take initiative, whereas the other group (say Y) are those who believe that people are responsible and will work hard if their personal needs are satisfied. In theory Y, there is hardly any difference between leader and following.
3. **Lippitt and White, IOWA Leadership Style (1939):** In this study, the leaders are categorized into three categories, namely autocratic, democratic and laissez faire (no control).
4. **Likert, Michigan Studies on Leadership Style (1961):** The studies conducted in the Michigan Survey Research Center have identified two major categories of leaders—one that is employee-oriented and the other that is productivity-oriented.

5. **Stodgil, Ohio State Studies on Leadership Style (1957):** The studies were based on a detailed questionnaire to find out the behavioural description of a leader. Two major dimensions emerged from the studies, one was "Consideration—relationship and mutual respect for subordinates, trust, feeling, warmth etc." and other was "Initiating the structure-defining role, goal attainment of subordinate".
6. **Kelly, Trait Theory of Leadership Style and Leadership (1974):** This is one of the very commonly accepted theories of leadership. In this theory, Kelly tried to classify the personal traits of a successful leader. These traits are divided into six major categories, namely physical characteristics, background, intelligence, personality (aggressive, alertness, dominance etc.), task-oriented and social characteristics. Many behavioural scientists take these traits as the indicators for successful leaders.
7. **Hollander and Julian, Group and Exchange Theory of Leadership (1969):** In this theory, the group dynamics is the basis for all the major leadership success. If in the group there is a positive exchange between the leaders and followers, the group goals can be achieved easily.
8. **Bandura, Social Learning Theory of Leadership (1977):** In this theory, leaders and subordinates have a negotiable and interactive relationship.
9. **House, Path Goal Theory of Leadership (1971):** This theory says that the leader is to smoothen the hurdles in the path of achieving the goal. Leader must be the person who has ability to persuade other to get the work done.
10. **Black and Mouton, Managerial Grid Theory (1978):** This theory is based on a perpetual mapping of the leader on two dimensions on a scale of 0.9; the two dimensions are task-oriented and person-oriented. If a leader is placed at 9, 1, he is primarily concerned about the task, whereas if a leader placed at 1, 9, he is primarily concerned with people.

5.2 TYPES OF POWERS ENJOYED BY A LEADER

Legitimate Power: It is the power that comes to the leader from the authority in the organization, for example, the chairman of a company has the power to recruit a new manager to improve the PR of the company. The power to recruit is a legitimate power of the chairman.

Expert Power: It is the power of knowledge and skill. When a leader is a skillful software professional, he would get the power to dictate terms in a software company, his decisions will be final. For example, a good surgeon has full powers to run the OT as per his choice he is the expertise and only he can run the show.

Charismatic Power: This is the power of attraction or devotion; people start admiring the leader. The great Indian leader, Indira Gandhi, had the charisma to attract large Indian masses. She was loved by all for her presence and enigmatic personality.

Reward Power: This is the present and potential ability of the leader to reward good and worthy behaviour and performance. Any leader who can reward a good work done by his subordinate will enjoy the power of rewarding. For example, a cricket captain who can select a player from his final eleven will exercise the power of reward in motivating young players to perform better.

Coercive Power: This is the ability to threaten or punish. The worst of all the powers to exercise control on the behaviour of another person is coercive power. For example, a mafia don commands the power to punish the local businessman, as the local businessman fears the unlawful muscle power of the don.

5.3 DIFFERENCE BETWEEN AUTHORITY AND POWER

The leadership process deals with different ways of influencing others, it is important for us to know power and authority differ, authority is the right to command and extract obedience from others, it generally comes with the post of chair you occupy. It comes from the organization you belong to and has very little to do with the individual concerned. Authority is the ability vested on a person to exercise control on the behaviour of other persons whereas the leadership of a person can influence others and control them, the authority does bring in with it some of the legitimate powers, but there are other powers that depend very much on the style of leadership.

5.4 THE MAJOR ATTRIBUTES OF LEADERSHIP

There are only two types of people in this world—a leader and a follower, yes, all people want to become leaders, but there will be only one who will lead a bunch of followers. Earlier people used to say that a leader is born and cannot be trained, but such concepts have considerably changed in the recent past. A leader who may have reached great heights and can motivate people to achieve high goals has very likely been a follower himself at one point of time, such people become leaders by closely planning.

Thinking and implementing the basic traits (like the ones mentioned below) which separate a leader from a follower.

1. **Courage:** No leader in this tough world can be thought of without the very basic trait of courage. If you lack the courage to take a calculated risk and lead the team for such an adventure, you will never gain in your life. The courage you show to the team members will motivate and inspire them to work harder to achieve the objective. Subhas Chandra Bose could inspire thousands of Indians only on one basic factor, which was his courage and confidence in his mission, the followers look at their leader as a security ring. The leader's courage should be based on knowledge of self, and of one's occupation. No follower wants to be dominated by a leader who lacks self-confidence and courage.
2. **Self-Control:** The man who has no control on himself can never control others. Set an example for others. Self-control is essential to show people what is expected of them.

3. **A Keen Sense of Justice and Fairness:** If you are not fair to all your followers, biased towards some of the hand-picked loyal and prefer to be surrounded by those people only, there is every possibility that your followers will not have any respect for you as a leader. No leader can command and retain the respect of followers if he is unfair and has no sense of justice. The large business houses such as Enron in USA could not sustain its prime position as people had little faith in the fairness of the leader.
4. **Definite Plan of Action:** Never be like a rudderless ship. Have a definite plan of action. The followers would like to see you as the one who can steer their ship even in stormy weather. If you do not have the correct road map and plan how can you think of reaching the goal that you have set and which may not be visible to your followers?
5. **The Habit of Doing more than Being Paid for:** As a leader you are the role model for others and whatever they see in their leader they will follow suit. If a leader is not putting his best efforts in his work, none of his followers will put in his best.
6. **A Pleasing Personality:** No leader is expected to be a rustic and rude person. People see the leader as their representative to the outside world. A corporate chairman and CEO who is representing an international IT company must have a pleasing personality.
7. **Sympathy and Understanding:** The people under you regard you as their guardian and expect your empathy just like a father in the joint family. The interest of the father has to take the back-seat if he desires his son to perform better.
8. **Mastery of Details:** The followers look up at their leader for guidance and direction towards the goal. Therefore, you are required to know the details of the work to be a true leader.

9. **Willingness to Assume Full Responsibility:** A leader is required to take up the responsibility for any mistakes of the subordinates. The leader should be ready to take more responsibility for the growth.
10. **Co-operation:** A leader is a leader as he is leading a team. If there is no team spirit, there is a possibility that his authority and his effectiveness will be questioned. The creation of conducive and cooperative environment is a must for an effective leadership.

Causes for major leadership failures:

(a) Inability to organize failures.
(b) Unwillingness to provide service.
(c) Fear of competition from followers.
(d) Lack of imagination.
(e) Selfishness.
(f) Disloyalty.
(g) Emphasis of the authority. A good leader must lead by encouraging.
(h) Emphasis of title. Generally, people, who lay more emphasis on their status and title, care very little for their followers.

5.5 PRINCIPLES OF INFLUENCING OTHERS

In a nutshell, we would like to list few of the behavioural qualities a person should have. A leader's job is to change people's attitude and behaviour. A famous behavioural scientist suggested a guideline that is still valid. These are to be practiced by those who aspire to become leaders of a group.

1. The relationship must begin with genuine praise and honest appreciation.
2. Never pinpoint mistakes directly.
3. Start by stating your own mistakes if you want to criticize others.
4. Direct orders may not be a welcome thing. Rather ask questions.

5. Other person must never be pushed to the wall.
6. Never be at a loss of words for praise of any improvement.
7. Encourage others to live up to a fine reputation.
8. Others must happily accept your suggestion.

5.6 MANAGEMENT INFORMATION SYSTEM (MIS)

In this age of information, all decisions are taken by top-level management based on the data and information available to them, the data collection, processing, analysis and decision support is greatly improved with better hardware available to today's manager. But still there is plenty of scope for improvement in the Managerial Information System. MIS refers to the system by which information is collected, processed and presented to the management. Accurate and proper information can lead to better decisions. The important aspect of effectiveness of any manager or an executive is his ability to take excellent, correct and timely decisions. This can be possible only if the right MIS supports it. The MIS has three major components:

1. Raw data from the field (Input).
2. Processing by the system (Processing).
3. Presenting the report, summaries to the management (Output).

Example: The sales figures collected from all the area managers for the General Manager (Marketing) is the MIS for the Sales Division of the company. An effective MIS should be:

1. **Timely:** The importance of any information can be of use only if it reaches the decision-making authority in time. The MIS is relevant if it is timely. Example: a company is trying to launch a shampoo in the Indian market. It engaged a market research firm that wanted to do an excellent report by a month. The company launched the product in the meantime. Of course, the report was of little use to the management.
2. **Accurate:** If the information presented is not accurate, it can lead to a wrong decision, therefore the MIS report must be accurate. Most MIS reports are used to take

decision that have an everlasting effect on the strategies adopted by the company. The decision is dependent on accuracy. Some of the less important decisions taken day-to-day activities may not be as badly affected even if the accuracy level is low.

Example: The Managing Director is interested in knowing the annual amount paid as wages to a particular production unit in order to find the fixed cost to the company. Even if the manager (Finance) gives a figure, which is less than 97 per cent accurate, the figure may be useful for the MD.

3. **Relevant:** There may be plenty of reports with volumes of data available in the office, but when a particular information is sought, the same is not available, storing unnecessary information is not going to help the management take any useful decision.

   Example: The HR department is maintaining the information of all the employees in a particular mill. The director (personnel) of the company, before launching a computer training programme, is interested in knowing how many of them are graduates. The personnel manager was unable to find the relevant information from the HR data.

MIS has different requirements for different levels of management in the organization. The top level is concerned about the external environment of the business and is expected to get all the relevant information from the external factors. The government policy, the competitors and information about inputs are critical for the survival and growth.

The middle-level manager has to utilize the resources at his disposal properly. Therefore, he has to get all the inventory level. Production planning and marketing information relevant to him in time so that any decision to change the planned schedule can be taken well in time.

The lower-level business executives have to take decisions based on the day-to-day information collected. They are not bothered about the previous records and long-term future of the company. The data and inputs from market sales figures can give him the deviation of sales from the target as per forecasted figures.

CASE STUDY I

Gopalan was the new administrative officer of the Hotel Continental, a five-star hotel famous for its grandeur. The new officer was trying to access the situation and the performance of each team member. There was a housekeeping team of eleven cleaners and two supervisors in the group. They were to look after the entire housekeeping job of the hotel. There was one person in the housekeeping team named Venu who was very calm and always preferred to be alone. Others informed that he was not a good worker and always delayed the work. The supervisor Mathew was critical of his behaviour too.

Gopalan called Venu to his room and asked him to speak for himself. Venu said that he was not very happy with the behaviour of his colleagues and was particularly distressed to the harsh words used by Mathew. He also informed Gopalan that when he wanted a week's leave to attend to his ailing mother, Mathew denied it saying that it was the peak season.

Gopalan took the case of Venu as the first task of his new assignment. He asked him to report to him the next day. He changed Venu's assignment from housekeeping of the kitchen to the front desk and main lobby (supposedly an important assignment). Venu seemed happy with the change. He went to lunch break at 2.30 on the first day, whereas the regular time was 1 p.m. When Gopalan went for a round at 3 p.m., he found Venu's colleague pulling Venu for not doing a nice cleaning. Gopalan saw that the job was not of high standard, but he appreciated him for his hard work and sincerity. Time went by fast and, with the encouragement from the new manager, Venu did improve his punctuality and quality of housekeeping. The transformation was commendable. The management recognized the efforts and recommended a cash prize for Venu.

Questions

1. What are the reasons for Venu's poor performance?

2. How did his peers' behaviour affect his performance?
3. Do you think Mathew was handling him correctly?
4. What is the main reason for Venu's transformation?

CASE STUDY II

The National Steel Company is the leading manufacturer of steel in private sector. The company was a pioneer in its field and was a profitable company since its inception by the legendary industrialist Manish Gupta. The company was on a decline since the last few years because the government had liberalized the import of steel from south Asian countries. The company engaged the leading international consultant Arthur Andersen to study the state of affairs in the company.

The consultant, after a detailed study, recommended few things including large-scale restructuring and a reduction of manpower through VRS. The twelve layers of executives must be flattered to four layers and the MBO (management by objective) style should be adopted with few key responsible person. Manoj Agarwal, 36, was working in the company as Sr. Manager (Marketing) since last seventeen years. He had always been a lovable boss and a peoples' Manager. But with the changing time, the attitude of the management changed drastically. They always felt Agarwal was more a relationship-oriented leader than the task-oriented type.

Agarwal wanted to change his style. He started behaving tougher with his juniors. The situation did not change for food; rather it deteriorated further as the juniors started doubting his intentions. He was under tremendous pressure of losing his job. He met a counsellor who advised him to pursue the interest of the company above his need of relationship. Manoj, after a few days, met his marketing chief and appraised him of the difficulty in the new work culture. The chief said that it is the organizational goals, therefore the team must strive to the organizational goal of working together and fighting the recession period. The chief also suggested that in such a flattened organization the role of the leader and follower change frequently and have to be flexible and that Manoj must switch over his role as per the job requirement.

Questions

1. What is your opinion about the difficulty being faced by a leader like Manoj?
2. Is the effort of change and transformation on part of Agarwal sufficient?
3. Was the chief right in saying that a flat organization has more flexibility than the conventional one?

6

Emotional Stress

6.1 INTRODUCTION

Emotional stress is a generalized state of heighted emotionally, which eventually becomes habitual. In some people, stress may come mainly from fear, while in other, it is a result of conflicts that give rise to anger, jealousy, envy, or some other unpleasant emotions. Stress is rarely characterized by a predominance of the pleasant emotions.

Stress differs from mood. A mood is temporary state of heightened emotionality which normally subsides after a relatively short time. Unless the preparation for action that accompanies a mood is expressed, however, a mood may persist and develop into stress.

Stress is more damaging to adjustment than moods because it is persistent. The person who is in a "bad mood" will be nervous and on edge, but these conditions will end when the mood passes. Not so with stress. The nervous mannerisms and the expression of stress on the face become habitual. Even when there is no apparent reason for stress, it will still be present, though in a less severe form than when there is a known reason.

6.2 EFFECTS OF STRESS ON PERSONALITY

Directly, stress affects the physical and mental well-being of the person by keeping him in a constant state of readiness for action related to the emotion that dominates his stress.

Chronic anxiety, for example, bring about an over-production of the adrenal steroids and they, in turn, inhibit growth by acting to antagonize the growth hormone from the pituitary gland. If chronic anxiety is present during the growth years, it may result in abnormal growth, especially in stunted growth. A disturbance to physical and mental health, as occurs in stress, affects the quality and quantity of the person's achievements and thus affects his self-concept if, in addition, the pattern of his growth is upset, the unfavourable effects on his concept will be intensified.

Since stress affects the quality of the person's behaviour, it indirectly influences his personality through the reactions it calls forth from others. A person who has learned to fear others acts in a defensive way, showing timidity and anxiety. Others react either by ignoring or by ridiculing him because of his immaturity. Similarly, a person who learns to act aggressively when frustrated in what he wants to do becomes hostile towards others. They react to his hostility by rejecting him. In both examples, the person's stress is intensified.

No one who suffers from emotional stress makes good personal and social adjustments. Nor is he happy, realizing how far short he falls of his capacities and of the expectations of the significant people in his life. People with low self-esteem are more adversely affected by stress than those with high self-esteem. Positive self-attitudes and "stress tolerance" are related.

Persisting intense stress may motivate the person to go to excesses in the hope of relieving it. He may try to dull intense feelings of insecurity by overeating or using drugs. Or he may try to prove his adequacy by compulsively engaging to reckless or self-destructive activities, such as drinking or even criminal behaviour. Women who experience severe stress during the menstrual period, when they are already undergoing an upset in homeostasis, have been reported to be more prone to commit suicide.

6.3 SOURCES OF STRESS

Stress comes from conflict. It occurs when the attainment of a goal is threatened by an environmental obstacle outside the person or by a physical or psychological obstacle from within him. How a person responds to obstacle is influenced by what he has learned will give him the greatest satisfaction.

External obstacles may derive from parental child-training methods that keep the person from expressing a strong drive, such as curiosity or aggression, for fear of punishment or loss of parental love. They may come from peer rejection, which thwarts the person's desire for acceptance and companionship. They may come from religious or moral restrictions on activities the person would like to engage in or they may come from group criticism and ridicule, which make the person feel inadequate to do what he wants to do.

Internal obstacles may drive from a physical handicap, such as blindness, or a chronic physical disturbance, such as asthma, which frustrates the person and prevents him from doing what he wants to do. Most often, internal obstacles are psychological. The person with unrealistically high levels of aspirations, for example, will suffer repeated failure in his attempt to reach his goals.

An excessively strong feeling of obligation to the family, an internalized puritanistic moral code, and obsessions of many kinds are further example of internal psychological obstacles.

Constant conflict over the satisfaction of drives results in a more or less steady state of heightened emotionally. Before the bodily changes that normally accompany emotions have subsided and before body homeostasis is restored, another conflict occurs and the bodily preparation of action is triggered once again. The person is in an almost continuous state of readiness for action. As a result, he responds the emotion provoking stimuli with greater intensity than a normal well-adjusted person would.

6.4 COMMON FORMS OF STRESS

In some people, emotional stress takes the form of anxiety, while in others, the stress is dominated by frustrations, jealousies, and envies. In some the emotions are expressed in overt actions, but in most, the expressions are inhibited or displaced. There variations contribute to the unique quality of each individual's personality pattern.

A brief description of anxiety, frustration, jealousy, and envy will show how differences in stress affect behaviour. Note how each particular kind of stress affects the person's characteristic patterns of adjustment and thus contributes to individuality.

6.5 ANXIETY

Anxiety has been described as a "painful uneasiness of the mind concerning impending or anticipated ill: it represents a danger or threat within the individual rather than an external danger". In anxiety, the disturbing stimulus does not physically precede or accompany the emotional state but is anticipated or expected or occur in the future. The response to this anticipated danger or threat is apprehension, uneasiness, or foreboding from which the person cannot immediately escape. Even more important, anxiety is accompanied by a sense of helplessness due to the person feeling blocked and unable to find a solution to his problem.

Anxiety differs from fear and worry, though it develops from them. It is vaguer than fear. Unlike fear, it does not come from a present situation which can be perceived but from some situation the person anticipates. Anxiety is more often stimulated by qualities within the person than by external stimuli. Frequently, the person is unaware of the conditions within himself which make him uneasy.

Like worry, anxiety is generally due to imaginary, often irrational, causes rather than real ones. Anxiety differs from worry, however, in two important respects: first worry is related to specific situations, such as examinations, parties, or money problems, while anxiety is a generalized emotional state; second, worry comes from an objective problem while anxiety comes from some subjective problem.

6.5.1 Causes of Anxiety

Feeling of inadequacy may come from any one of a number of common causes, such as parental over protectiveness, which results in the person's inability to handle his problems successfully without help; criticism and belittling attitudes of significant people toward the person's achievements, which make him question his abilities; unrealistically high levels of aspiration, which cause the person to suffer repeated failure and undermine his self-confidence.

A person with a well-developed feeling of insecurity faces even the normal uncertainties of life and the problem associated with adjusting to new situations with little confidence that he can handle them successfully. As a result, he often fails, thus adding to his lack of self-confidence and increasing his anxiety.

Experiences that undermine self-confidence and make the persons feel inadequate lead to anxiety. Students who in the past received grades below their expectations face a test situation with greater anxiety than those whose achievements were nearer their goals and who, as a result, have greater confidence in their ability to meet new challenges successfully. Older people who recall embarrassing experiences that occurred in their youth often shun social situation and refuse to talk in public for fear of future embarrassments.

At certain times during the lifespan, stress is almost universal "stress periods" commonly occur when radical physical changes take place, as at puberty or middle age, and when the pattern of life changes radically, as after the death of a spouse, divorce, or retirement. Stress is also common when there is a family crisis or business reversal. A person who suffers from feelings of inadequacy will meet challenges with far greater anxiety than one whose past successes have given him self-confidence.

6.5.2 Variations in Anxiety

Anxiety varies in quantity and quality from one person to another and within the same person from one time to another. Shaffer and Shoben write, "Anxieties vary greatly in intensity from a mere qualm in a transient situational conflict to a permeating distress that affect all of a person's social adjustments."

Those who worry more than usual, especially during period of adjustment when worry is common, are more likely to develop anxiety than those whose worries are less frequent and less intense. Sex differences in anxiety are not so great as are the methods members of the two sexes use to handle anxiety.

Girls defend themselves against anxiety by daydreaming and expressing feeling of inferiority while boys handle their anxieties by being rebellions and engaging in annoying activities. The more intelligent the person, the more likely he is to suffer from anxiety and to resort to defense mechanisms to decrease his self-dissatisfaction. Birth order affects anxiety through its effect on dependency. Since first-borns and only children tend to be more dependent than other children, their anxiety is greater both in amount and in intensity. Anxiety is higher among members of the minority group at all ages because of the feeling of inadequacy engendered by prejudice. Regardless of social, religious, racial, or economic group status, people who are popular feeling more secure and consequently, less anxious than those who lack social acceptance.

6.5.3 Effects of Anxiety Personality

Anxiety affects personality through its effect on behaviour. How the person judges his own behaviour and the satisfaction he gets out of its determines how he will evaluate himself. This evaluation of self-forms the core of his self-concept. His behaviour likewise affects the judgement other make of him and their treatment of him. Indirectly, the judgement and treatment of others influence his self-judgements.

When an anxious person speaks, for example he often breaks his speech with “ah”, “er”, “um”, and other non-speech variants. Others get the impression that he is unsure of himself and make unfavourable judgements of him.

Mild anxiety may be a source of motivation to improve. An anxious student is motivated to prepare his work before he goes to class and the anxious worker is motivated to do the best he can in the hope of retaining his job.

Anxiety of great strength may motivate some people to greater achievement. Most often, however, it leads to vacillation and indecision, thus lowering the level of achievement. Furthermore, the actions of highly anxious person and his mixture of over concern and under concern often seem irrational to others and even to himself.

One of the marks of an anxious person is that he tends to overdo or to underdo. A slight affront or criticism may send him into a rage, or he may have what seems like an excess of calm when there really is something to get emotional about, as though he were under duress to put a tight lid on his feelings.

An anxious person often behaves in a manner that is curiously "out of character", as when a usually friendly person shows streaks of cruelty or when the "best boy in town" commits a brutal act that no one is able to understand. As Shaffer and Shoben have explained: (when a person) behaves irrationally, and contrary to his own best interests, his needs to escape from anxiety is likely to lie at the root of it...there is no specific effective adjustment to anxiety. When you are anxious, you are merely stripped up, unhappy, and driven to do something when there is really little to do. Anxiety is therefore primary evidence of a lack of adjustment and is a key concept in the study of adjustive difficulties.

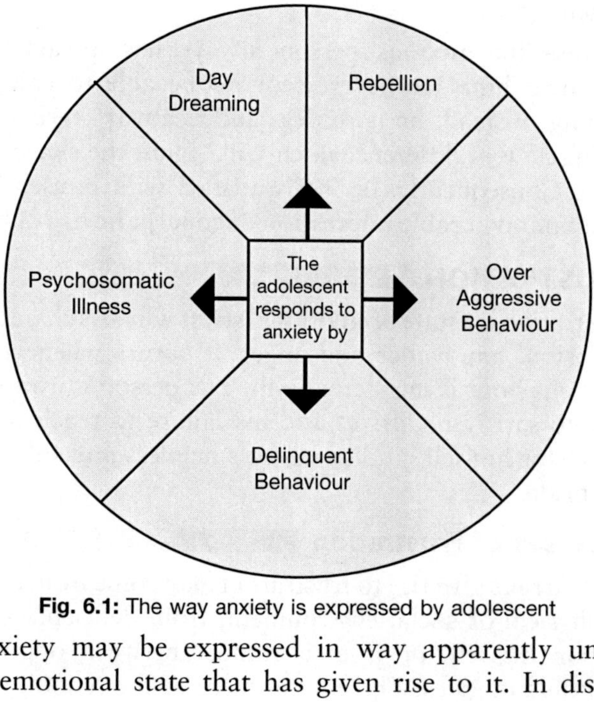

Fig. 6.1: The way anxiety is expressed by adolescent

Anxiety may be expressed in way apparently unrelated to the emotional state that has given rise to it. In discussing adolescent anxiety, Hornick remarks, "one of the commonest paths of anxiety in adolescence is acting up, or just plain action". In Fig. 6.1 some of the way anxiety is expressed by adolescents.

Some of the common ways, adolescents respond to anxiety producing stimuli. At any age, the person expresses wild anxiety in readily recognizable ways, he is worried and depressed or unaccountably edgy and nervous, he becomes angry very easily, or he gets his feelings hurt easily. The anxious person is easily influenced by what others say and he tends to be gullible. In addition, he often feels that he is misunderstood and is highly sensitive to criticism.

Strong anxiety may be so cloaked that it is not easily recognized. The highly anxious person, for example, may be a boisterous show-off, secretly trying to convince himself and other that he has no doubts about his ability to do anything he wishes. He may, on the other hand, appear to be bored and restless. Going from one activity to another and being ill at ease when alone.

Because the anxious person always has a vague threat hanging over him. He never seems to be able to enjoy what he is doing. Instead, he is restless and is always trying to find something new of different which will "blunt the sharp edge of anxiety". Consequently, he is dissatisfied with himself and he creates an unfavourable impression of concept he has of himself.

6.6 FRUSTRATION

Frustration is a state of emotional stress which is characterized by confusion, annoyance and anger. It occurs whenever goal-seeking behaviour is interfered with. The person is aware of his inability to satisfy his drives and his failure to reach the goals he has set for himself, and so he feels helpless and suffers from injured pride.

6.6.1 Causes of Frustration

The barriers give rise to frustration may come from obstacles in the physical or social environment, from deficiencies within the person himself, or from a conflict between opposing or incompatible motives. The environment of the school, planned to meet the ends of children of average intelligence, often prove to be frustrating to both bright and dull children. The adult who derived keen enjoyment from sports and outdoor activities when he was young may find confinement to an office desk so frustrating that he makes a poor adjustment to work and is constantly looking for a new job where he will be able to engage in the activities he formerly enjoyed.

Demands by people in the environment place even greater barriers in the way of satisfying derives. When parents and teachers insist that a child do what they think best rather than what he wants to do, the child suffers from frustrations.

By the time he reaches adolescence, annoyance and anger may dominate his usual pattern or response to all in authority. Frustration is at the basis of the revolt which has now become one common so characteristic of the adolescent years.

Frustrations frequently come from excessive demands the person places on himself. Personal deficiencies—physical shortcomings, lack of intellectual ability, or skills inadequate to enable him to do what he wants to do, all place barriers in the way of goal satisfaction. The adolescent whose vocational aspirations are too high for his intellectual capacities, whose social aspirations are blocked by lack of physical attractiveness and social skills and whose aspirations for independence are thwarted by economic dependence experiences constant tension.

Many frustrations trace their origin to a conflict in motives. When a young person is confronted with a conflict between wanting to go along with his friends in their forbidden activities and wanting to do what he knows he morally is right, he meets with frustration every time a choice must be made. A girl experiences stress when she must choose between being popular with boys and petting to extremes she disapproves of, just as boy experiences stress when he masturbates to gain relief from sexual tension, knowing that masturbation is socially disapproved.

6.6.2 Variations in Frustration

People differ greatly in their frustration thresholds, the level of tension below which they can think rationally and act effectively. Not only does the frustration threshold differ for different people but is varies in the same person from time to time and for different needs. Shaffer and Shoben have discussed the variation of the same need at different times:

A housewife "needs" her house to be very neat, orderly and clean. In the forenoon, her three-year-old son might spill a glass of milk, leave his toys in dismay and scatter magazines all over the new-cleaned living room. Her reaction at that time is one of mild anger, followed by efficient attempts to set things straight. At five-thirty in the evening the child repeats his efforts at messing up the house. This time the mother "explodes"—she spanks the child hurls some chinaware himself, and is unable to begin preparation for supper until she has vented all the tension the mess has provoked.

At all ages, people from the lower socio-economic groups have their needs thwarted or only partially met more often than those from other groups. They thus suffer more from frustration, which is expressed in hostility and often in aggression. Girls and women have greater social restraints on their behaviour, and they suffer more from frustration than boys and men. With advancing age, frustrations are less troublesome than they were earlier. Whether this is due to a general dulling of emotionality or to the elderly becoming more self-bound and thus less influenced by external conditions or to some other cause is not known.

Reactions following frustration vary also according to the intensity of the frustrating experience, how the person perceives the situation, what social restrictions there are on his behaviour, and what methods of expression he has previously found to be satisfactory in copying with his frustrations. Moderate frustration usually strengthens the person's drive because a goal that is hard to reach seems to be more attractive than one that is easy to reach. If the drive is weak, however, and the barriers seem insurmountable, frustration generally decreases effort. If the drive is strong, Insurmountable barriers generally lead to disorganized behaviour.

6.6.3 Effects of Frustration on Personality

How a person reacts to frustration influences the judgement of others and, in turn, the way he judge himself. Furthermore a person's manner of reaction to frustrations tends to be consistent, and so he soon acquires the reputation of being an immature or a mature person.

One of the commonest and earlier-to-appear patterns of reaction to frustration is aggression in which the frustrated person strikes out at an offending person or object, either physically or verbally and with varying degrees of intensity. While most aggression is extra punitive, in the sense that it is directed toward others, some is intro-punitive or directed toward the person himself. Most often, however, aggression is displaced. Instead of attacking the person or obstacle responsible for the frustration or blaming himself, the aggressive person directs his attack toward an innocent person or group.

Even intense frustration may not be expressed directly or displaced because the channels for expression are blocked by fear of punishment or social disapproval. The frustrated person then withdraws into himself and becomes inactive, inattentive, and apathetic. He gives the impression that he either is indifferent to frustration and lacking in emotional responsiveness or is "weak or spineless".

Some people regress by not "acting their ages" when faced with frustration. They long for the good old days when they felt capable of meeting life's challenges and were not frustrated by feeling of inadequacy. The married woman who feels incapable of meeting the responsibilities of home and family runs home to her mother for help. The man, feeling that running the home to mother is "childish", goes to his pals where he can get his gripes off his chest as he did during the gang days of childhood.

Frustration from thwarted drivers has long been regarded as a precipitating factor in personality maladjustment. But there has not been universal agreement about exactly how the personality is affected because frustrations are not expressed in just one way.

Freud placed emphasis on regression to infinite modes of response as the usual reaction to frustration, hung contended that continual thwarting resulted in a turning inward of the libido or like urge, thus causing the person to become self-centered and reflective rather than overtly expressive—characteristic behaviour of the extrovert. Adler maintained that thwarting leads to compensation in which the person is motivated to overcome barriers either by overt behaviour or by symbolic expression in fantasy. More recently, Lewin has claimed that the person who encounters seemingly insurmountable barriers will insulate himself from his environment by withdrawing into himself and showing the characteristic behaviour of the introvert.

These and similar observations of the behaviour of people in frustrating situations have emphasizing two things: first, that there are marked individual differences in the way people react to frustration, with each person learning a pattern of behaviour which he has found to fit his needs best, and second, that most patterns of behaviour learned to frustrating situations result in maladjustive forms of behaviour.

It is important to recognize, however, that frustration does not always lead to maladjustment. Some people try to relieve the emotional stress caused by continued frustration by making a rational attack on the problem. If they fail, they will probably resort to the use of defense mechanisms, "such as rationalization, projection of the blame on other, and fantasy, or some other stress-relieving mechanism. Under such conditions, maladjustive behaviour develops with its unfavourable effects on personality.

6.7 JEALOUSY AND ENVY

As a forms of emotional stress, jealousy and envy have much a common with anxiety and frustration. Jealousy and envy come from feelings of insecurity and inadequacy in situations the person regards as crucial to his happiness and welfare, as anxiety does. Both involve hostility, as frustration does. Both keep the person in a more or less constant state of emotional stress, as do anxiety and frustration. And both are expressed in behaviour patterns combining the usual expression of anxiety and frustration.

Jealousy and envy are separate and distinct emotional patterns, though they usually occur together. They are directed against people only, unlike anxiety and frustration, which may be directed also against objects. In jealousy, there are people involved while in envy, only two are, jealousy generally develop. Either than envy and it develops because the person is unable to understand meaning and values, envy on the other hand, develops because the person is able to understand meanings and values.

In jealousy, anxiety is usually stronger than frustration though both contributes something to the jealousy pattern. In envy, the reverse is true; frustration is stronger than anxiety though certain characteristics of anxiety are involved in the envy pattern. The patterns of response are often difficult to distinguish, especially when the stress comes from a combination of envy and jealousy.

As in anxiety and frustration, people discover from past experience what methods of expressing jealousy and envy provide the maximum of satisfaction and the minimum of social disapproval. Consequently, each person has his own way of expression these forms of emotional stress, and the contributes to the unique of his personality pattern.

6.7.1 Jealousy

Jealousy grows out of fear and anger. The jealous person feels that he has been deprived of something that is rightfully his and that he is incapable of defending himself against this threat to his security. Jealousy develops over a period of time, beginning in babyhood, it may gradually become a generalized form of stress which, if intense, can play havoc with the person's physical and mental well-being.

6.7.2 Causes of Jealousy

Most babies, because of the constant care and attention their helplessness demands, develop proprietary attitude towards the mother. Often before they can find a satisfactory substitute for the affection they expect the mother to apply, they find themselves displaced by a newly arrived sibling. Not understanding why this newcomer has usurped the status they regarded as rightly theirs, they become angry at the interloper and lose the sense of security they formerly enjoyed.

The anger and sense of insecurity of the young child are intensified when he observes that order siblings get privilege denied him, that a sick sibling gets more time and attention than he, and that his father becomes the centre of his mother's attention when he is at home. Experiences of this kind soon convince the child, too inexperienced and too immature mentally to understand them. That every family member is a threat to his security. This both angers and frightens him. If parents hold up and older sibling as a model for the child to imitate they unwittingly increase the child's jealousy by implying that they favour the older sibling.

At school, if the child does not receive from his teacher the affection and attention that he has been accustomed to receiving at home, he feels insecure. To safeguard his security, he may take a proprietary attitude towards the teacher and the children he selects as playmates. While jealousy normally wanes when the child makes good adjustments to school, it often flares up again in adolescence when he is faced with the difficulties and uncertainties of dealings with members of the opposite sex. The strong desire for popularity, combined with feelings of insecurity, causes the adolescent to be jealous of those who are more popular than he or whom he regards as a threat to his popularity.

Before adolescence is over, the person may develop the habit of being jealous—a generalized pattern of viewing everyone as a threat. Many adults do not know why they feel uneasy about people and unable to trust them. Their reactions are so habitual that they fail to recognize the underlying jealousy that gives rise to their stress. As Jersild has explained:

Among adults, the degree of jealousy a person exhibits frequently bears little relationship to his relative status of power as compared with others. The person who has "arrived" and has achieved the outward semblances of success will sometimes begrudge the recognition bestowed upon an underling, much as a big bound bristles when his master pets a forlorn poodle.

6.7.3 Effects of Jealousy on Personality

The intensity of jealousy determines how greatly it will upset physical and mental homeostasis undermine the person's feeling of security. Indirectly jealousy affects personality inviting unfavourable judgement from others, especially when the person expresses his jealousy in socially disapproved ways.

Regardless of how the individual expresses his jealous, either in physical or in verbal aggression, he is likely to be judged as immature. Most people, even young children, sense the unfavourable social attitudes toward their jealousy. This adversely affects their self-attitudes and is damaging to their self-concepts.

6.8 ENVY

Like jealousy, envy develops from anger and fear. It differs from jealousy in that the immediate stimulus is a possession of another person—a quality of that person, such as intelligence or skill in sports, or a material possession, such as clothes or a car. Envy is a form of covetousness of wanting what someone else has, not so much because of the possession itself but because it is highly valued by the social group.

Normally, envy develops later than jealousy because it depends upon the ability to recognize values and know the relative amount of social prestige attached to them. Envy often gives rise to jealousy. A man who had no feelings of jealousy toward a classmate who was regarded as a "brain" may, as the years pass, envy the "brain's" financial success, his manner of living, and his status in the community and also come to be jealous of him.

Like jealousy, envy may be either sporadic or continuous. It may occur only when the envied person gets a new car has a new honour bestowed upon him, or announces the birth of a new son. On the other hand, it may become an obsession. A person who suffers from feelings of inadequacy, insecurity, or inferiority can interpret anything other have as superior and consequently never really be free from envy.

6.8.1 Effects of Envy on Personality

Obsessive envy is far more upsetting to physical and mental homeostasis than sporadic envy. Indirectly, envy affects personality through its influence on behaviour and how the social group judges this behaviour. If envy motivates the person to secure things others have, and to secure them by socially approved action, the person will be favourably judged by members of the social group.

If he resorts to socially disapproved actions, and succeeds in their not being discovered, he is likely to feel guilty. If his actions are discovered, he will be judged unfavourably and will feel ashamed.

Inability to relieve the emotional tension of envy in direct action may lead to indirect, usually verbal, modes of expression. Some people express their envy by complaining about their lot, feeling sorry for themselves, and thus hoping to win the attention and sympathy they crave. Others defined themselves against feelings of inadequacy by rationalizing their lack of material possessions on the grounds that they have had "bad luck".

Others defend themselves by the "sour grapes mechanism," making critical and disparaging remarks about the very material possessions they crave. By so doing, they relieve themselves, temporarily at least, of the emotional stress of envy. Still others displace their reactions, blaming others for their lack of success. Whatever form of expression envy may take, it is not easily camouflaged and is likely to be detected. And as envy is not a socially approved emotional reaction, the envious person is unfavourably judged by others, and consequently makes unfavourable judgements of self.

CASE STUDY I

Ravi Tikku, 28, is a software professional in a leading MNC software company. He is heading a team of software developer who are responsible for implementing a package in a reputed Indian business corporate. Ravi is a very intelligent person and has proved his worth for his sharpness and wits. In the previous organization where he worked, he was a programmer himself and used to contribute a lot, as he was independently responsible for his performance. But in this new assignment he was not finding his team members as sincere as he expected them to be. He was not finding himself in a very comfortable position to get the work done and meet the deadlines set by the Project Manager.

During one of the interactive sessions, Ravi was very critical of the performance of one of his team members Asutosh. The discussion turned into blame and counter blame. Asutosh was very harsh and in the presence of all other superiors blamed Ravi for his autocratic attitude and hiding all important information from his team members. He was also charged with not allowing others to contribute significantly. Asutosh was ready to tender his resignation in case he was not assigned a different job in which he was not required to report to Ravi.

The company did not want to lose a good developer such as Ravi. To end the stalemate the General Manager had to intervene. He was not happy with the co-operation effects of Ravi and asked him to improve the situation by taking up open feedback session with his team members.

Questions

1. What went wrong for Ravi?
2. Was he delegating to his team members properly?
3. What is your opinion to improve the effectiveness of the team?
4. Whether blaming his boss in a meeting was the right approach by Asutosh?

CASE STUDY II

Indu Jain was the youngest in a family of four sisters. The family was a traditional Jain family from Rajasthan and believed in conservation traditions. She was rebellious by nature since childhood and was very harsh on any cultural values, especially those which reminded her of Indian tradition. She did her schooling from St James School in the capital. In school, all her friends were from affluent families. She was suffering from a complex as she always wished to have all the goodies that her friend used to bring to school. Her school bag, water bottle, dress and shoes were always of cheaper quality compared to her peer group.

After her schooling she joined a college of repute in Delhi. The parents were happy that the girl was doing well in her college and was going in the right direction to achieve a good career. But little did they knew that the small girl from whom they had a lot of expectations was hardly attending any classes. She joined a group of girls who had no interest in academics. They used to spend hours sitting in canteens and bunking classes to watch movies. On one occasion, one of her neighbours saw Indu in the city cinema hall, but she convinced her parents that it was not she.

In a short span of time she was finding it difficult to meet the extra expenditure from her pocket money. She invented a very innovative way of picking the pockets of others. She started it just as fun with a few of her friends, but after some time it became a hobby. Time went by and the small Indu was a clever pick-pocketer on Delhi roads. She picket up the horrible habit of taking drugs and insisted on shifting to the college hostel on the basis that she found it a waste of time travelling on the college bus. Her parents thought it was good for her. But it turned out to be worse.

One day Jain was informed that his daughter was in the police lock-up at Kotwali Thana. It was a shock for him, but he had little choice and arranged for her bail. She is now a drug addict, suffering from mental dysfunction. She is undergoing anti-drug treatment in a hospital in Dehradun.

Questions

1. Was it a matter of social complex that turned Indu rebellious?
2. Do you find it justified for her parents in sending her to a school not within their means?
3. How do you rate Indu's development as a young woman? Key actions could she have taken to avoid such as embarrassment for her and her family?

7

Handling of Conflicts

7.1 CONCEPT OF CONFLICTS

The term conflict may mean different things to the different persons. It may be regarded as the disagreement or hostility between individuals or groups in the organization. It may even mean rivalry or competition or may be viewed as the perception of disagreement in the individuals. Pondy has described that the term conflict is used in four ways in the literature to describe:

1. Antecedent conditions of conflictual behaviour, such as scarcity of resources or policy differences.
2. Affective states of individuals involved, such as stress, tension, hostility, anxiety, etc.
3. Cognitive states of individuals, that is, their perception or conflictual situation.
4. Conflictual behaviour ranging from passive resistance to overt aggression.

The attempt to classify to which classes of situations are conflict may not be meaningful from practical point of view, since each of these may be relevant stage in the development of a conflict episode. Considering the various stages in a conflict episode, Pondy has defined conflict broadly as a breakdown in the standard of decision-making. A Comprehensive review of the literature on conflict notes the extreme diversity of the definitions of conflict.

Conflict has been defined as the condition of objective incompatibility between values and goals; as the behaviour of deliberately interfering with an other's goal achievement; and as emotionally in terms of hostility. Descriptive theorists have explained conflict behaviour in terms of objective conflict of interest, personal styles, reactions to threats and cognitive distortions.

7.1.1 Features of Conflict

1. Conflict arises because of incompatibility of two or more aspects of an element; it may be goals, interests, methods of working or any other features.
2. Conflict occurs when an individual is not able to choose among the available course of action.
3. Conflict is a dynamic process as it indicates a series of events; each conflict is made up of series of interlocking conflict episodes.
4. Conflict must be perceived and expressed by the parties to it. If no one is aware of a conflict, it is generally agreed that conflict does not exist though there may be incompatibility in some respect.

7.1.2 Issue Involved in Conflict

Issue which help in understanding the nature of conflict are the issues involved in the conflict and conflicts may arise because of several factors like economic, social and psychological. Sometimes, these factors may exist in such a way that a person may feel tension and conflict; at other times, the person may perceive these factors incorrectly and the feeling of tension and conflict arises. Thus, diagnosing the issues in a necessary pre-condition for handling conflicts successfully. There are four basic issues which may be involved in a conflict either exclusively or jointly with others. These are facts, goals, methods and values.

1. **Facts:** Conflicts may occur because of disagreement that the persons have over the definitions of a problem, relevant factors related to the problem, or their authority and power.

2. **Goals:** Sometimes, there may be disagreement over the goals which two parties want to achieve. The relationship between goals of the parties may be viewed as incompatible with the result that one party may achieve the goal at the cost of the other.
3. **Methods:** Even if goals are perceived to be the same, there may be difference over the methods—procedures, strategies, tactics, etc. through which goals may be achieved.
4. **Values:** There may be differences over the values—ethical, standards, considerations for fairness, justice, etc. These differences are of more intrinsic nature in persons and may effect the choice of goals or methods of achieving them.

7.1.3 Conflict and Defense

According to Freud, all psychopathology relates to an effort gratify instincts that have been fixated at an earlier stage of development. Thus, in psychopathology the individual still seeks sexual and aggressive gratification in infantile forms. However, because of its association with past trauma, expression of this wish may signal danger to the ego and lead to the experience of anxiety. As a result, there is conflict situation in which the same behaviours are associated with both pleasure and pain.

For example, a wish to indulge in sexual behaviour that is blocked by feeling of guilt and fear of punishment or injury. A third example is the conflict between a wish to retaliate against powerful, other representing the parents—and a fear that these figures will themselves retaliate with force and destruction. In each case there is a conflict between a wish and anxiety. In such a situation the result is often that the individual cannot "say no", cannot be assertive or otherwise feels blocked and unhappy (see Table 7.1).

A critical part of the conflict is anxiety. To reduce the painful experience of anxiety, defense mechanisms, are brought, into play. For example, the person may deny his or her aggressive feelings or project them onto others. In either case, the person no longer has to be afraid of the aggressive feelings. In sum, in psychopathology there is a conflict between a drive or wish (instinct) and the ego's sense (anxiety) that danger will ensure if the wish is expressed (discharged). To guard against this and to ward off anxiety, defense mechanisms are used. In structural terms, a neurosis is a result of conflict between the *id* and the *ego*. In process terms, an instinct striving for discharge triggers anxiety, leading to a defense mechanism.

Table 7.1: Psychoanalytic Theory of Psychopathology

Illustrative Conflicts	**Behaviour Consequences of Defense Mechanisms**	
Wish	**Anxiety**	**Defense**
I would like to have sex with that person.	Such feelings are bad and will be published.	Denial of all sexual behaviour obsessive preoccupation with the sexual behaviour of other.
I would like to strike out at all those people who make me feel inferior.	If I am hostile they will retaliate and really hurt me.	Denial of wish "I never feel angry." "I'm raid of anyone or anything."
I would like to get close to people and have them feed me or take care of me.	If I do they will smother me or leave me.	Excessive independence and avoidance of getting close to people or fluctuations between approaching people and moving away from them, excessive need to take care of others.

In many cases, the conflict between the *id* and *ego*, between instinct and defense, leads to the development of a symptom. A symptom, such as a tic, psychological paralysis, or compulsion, represents a disguised expression of repressed impulse. The meaning of the symptom, the nature of the dangerous instinct, and the nature of the defense all remain unconscious. For example, a mother may be painfully obsessed with the fear that something will happen to her child. Underlying the obsession may be rage at her child and anxiety about the harm she may do to the child. The symptom of the obsession expresses both the mother's feeling that she may harm or injure the child and her defense against it in terms of excessive preoccupation with the child's welfare.

To take another example, in a hand-washing compulsion—in which a person feels compelled to wash his or her hands continuously—the symptom may express both the wish to be dirty or do "dirty" things and the defense against the wish in terms of excessive cleanliness. In both of these cases the person is unaware of the wish or the defense and is troubled only by the symptom. Many people do not suffer from such specific problems or symptoms, but analysts that all psychological problems can still be understood in these terms.

To summarize the psychoanalytic theory of psychopathology, there is an arrest in the development of the person that is associated with conflicts between wishes and fears. The wishes and fears that were parts of a specific time period in childhood are now carried over into adolescence and adulthood. The person attempts to handle the anxiety that is a painful part of this conflict by using defense mechanisms. However, if the conflict becomes too great, the use of defense mechanisms can lead to neurotic symptoms or psychotic withdrawal from reality. Symptoms express the unconscious conflict between the wish or drive and anxiety. In case of abnormal behaviour there is an unconscious conflict a wish and a fear that dates back to an earlier period in childhood. So as adults they continue to be childlike parts of us which—under stress and some other conditions—may become more active and troublesome.

7.2 BEHAVIOUR CHANGE

How does behaviour change come about? Once a person has established a behavioural pattern, a way of thinking about and responding to situations, through what process does a change in personality take place? The psycho-analytic theory of growth suggests that there is a normal course of develop a standard test that will tap the uniqueness of each individual. A second problem concerns the extent to which subjects are willing to give, or are capable of giving, honest self-reports. There is considerable evidence that self-reports can be influenced by conscious efforts to present oneself in socially desirable ways as well as by unconscious defensive processes. It is assessment problems such as these that have frustrated so many investigators and left so many questions unanswered.

The concept of self has a long history in psychology, receiving major attention during some periods and virtually disappearing from the literature during others. Because of the difficulties in conceptualization and measurement, some psychologists have concluded that the relevant research has led us toward intellectual bankruptcy. Still, despite the many conceptual and methodological problems, the concept of self remains important to the layperson and to the field of psychology. Rogers, more than any other theorist, gave it the attention it deserves in theory, research, and clinical work.

7.3 CONFLICT, ANXIETY AND DEFENSE

Critical attention has been given to Roger's concepts of congruence, anxiety, and defense, and we have already compared these process concepts with the Freudian model of anxiety and defense. We can recall that, according to the theory, the individual may prevent awareness (through denial or distortion) of experiences that are succeeded as threatening to the current structure of the self. Anxiety is the response of the organism to the subception that an experience in-congruent with the self-structure may enter awareness, thus forcing a change in the self-concept. The incongruence between self and experience remains as a constant source of tension and threat. The constant need to use defensive processes results in a restriction of awareness and freedom to respond.

We have, then, a model in which the essential ingredients are conflict (incongruence), anxiety, and defense. Both the Freudian and Rogerian theories involve conflict, anxiety, and defense. In both theories the defenses are used to reduce anxiety. However, the sources of anxiety and, therefore, the processes through which anxiety is reduced are different in the two theories, for Freud, the conflict leading to anxiety is generally between the drives and some other part of the personality the ego, or the superego as mediated by the ego. For Freud, the defenses are used to deal with the threatening nature of the instincts. The result may be formation of symptoms—symptoms representing partial expressions of the instinct and partial drive reduction. Rogers rejects the assumption that the defenses involve forbidden or socially taboo impulses such as those that Freud describes as coming from the *id*. Instead, he emphasizes perceptual consistency. Experiences that are in-congruent or inconsistent with the self-concept are rejected, whatever their social character.

As observed previously, according to Rogers, favourable aspects of the self may be rejected because they are inconsistent or discrepant with the self-concept. Whereas Freud emphasized instincts and drive reduction. Rogers stressed experiences and their perceptual inconsistency with the self-concept. The ultimate goal for Freud was the proper channeling of the drives. The ultimate goal for Rogers was a state of congruence between organism and self. Rogers' description of possible modes of defense was similar to Frued's and was undoubtedly influenced by psychoanalytic theory. Generally, however, Rogers gave much less attention to differences in types of defense and did not try to relate the type of defense used to other personality variables, as is the case in psychoanalytic theory.

The preceding distinctions seem fairly clear until Rogers attempts to account for the development of a rift between organismic experience and self and introduces the concept of the need for positive regard. According to Rogers, if parents make positive regard conditional, their children will not accept certain values or experiences as their own. In other words, children keep out of awareness experiences that, if they were to accept them, might result in the loss of love. According to Rogers, the basic estrangement in human—between self and experience, and this estrangement has come about because humans falsify their values for the sake of preserving the positive regard of others. This statement complicates Roger's position, since it suggests that the individual disregards experiences that formerly were associated with pain (loss of love). The view is not unlike that of Freud's concerning trauma and the development of anxiety. In essence, one can again see a conflict model, in which experiences that were associated in the past with pain later become sources of anxiety and defense.

In the theoretical formulations of both Freud and Rogers, the concepts of conflict, anxiety, and defense play a major role in the dynamics of behaviour. Both view well-adjusted people as less concerned with these processes and neurotic people as more concerned with them. For Freud, the process aspects of behaviour involve the interplay among drives and the efforts of the defenses to reduce anxiety and to achieve drive redaction. For Rogers, the process aspects of behaviour involve the efforts of the individual towards actualization and towards self-consistency. Although at time Rogers appears to be on the maintenance of congruence, which includes disregarding positive characteristics that are inconsistent with a negative self-concept and accepting negative characteristics that are consistent with this self-concept.

7.3.1 Types of Conflict

In the course of development, the same stimulus may come to elicit both an approach response and an avoidance response. At this point the individual experiences an approach-avoidance conflict. Thus, a boy may be torn between making sexual advances toward a girl (approach) and the fear of doing so (avoidance). Or an individual might wish to express anger but he is afraid to do so because of past punishment for this behaviour. Most people can think of many such approach-avoidance conflicts they face in their daily lives.

The approach-avoidance conflict between two drives is the basic ingredient for the development of neurotic behaviour. As a result of the conflict and the anxiety involved, the individual develops a symptom. The symptom reduces the anxiety and relieves the pressure of the conflict, for example, Dollard and Miller described the case of 23-year-old married woman who had developed a number of fears, one of which was that her heart would stop beating if she did not concentrate on counting the beats, the difficulties started with her feeling faint in a store, then developed into a fear of going out alone, and then into a fear of heart trouble. Dollard and Miller interpreted her symptoms an involving a sex-fear conflict. When on the streets along, the woman was afraid of sexual temptation. She felt that someone might try to seduce her and that she would be vulnerable to the seduction. The increased sex desire accompanying the fantasized seduction touched off anxiety and guilt, leading to the sex-anxiety conflict. Going home and avoiding being along on the streets were reinforced because they reduced the anxiety and relieved the conflict. The counting of heartbeats was similarly reinforcing because it preoccupied her and did not allow her to think of possible reduction. The counting habit was reinforced by the drop in anxiety.

The case illustrates how Dollard and Miller used the concepts of drive, drive conflict, anxiety, and reinforcement through drive reduction to account for the development of a neurosis. Although the details are sketchy, the case also illustrates how Dollard and Miller attempted to use Hullian theory in a way that was consistent with psychoanalytic theory.

Although most attention has been given to approach-avoidance conflicts in the development of neuroses, Dollard and Miller also emphasized the importance of approach and avoidance-avoidance conflicts. In an approach-approach conflict a person is torn between two desirable alternatives. Should a person date one or another attractive individual, watch this or the other great movie, buy this or that car? In an avoidance-avoidance conflict a person is torn between undesirable, unpleasant alternatives. Should a person pay the bill now and be without money or pay a larger bill later, is divorce or living in an unpleasant situation worse, should a child tell his or her parent the risk punishment or stay silent and feel guilty?

7.3.2 Conflict Resolution

Whenever conflicts arise, these have to be resolved by some specific actions, known as conflict-resolution actions, there may be many such actions. For example, March and Simon say that an organization may react to conflict by problem-solving, persuasion, bargaining and politics. Rube and Thomas have identified five types of actions: competing, avoiding, accommodating, compromising and collaborating. Lawrence and Lorsch have identified three types of behaviour in conflict resolution: confrontation, smoothing, and forcing. Some major actions in conflict resolution take place in the following ways:

1. **Problem-solving:** The problem-solving technique is considered to be the most positive technique available for conflict resolution because it emphasizes the attaining of the common interests of both conflicting parties, in mutual problem-solving process, the conflicting

parties must come together with the responsibilities of solving the mutual problem that faces rather than merely finding a way to accommodate their different perspectives. Questions of who is right or wrong are generally avoided, but sharing and communicating are required in order to find areas of common interest, this process causes the doubts and misunderstandings that underlie the conflict to become more obvious to the parties so that they may more effectively deal with them. Problem-solving technique can be applied effectively where conflict is based on misunderstanding of the parties concerned. However, this technique is not effective when conflicts stem from value system that differ and that are the one of the major sources of conflicts.

2. **Avoidance:** Another method of overcoming conflict is its avoidance, that is parties to the conflict may either withdraw from the conflict or conceal the incompatibility. Withdrawal may be observed when one party leaves the field of conflict so that other party may win by being in sole possession of the goal in dispute. Alternatively, the goal may be redefined through mutual withdrawal from the field and the redefinition of other and non-overlapping goal priorities. Concealing the incompatibility is another form of conflict resolution when it is not possible for any party to withdraw from the conflict. In such a case, the conflict may be eliminated by withholding the information from the parties in conflict because of goal incompatibilities. However, these are the methods for avoiding conflicts rather than solving the actual conflicts.
3. **Smoothing:** Smoothing can be defined as the process of playing down differences that exist between individual or group while emphasizing common interests. Differences are suppressed and similarities are accentuated in smoothing process. Finding and emphasizing similarities between conflicting parties, while suppressing differences, can eventually lead the

parties to realize that they are not far apart as was first believed. With shared viewpoints on an issue, the ability to work together towards a commonly held goal must be facilitated. This again, however, is not a long-term solution for the conflicts.

4. **Compromise:** Compromise is a well-accepted technique for resolving conflict, yielding neither a definite loser nor a distinct winner. Included here are external or third-party intervention, plus internal compromise between conflicting parties through both total-group and representative negotiation and voting. Such a compromise may be achieved either through the intervention of third party, the process is commonly known as mediation, or without the intervention of the external parties, the method known as bargaining. In both such case, the conflicting parties arrive at some compromise which is mostly mutual give-and-take situation. Compromise may be effectively used when the goal object may be divided up in some way among the competing parties. In case where this is not possible, one group may yield to the other something of value in exchange for a concession of value. Both parties then give something up. In a compromise situation, the outcome depends primarily on the relative strength of the parties. In situations in which one of the parties in much stronger than the other, little actual compromising may occur, and one side dictates the other. This is quite effective method of conflict resolution between management and workers.
5. **Confrontation:** The various action enumerated above may not be the resolution of conflict between parties if they take very rigid stand. In such a case, the parties are left to confrontation to settle the conflict themselves. This strategy may result into win-lose situation. The parties concerned may settle their score by applying their strength against each other. Confrontation may be used for organization development and increasing organizational effectiveness. Lawrence and I. Lorsch

have observed that high-performing organizations use confrontation techniques far more frequently than do the lower-performing organizations. However, confrontation may not be treated as ideal technique for most of the organizations specially if they are not equipped with taking the advantages of confrontation. It can be desirable only if the organization is working on competitive spirit basis. Since this is the part of organizational climate and if organizational climate may not be developed on this basis, it is not desirable to go for confrontation.

The parties involved in conflict may analyse certain aspects before going for confrontation. The first basic questions are: What are the issues of conflict? What are the costs for achieving a particular thing? Often, conflict is based not on actual issues but on misperception which may aggravate the situation leading to conflictual behaviour. In such a case, self-introspection provides the real understanding of conflict phenomenon. The second aspect, which must be analysed is the cost involved. Thing is obtained by paying cost for it. Often, the cost involved is much more than the achievement in confrontation. Therefore, it cannot always be relied upon.

What type of conflict, resolution actions would be taken depends on a variety of factors like nature of the conflict, nature of the parties involved in the conflict, and behavioural strategies adopted in conflict resolution. In this context, Wall and Callister have presented some interesting conclusions:

1. Males tend to use the forcing approach as their dominate styles; females use forcing less and often rely on a range of others tactics.
2. Managers tend to use forcing approach; employees prefer avoiding, smoothing, or compromising.
3. American managers tend to be competitive; Japanese managers prefer a cooperative approach.
4. Each party tries to mimic the style of the other-forcing induces forcing; accommodating induces accommodating and so on.

5. People tend to use different resolution styles for different issues: confrontation is used in performance appraisals, compromise is used in issues involving habits and mannerisms.

Another issue which is important in conflict resolution is the outcome of conflict resolution. Conflict resolution outcome is presented in Fig. 7.1.

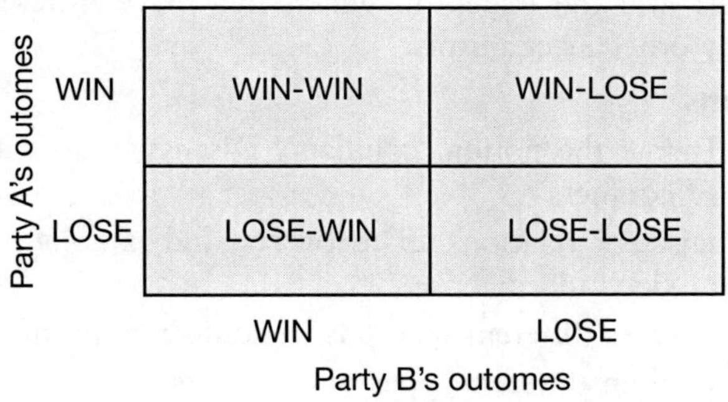

Fig. 7.1

Out of the four possible outcomes of conflict resolution, win-win situation is ideal as both the parties feel satisfied. In lose-lose outcome, both the parties feel cheated. In other two alternatives, only one party wins at the cost of the other, and the conflict becomes a zero-sum game. Such a situation may generate more conflicts in future.

Negotiation

We have seen above that compromise is a well-accepted technique for resolving conflicts. This compromise is arrived at through negotiation. Therefore, understanding of negotiation and how it works is important for conflict management. Wall has defined negotiation as follows:

> Negotiation is a process in which two or more parties exchange goods or services and attempt to agree on the exchange rate for them.

Negotiation basically involves bargaining. The dictionary meaning of negotiation is bargaining for the purchase of mutual agreement. Thus, negotiation may be defined as follows:

> Negotiation is the process in which two or more parties (individuals or groups) attempt to reach agreement on issues on which they have differences.

It may be seen that negotiation is an attempt to settle differences among parties; it is not necessary that the difference are actually settled. For example, many times, negotiations between management and workers do not bring desired outcomes, and the issues on which they have difference are settled by other mechanisms.

Questions

1. Define the notion 'conflicts'. Discuss various features of conflicts.
2. Discuss relationship between and among conflict, anxiety and defense.
3. Discuss different methods of conflict resolution.
4. Explain different types of "conflicts".

8

Etiquette and Mannerism

8.1 INTRODUCTION

Etiquette is necessary to have an effective and well-groomed personality. Public mannerisms and etiquette should be such that they can create an everlasting impression on the people you meet. We must possess qualities to build a personality that is charming, decent, lovable and welcome wherever we go. Therefore, we cannot ignore it. Certain people pick up these habits while still at school, but there are many of us who never had such an opportunity or exposure. The doors are not shut for them also. There is no age, time of the year or period of life when you cannot learn the art of better public mannerisms. We may be well-trained by our parents and teachers who try and instill in us the importance of being well-mannered. Our manners are categorized as good or bad depending on the kind of society we live in. If we are not toilet trained and do not hesitate to pee in the open facing the wall of a public building, it is because we have been trained since childhood like that. We have seen all our senior in the society behaving the same way. Can we do the same thing that we do in the city of Kolkata or Patna or in places like London or Frankfurt? Of course not!

Some very poor mannerisms often noticed in Indian youth are:

1. Biting nails when under stress.
2. Picking teeth in public.

3. Making slurping sounds while drinking and eating.
4. Picking of nose with fingers.
5. Spitting in public places.
6. Shouting and talking loudly over the telephone much to the discomfort of others.
7. Crossing the road wherever you feel like.
8. Sitting with your back facing someone.
9. Sitting on the office table.
10. Mailing rude and vulgar jokes in front of a lady colleague.
11. Ridiculing someone for his physical limitations and shortcomings.
12. Treading on grass in the park.
13. Occupying the street in a group while walking on the pavement.
14. Jumping queues.
15. Not allowing others to complete their sentences.
16. Not leaving seats reserved for ladies and disabled persons.
17. Smoking at a prohibited place.
18. Braging into someone's room without permission.
19. Participating in spreading rumours.

The general reason for making us branch the code of civility or forget social courtesies is sidetracked conduct, cultural heritage, and states of morality we follow or simply, eccentricity. If you want to be respected in society, you must also respect society.

One good thing about a human being is the capability to change. An Indian in a few years' time can learn French better than a French national or a Britisher who lives in India for years and starts behaving like an Indian. Therefore, we can always change our behavioural mannerisms for the better any impressive personality whether in India or America has to follow a code of conduct which is applicable not only in a particular state or a country but throughout the globe.

The breeding ground of all good and bad manners is the home. If a young boy has always seen his elders in the family abusing the female members, he will never hesitate in doing that, many people are in the habit of walking around in shorts or a dress that is not presentable while they are at home. They must have learnt all this from their parents. Of course, all good manners must start at home. If Mr. Lal walks across to the balcony of his second-floor flat to spit out a jet of betel juice, why would his teen-aged son bother to throw his coke can into a bin?

There are many educated people with their children attending good public schools. When they arrive into a movie hall in full family strength, their kids clamber onto the seats and spill popcorn all over while the adults constantly guffaw in the darkness. These are not acceptable in any civilized society. To each person his set of codes, traits and notions of civility are the reference of the mannerism. An Indian would find it discourteous to unwrap a gift as soon as he receive one, while an American would deem it ill-mannered not to open it and express his delight.

The use of toilet and using fingers to eat your meal are some of the common points we generally consider important for behaving nicely in public places. It surely can get sticky in a melting pot. The radicals would beg to differ. Being gallant to women and graceful to men is find, but why be finicky about how to use the potty or how to handle a fork, they ask. Are not some principles too trivial?

If the host removes his jacket at the eating table, must you remove your too? Must you make sure you do not slouch or look casual while eating?

Ask Judith Martin, who writes the globally syndicated column, 'Miss Manners', and has published several books on etiquette. Says she: "Even the most apparently trivial etiquette rules are dictated by principals of manners which are related to, and sometimes overlap with moral principals. Respect and dignity, for example, are two big principles of manners from which a lot of etiquette rules are derived."

But manners are more about considering the feelings of others than just about blending with the best. And it's also about taking responsibility. Have you not heard these sentences when you are using some public services? The poor unkeep of railways is always in question. The government is to take all the blame for the condition of hospitals, public parks and roads. Why are we so unperturbed and participate in these dirty games of blaming other for all the bad things we get? To begin with a better etiquette and responsible behaviour to society, you must think twice next time when you are asking these questions:

1. Is not upkeep of roads the government's job?
2. What is the benefit of following rules when none is doing so?
3. This country and society is not civilized.
4. Where are the public toilets?
5. Who the hell follows rules anyway?
6. So, what if my nephews are raising hell in the neighbourhood's? After all, 'boy will be boys'.

If you think the world is your own, you will be more careful of people and their belongings, if you feel like an alien you will behave like one. It just goes to show that the ones exhibiting had manners and I don't care a damn attitude are the ones who are the real social outcasts while the polished ladies and gentlemen are the people everybody gravitates towards.

We must try to avoid the following things in public:

8.2 EATING HABITS

A gentleman is identified when he is eating and a lady when she is talking. This is an old say, but very true at my point of time. Uncouth and bad table manners can send a very sorry message to the people sharing the table with you. Nobody will complain about this, but people do mind such behaviour.

1. Take as much as you can eat. Wasting and spilling food is not an accepted behaviour anywhere in the world.
2. Slurping, belching while eating in public is considered bad manners. If per chance you have picked up this bad habit, try to discontinue it. Practice eating with a

closed mouth and avoid slow eating, it will help you to give up the slurping while eating.

3. Hunching over one's food at the table must be avoided, as this is an awkward posture for eating.
4. Try not to eat and chew with one's mouth upon. The unpleasant sound and scene is repelling for others. This will pose a poor picture of your behaviour.
5. Picking one's teeth in public after food is a very common sight after a heavy meal in Indian homes. If it is must to pick something, you can use a toothpick and must not do I in public.

8.3 PUBLIC SPEAKING

The art of public speaking was discussed in detail when we were discussing effective communication skills, but as far as etiquettes are concerned we must identity few habits which are not acceptable in any society.

We must not interrupt someone when he is talking. It is considered highly ill-mannered if you do not allow the other person to complete his sentence.

Public Behaviour

1. We must care for the privacy of others and if we are travelling in a public transport, such as a bus or train, we must not talk or laugh loudly to distract other. Talking and laughing loudly in public is not considered good behaviour.
2. You are free to listen to the music of your choice, but blaring music from your car or home can be a cause of disturbance to others. Such behaviour must be avoided.
3. When we are attending a call, the person at the other end perceives you and your personality based on what you say and how you say it.
4. We may dial a wrong number. It is a human error. But not apologizing when one dials a wrong number is uncouth.

5. We know that it is an art to be a good listener and for successful communication you need to be attentive to what the other person is saying. Not looking at a person when he or she is talking is one thing that can spoil the essence of good communication.

Hygienic Behaviour

By your hygienic habits in public your behaviour will be perceived. We must never ignore the smaller hygiene issues such as:

1. The smaller habits make the man what he is. When you are spitting in a public place you are not only allowing others to be affected by the germs in your mouth, but you also portray a very poor image of yourself. Mend your ways.
2. Blowing one's nose in public must be avoided.
3. If you are not organized at your home front and are in the habit of littering your house, people will certainly not have a very high opinion about you.
4. It is nice to distribute your love to your pet, but a pet is your responsibility and if you are habituated of leaving pet excreta on the pavement you have a scope for improvement in your hygiene behaviour.
5. We all need to attend to the call of nature. In civilized society we have identified places for that, easing oneself in public must be avoided. Just imagine a familiar face seeing you doing that in a public place. It can be a cause of great embarrassment and dent you image.

Behaviour on Road

The road is a place where we behave unconsciously and without realizing what we are up to. If we can improve our road and traffic behaviour we can improve our public behaviour to a great extent.

1. Why do we try to float traffic signals and jump queues? Does it save some time for us? There answer is no. This is an attitude and poor public mannerism. If you find someone jumping the queue, you immediately perceive

him to be arrogant and indisciplined. We must avoid these poor habits.

2. Blowing the horn unnecessarily is one aspect in which we Indians are much ahead of any nation in the world. We keep one hand on the horn and never spare a moment to use it. It is certainly an area we Indians must try to improve.
3. We do not respect others and their rights. If we are on the roads or even on a pavement we like walking in a group abreast on the sidewalk. This is certainly avoidable.

Behaviour in a Meeting

When we are in a meeting there are a few basic etiquettes which need to be followed, these are:

1. Introducing a friend. It is always bad manners not to introduce someone when they are in a meeting.
2. In India, which is a multilingual country, it is highly undesirable to start discussions in a language that is not known to all.
3. When there is a large group discussing something, avoid parallel smaller group gossiping.
4. Try not to speak when someone else is addressing. If it is an urgent interruption, take permission from the speaker, even if he is a junior colleague of yours.
5. Avoid chewing gutka, smoking or eating during a meeting.
6. Never shout or talk loudly to impress the gathering or to score a few points. Try to stick to the agenda of the meeting. Never talk only about you, your company or your own agenda, but allow others also to express their viewpoints if they are invited for the meeting.
7. Disregarding RSVPs is a very poor habit and somehow an inbuilt defect of the Indian psyche. Try to mend it as soon as possible as it will stand you in good stead.

CASE STUDY I

Johnson had to appear for GD (group discussion) for the campus recruitment for CSC, a reputed software company in Eastern India. Johnson had always secured top slot in the class. He was confined that the company would choose him. The GD was scheduled at eleven in the morning. Rest of the boys arrived fifteen minutes in advance, but Johnson arrived just at eleven. The recruitment consultant had already intimated about the rules and the time for the GD. Johnson had to ask the rules again as he could not listen to it in the first instance. Mr. Bhatia, the consultant, was not happy to repeat it. The first thing he did was to identify a team leader for the GD. He identified Karan, a polished and cheerful candidate, as the leader; the topic was 'impact of MNCs Arrival on Indian Industries'.

Johnson had always considered himself superior to others in the class. He did not find it comfortable to accept Karan as the moderator. When the GD started he was intervening every now and then. At one point or time when Romesh was expressing his viewpoint, Johnson lost his temper and virtually started shouting to impress his awareness. The discussion was virtually reduced towards of war between Johnson and rest of the boys. Finally, after the stipulated time, the discussion came to an end.

Johnson was happy, that he could dominate the proceedings. Karan remained cool till the end he summed up the discussion in three lines in clear terms. In the evening the results were declared on the main placement notice board. Johnson could not believe his eyes when he did not find his name in the list. Karan was very much in the list and perhaps was rewarded for his cool moderation.

Questions

1. What reason do you think is attributable to Karan's selection?
2. Why was Johnson's potential and competence neglected?
3. What is your opinion about time management of Johnson?

CASE STUDY II

Mr. Bhatia was travelling in a train; the compartment he was travelling in was a second-class reserved bogey. He had reservation for his family consisting of four members. He was a religious person and a strong believer in God. He was very upset to see that some local travellers occupied the seats booked by him. Mr. Bhatia was travelling with a lot of luggage. As soon as he entered, there was a big scuffle between Bhatia and daily passengers. The scuffle started becoming physical with a few pushes from each side. The local travellers cooled down when an old person intervened and offered them some other seat. Mr. Bhatia was no longer in good mood.

The train crossed many stations and different places. It was hot and humid. Then there were a few moments of tension growing between the two groups again when there was a discussion regarding the policies concerning religions being followed by the Central Government. There were two sets of people from different communities in the compartment. The discussion started as a debate, but the pitch of discussion became harsh and ended in a hot exchange of words from both sides. Once the issue was at its peak, there was a shout from the other end of the compartment, a robber snatched the gold chain of a lady and ran away.

People were consoling the lady telling her that the unfortunate moment as the result of bad luck. The lady was crying as she said it was the only memory of her late mother. The train journey for Bhatia's family ended with the entire family soaked in depression of the sorrowful with train environment.

Questions

1. What are the other ways to improve the quality of discussion in such a heated environment?
2. What are the troubles that could have been avoided?
3. Was the area of concern and area of influence for travelling of passengers the same?
4. Why did Bhatia lose the opportunity of an enjoyable train journey?

5. You think these was any scope of reducing the tension of co-passengers?

CASE STUDY III

Mohit is young lad in the first year of a private Medical college in Pune. He belongs to a rich family from Gujarat. His parents have several tea estates in North-eastern India and his father has sent him to Pune only to acquire some qualification. His monthly expenditure is more than the salary of the Dean of the college. He has a Ford Ikon for his personal use. He feels proud to park his car next to the Dean's old Maruti 800. He stays in a luxury flat in a posh locality of the town. With the kind of living standard he has, he has little respect for the teacher in the college.

He is very casual in his approach towards studies. He hardly attends the first class of the day. He is used to wearing casuals and has very strange kind of hairstyle. Since his arrival in the college this year he has started violating the stringent rules laid down in the college. He says that he does not believe in any rules. He had once gone to the college Welfare Section with the idea of allowing the local fast food owner to start a fun-centre in the campus. His argument was, all work and no play makes Jack a dull boy, a good doctor has to have a pleasing personality and can learn medicine only if he is given a refreshing environment of learning. In a few months of his stay in the college he had a strong following. He was very popular among the girls.

Mohit had to appear in the first term exams for which he was under pressure, as he had not devoted sufficient time to studies. He went to his close friend Amit for help, but he too was also not of much help. All the students themselves were nervous, as it was the first exam for them. He went to the Registrar to postpone the exam for a fortnight. The Dean was not willing of the class in the canteen and they decided to boycott the exams protesting again what they called the inflexible attitude of the Dean.

Ramesh, a sincere student of the class from a middle-class family, did not want to lose a single day for the whims of Mohit. He went to the Dean and told him the plans of the students to boycott the exams. The Dean was annoyed with Mohit from the very beginning and he rusticated him from the college. But Mohit took this as his personal animosity with Ramesh; he made it a point that the class socially boycotted Ramesh. The rift between the two, turned violent and college was closed sine die.

Questions

1. Was the discipline in college affected by students like Mohit?
2. Was the new concept of fun with studies propagated by Mohit right for a country like India?
3. Was it ethically right on the part of Ramesh to inform the Dean of what happened in the college canteen?

9

Sense of Humour

9.1 INTRODUCTION

The world is full of sorrows and everyone is facing some problem or the other. If there is some escape from these sorrows, it is the lighter moments in our life when we can forget the moments of our worry, and tension of life. The person who can bring such a relief is always welcome. When we are doing something in which success is far away and we are down with failure we need a break from the gloom and sorrow of not getting what we wanted, this is the time when we must give a thought to assess which is a better way to lead our life. Is it better to carry with us gloominess to the places we visit, people we meet and make the surrounding gloomy, or take with us a sense of refreshing personality which is symbolic of happiness and positive change? There are a few people you must have met who are living example of all the sorrow in this world, they are always complaining about everyone including their own self. They will say that they are born with misfortune and are not successful for the simple reason that they have not been granted the fate of a successful man, whereas there are people who will be smiling even when they are undergoing tremendous pain. A humorous person met with an accident and suffered several broken bones and bruises on the face. When his friends went to see him and asked how he was, he replied that he was just fine and laughed wondering how funny he must be looking with the bandages all over his face.

The great Indian Mughal king Akbar was so pleased with the sense of humour of Birbal that he appointed him as a Minister in his Cabinet. His sense of humour used to bring in the much-needed relief from the most difficult job of governing such a big and difficult kingdom like India. A sense of humour should be very clearly different from mockery and cheap jokes. You must differentiate between mockery and ridiculing someone and a sense of humour that can make even your enemy your friend. The best example of the true sense of humour is cartoonist R.K. Laxman who has excelled in making cartoons of almost all great personalities of our generation. The aim of these works is to make these people laugh at themselves.

If the intentions of the person is to make the dull environment lighter and not hurt the sentiments, it has to be pleasant. If you have a real sense of humour you may save your face at the most difficult period of life.

It may not be so easy to learn the art of having a perfect sense of humour, as the line between humour and mockery is very thin and the only difference is the motive and intention. But once you know it you have enhanced your personality. Learn the art of laughing at your own self. If you have learned the art of admitting your blunders and laughing at your own foolishness you have automatically stopped others from laughing at you. Mahatma Gandhi, when he said about himself that he was the naked fakir, stopped the British Government from commenting on his physical traits and dress.

Some people may suggest that you need to be serious with whatever you do, but these suggestions are wrongly taken as if the person should be straight-faced devoid of a smile and must talk only business. There are many successful businessmen throughout the world who have a perfect sense of humour. The Virgin Airlines chief is remembered for his sense of humour and he does business better than many of the other Airlines.

Let us see in what way we can enhance our personality traits by the right sense of humour:

1. Sense of humour brings down the communication barrier and allows others to consider you as approachable.

2. It can reduce ill-feeling and can create a friendly environment.
3. It can inculcate a sense of confidence to penetrate the ego fence of the other.
4. The right sense of humour can help you to convey some messages without hurting other's feelings.
5. Humour is a terrific guard against hostility and difficult situations.
6. It gives a positive attitude towards others.

If there are so many advantages of being humorous then why can we not try it? There are certain easy ways to make it a part of our life, but it is not always possible to use it at the right time and moment. Prepare yourself for such an effort.

1. When you get ready for a party wearing a smart dress, prepare a mental frame of mind to share a moment of laughter with other.
2. Whenever you are using humour to bring down the communication barrier make it a point not to use harsh words that can hurt others.
3. Prepare yourself with few one-liners that can bring in laughter. It is a way of better communication.
4. Do not laugh at your own jokes, allow others to enjoy them too.
5. Use old jokes, quotes, cartoons, analogies, observations etc. to bring in the much needed humour.
6. One should never give notice to your audience that you are going to share a joke with them.
7. Never pause to give the punch line; you may not get the laugh from your audience.
8. Make it a point not to use it when someone is making a serious proposal or viewpoint and he is expecting others to listen carefully.

CASE STUDY I

Romesh 'Lucky' was the owner of a very popular eating-place "EAT and FUN", in Pune. Lucky was a local resident who was very fortunate to reach upto this level. He started as a small tea shop owner in the highway. But in a span of twenty years he made a big fortune and his eating point was one of the most popular ones in the city. He was very popular since his college days and was always a welcome personality in each and every group in the college. He had the capability to make people laugh. When he first opened the tea shop, everybody in town was laughing at him for choosing such a career. His tea stall became a favourite place for all commuters to stop and have some snacks and tea. The tea was less important for everyone who stopped, but the hearty laughter they shared was all that drew them. Lucky used to be the centre of attraction for even the older people who visited the shop.

The tea stall became a place of reducing the tension of driving on the highway. Lucky never left the great asset he had. He was gifted with a great sense of humour. His competitors were very upset and used all the sales promotion through various means, but the personality of lucky was the single most important USP for his business. He never allowed success to dictate his behaviour and manned the front desk himself. The excellent behavioural skills of lucky also motivated other staff members in the restaurant to behave nicely. As the name of the hotel reflected, it was a place of fun for all. There was a nice business environment. It has been heard that the Government of Maharashtra is planning to lease out all the State-owned tourism development hotels to Lucky.

Questions

1. What was the secret of Lucky?
2. Why cannot the other shopkeepers follow the success route of 'Eat and Fun'?
3. Should Lucky expand his business to other cities?

10

Develop a Hobby

10.1 INTRODUCTION

We need to have a constant source of energy. This source can be the mental strength. Our physical limitation is very much affected by how we think and how we feel. If our mind tells us that we are tired, the body mechanism, the nerves and the muscles accept the fact. If your mind is interested in any activity, you can keep on doing that activity without ever feeling tired of it. Therefore it is essential for us to make our activity without ever feeling tired of it. Therefore it is essential for us to make out activities interesting to our mind. Persons who are energetic and full of vigour and vitality are those who get the battery regularly charged by imposing self-faith in what they are doing. The other source of this vitality and energy is proper care and nurturing the body, taking simple care of it and not abusing it. Norman Vincent has suggested the formula of "believe in whatever you do and say. Be enthusiastic about your convictions." The mixing of the necessary pleasure with your activities can be achieved by developing a hobby.

Hobbies can help you to build a fine personality. We all have some time to relax. Some spend it watching TV, others spend in gossiping and some other reading books. Before we start discussing what we need to do as a hobby to improve our personality. I would like you to do a small exercise. We may spend a few minutes before we do to the next section to find out how we have spent the day in the last seven days and what was our routine.

10.2 ACTION I

Take a piece of paper. Sit at a desolate and peaceful place. Spend a few minutes in recalling the way you have spent the last week. We may exclude the time we spent in doing daily work such as eating, daily hygiene, etc. list out the work you have done and how you spent your time during your leisure hours. What is generally your favourite pastime?

If you are watching too much TV and/or gossiping with your friends, it is time to reorient your thinking. Watching TV does not keep your brain in use as we only see and listen. Therefore, persistent viewers become dull after a period. Similarly, gossiping with your friends always involves criticizing someone. We must avoid such situations. We may categorise three types of people.

Category I: persons who discuss people.

Category II: persons who discuss events.

Category III: persons who discuss philosophy.

The worst of all the gossipers are the ones who discusses persons and their shortcomings. The more intellectual person will discuss an event and if you are great you will discuss philosophy. God has made us all with some shortcomings, why find it in others when there are many in ourselves? Few of the good habits to be inculcated in the younger people are:

10.2.1 Book Reading

Book reading makes you think. The more you think, the more you know how better you can do the job. Joining a good public library is the ideal way of spending your free time constructively. Never read a book for immediate gain. The knowledge you acquire never goes waste.

Reading is to the mind, what exercise is to the body.

—*Joseph Addison*, English Essayist and Poet

10.2.2 Close to Nature

If nature inspires you, spending your time on your plants and pots, doing horticulture is an excellent hobby. In cities, people do not get sufficient space to pursue this hobby. But if you begin with a few pots it is good constructive work. You can find out what your talents are. Many great people grew famous from what began as a hobby, Jagdish Chandra Bose's hobby was keeping rats, snakes and other animals in his house. He used to compare them with plants and other living bodies; this study later on make him a great scientist. Many writers like Enid Blyton wrote stories as a hobby; but soon they became great writers and people still red their books.

CASE STUDY I

Deepa was a post-graduate student in Chennai University. She always considered that education was not her first priority. Her parents were from a famous family from Chennai. She had always done whatever she thought was interesting. Deepa took social service as her main pastime. She was greatly inspired by the great work done by mother Teresa for the poor and helpless in Kolkata. There were many instances in which her parents also supported her to pursue extra-curricular activities. She took the initiative in forming a non-profit NGO (non-governmental organization) for social service with the help of family friends. She was spending two hours everyday in organizing evening adult education classes for the poor women in nearby village.

Deepa had to compromise with her studies to pursue this hobby, but the response she got was really encouraging. Even the government was supporting response she got was really encouraging. Even the government was supporting her initiative with a special grant for her evening school. She took the hobby more seriously and desired to become a social worker. The long cherished dream of Deepa was fulfilled when UNESCO recognized her social welfare scheme as a unique model for semi-urban villages.

She could not complete her PG course and left it for the UNESCO pilot project which came her way.

Questions

1. Was the taking up of social work as hobby by Deepa a correct step?
2. To accommodate the hobby of social service, can Deepa cope with her studies too?
3. Has she achieved the final goal?

11
Ethics and Values

11.1 INTRODUCTION

There is a great need to have a strong foundation to any big structure. Never forget that the height of the building we see is only the visible half. The great monuments which are there for hundreds of years is due to the bottom half of their strong foundation. If you are to develop your personality, you are also required to give a fresh look to your character.

When we were small and our teachers and parents told what the character of a great man should be, we used to think of all these traits as very simple. Nothing difficult to follow as principles in life. Give a few minutes to yourself and try to think if at all we are on the right path. Now we will see in this chapter the hard work and the sacrifice of a few great persons in history to keep their character traits at high standards.

Mohandas as he was known in his childhood, was a staunch supporter of truth and honesty. He attended a school in a small town of Gujarat. Once the Inspector of schools was scheduled to inspect. Everybody was very alert and the headmaster was especially keen to present a better image of the school. The inspector went to the class in which Mohandas was a student. To ascertain the knowledge of the students, he gave them a few dictations. The spelling Mohandas wrote was not right, the teacher was standing in front of him, he hinted to Mohandas to copy the right one from the boy next to him. Mohandas refused to budge knowing well that the teacher would not spare him for his refusal once the inspector left the class, this was an ordinary incident but the foundation that was based on such truth and honesty was good enough to make Gandhi out of little boy. He deserved to become the Father of the Nation.

For very long years, life of Abraham Lincoln has inspired me a lot. I feel very deeply that all of us can derive lots and lots of inspiration from Lincoln's life. So, I have devoted this essay on Lincoln's life.

American President Lincoln's life was remarkable in many respects. He came up with great patience against many odds—against many trying times. He had many failures in his name, before emerging out very successfully in his career.

He saw many failures, frustrations and defeats. His life truly represents the quotation he linked to the core of his heart our greatest glory does not lie in never failing; but lies in rising every time we fall.

He was born on 12th February 1809 and was shot dead on 4th April 1865. During his life of 56 years, he lived in a sublime manner. He did all petty works like feeding animals, harvesting crops, planting, and chopping trees to earn enough to go to school. He did not have money to buy books; he borrowed and copied them in the candlelight.

His life of 56 years can be divided in 8 equal parts of 7 years each. For first 7 parts of his life, namely for first 49 years, he suffered many setbacks and failures.

In such trying circumstances for 49 years, it demanded very great stamina, guts, efforts, optimistic outlook and staying power to withstand that. In the face of all these adverse factors he came up. We can draw deep-deep inspiration to fight against our own but odd personal circumstances of life. "With malice towards none—with charity for all." This was his approach even towards his very bitter enemies. He did not hate them. Far from that, he respected his enemies for their good qualities. He sought co-operation from them.

He had great respect for his stepmother who made a lot of sacrifices to bring him up in life. Lincoln once said for her,

"What I am and what I will be. I owe everything to her." Lincoln suffered much in his married life.

Once Lincoln was asked a question about his viewpoint on religion. He said, when I do good, I feel good. When I do bad, I feel bad. That is my religion. Lincoln had infinite capacity to stick up to his conviction. Once he said, I am not bound to win. I am bound to make my best attempt. I am not bound to success, but I am bound to live up to the light I have. On the significance of success in life he once said. When I am gone, I hope it can be said of me that I plucked a thorn and planted a flower, where I thought a flower could grow.

In his lifetime Lincoln was very much criticized by Mr. Statonton. But when Lincoln was lying dead, the latter paid a fine tribute "There, lies the most perfect ruler of mankind the world has ever seen."

Dale Carnegic has written very nice biography on Lincoln's life entitled *Lincoln the Unknown*.

Lincoln's peculiar ambition led him to become a reputed layer, and eventually the president of USA. Not many people believed he would achieve either of his goals. He had farfetched peculiar ambition, which he strived for and succeeded.

Ethics—Do Not Compromise on This

During the devastating earthquake in Dobe, Japan, an American newscaster saw a Japanese woman selling flashlights and batteries in a small makeshift shop, which was made up of wooden boxes. There was a great demand for batteries and flashlight torches as there was no electricity. The newscaster went to the lady and asked why she was not selling the essential items for more than the regular price. The woman answered, "why would I want to profit from someone else's suffering?", these are the Ethical values of citizens of a great country like Japan.

Character Ethics

Character ethics has nine dimensions as suggested by Behavioural Scientists. In the initial years, character ethics was considered the foundation of success. The important issues were:

1. **Integrity:** The Oxford Dictionary defines it as honesty, the oneness of honest approach, which cannot be disintegrated.
2. **Humility:** Person having a low opinion of one's importance, less proud.
3. **Fidelity:** The faithfulness and loyalty of a person.
4. **Temperance:** It is the quality of self-restraint, moderation, and total abstinence from alcohol.
5. **Courage:** It is the ability to control fear when facing danger or pain.
6. **Justice:** The quality of being just or fair.
7. **Patience:** It is the ability of calm tolerance.
8. **Simplicity:** It is the quality of a man who is not showy, proud or extravagant.
9. **Modesty:** Now behaving boastfully and avoiding indecency.

Covey had said that character ethics teach that there are basic principles of effective living and that people can only experience true success and enduring happiness as they learn and integrate these principles into their character.

People like Covey, Gandhi and Lincoln are examples of strong followers of character ethics.

The above followers have identified four basic qualities or traits:

1. Character
2. Competence
3. Integrity
4. Acceptance

1. Character: For any relationship to proper, character is the prime quality, which a man must possess. A person may have all the good qualities in him. But without character, he cannot be trusted and therefore can never ever build a sound platform of relationship. A fox is cunning by character and will behave so when it gets an opportunity even with the best of friends, it is character that communicates most eloquently. Generally to improve a relationship a person uses human influence, strategies and tactics to get people to do what he wants, to motivate them, to influence them to work better, to like him and each other without focusing on character building which is not going to last long. The flawed character marked with insincerity in a relationship cannot be successful. Duplicity in a relationship will breed distrust and the best of human relationship techniques. The most modern inventions of man that has changed human life and his way of thinking, that its computers, also could not change this natural law, i.e., 'Garbage In, Garbage Out'.

Duplicity in behaviour and double standards in dealing with people cannot be sustained forever. When such dubious behaviour is exposed, the people around will never forgive you, no man in this world ever wants to be cheated and the worst wounds a person can inflict on other is by cheating. Character is one trait, which comes to its own, when a person is at ease and not under any pressure to buckle. Out of all the major personality traits of a man is the most difficult to change the character building. Character is the structure of the building and is developed on several layers of time-tested concrete. The character of a man comes to its fore at times of distress. People generally resort to unfair and easy path at the time of goods against him. Including his own relatives and friends not willing to come forward for any help. But it is equally true that people who have experienced such kind of trauma with grace, stand in high esteem of those around. It is at a time when loneliness is the only companion of a man with hurdles around, that the true strong character comes out to overcome the problems.

2. Competence: It comes when a person has the right kind of ability complemented with attitude to serve, the best of knowledge and skills without the right kind of attitude does not make a man competent.

If we cannot believe in ourselves, who else will. There is only one winner amongst several contenders having the same strength, same caliber and skills. A loser gives up the race before it starts, thinking that it cannot be won. I know many of my friends, who did well during their school days. Nobody had any doubts about their competence. But to tell my readers, very few of them have really achieved any to mention about afterwards. The reason for their losing before they started playing was complacency can bring success if, and only if the person is strong and resolute. You yourself should be convinced first and then only you can cross the hurdles.

The famous book *Think and Grow Rich* by Napolean Hill has taught an invaluable lesson that one should not give up the fight on the ground that one would loose. There are several people in our society who are symbols of gloom and who advise not to venture in any new field. They will never try anything new themselves nor allow others to think or try something new. Their plea for not venturing into something new may be one of the following:

(a) It has been attempted before but without success.

(b) It is a risky proposition.

(c) what society will say; they will not accept it.

(d) It goes against government policy.

(e) I do not have time to try something new.

3. Integrity: Integrity is based on the principles of fairness, the principle which gives birth to equity and justice. No example can be better than the sense of fairness prevailing in children. Even in adverse conditions the definition of fairness remains the same. Steven Covey has showed personal integrity as the basis of creating goodwill, which generates trust. Lack of integrity can undermine any effort to create trust in relationships. Even people who seek to understand, remember the little, things, keep their promise, clarify and fulfill expectations, fail to build a relationship because they are inwardly duplications. Integrity is more than honesty.

Honesty in simple words is telling the truth, or in other words, is conforming our words to reality. Integrity is conforming reality to our words or in other words keeping promises and fulfilling the expectations.

One of the best ways to explain integrity is to be loyal to those who are not present. In doing so we build the trust of those who are present. When you defend those who are absent you retain the trust of those who are present. Never sweet-talk in somebody's face and bad mouth behind his back. That's the essence of duplicity.

4. Acceptance: If we want to have a good relationship we must know the importance of accepting each other with all the plus and minus points we have. Changing a person as per your own requirement will always create a strained relationship.

Questions

1. What do you mean by the term, Ethics? How does it differ from values?
2. Discuss key characteristics of Ethics.

12

Personality of Face Value

12.1 INTRODUCTION

While observing personality of a person, attention generally focuses on the face first and there a whole gallery of expressions waits for us—cheerful, grieving, angry, irritated, smug, determined, and so on. Even a 'poker face' conveys just that expression, although it intends to presents a blank. The muscles of the human face are extremely flexible and mobile and even feeble variations of mood or sentimental get registered on the face.

12.2 EYES

Looking one straight in the eye may denote frankness, honesty, uprightness, or steadfastness. But the same glance may be widened into a fixed stare of hostility, indifference, or social insult.

When the eyes are dilated and the eyebrows raised simultaneously, the expression may convey surprise, disbelief or envy. When eyes glare at the opponent, and the chin is thrust forward defiantly, it is a real 'eyeball to eyeball' confrontation, or the jaw muscles may tighten as well as the lips, to express disapproval in every rigid muscle.

Another type of eye-to-eye contact produces the gentle and tender looks of love and affection. Love and happiness, and faith in the future, give a 'starry-eyed' or 'dreamy-eyed' look to the person. People like sailors, air-pilots, and ranchers, who are accustomed to gazing into distant horizons and spaces, develop a keen yet faraway look, with perhaps a slight squinting of the eyes, this sort of remote look also comes into the eyes while one is concentrating on a deep problem, though one avoiding or shunning direct eye-to-eye contact may be caused by bashfulness in a young girl. In others it may be prompted by a sense of guilt, deceit, prevarication. It is the obvious sign of a lair.

Fluttering of eye-lashes, looking up through the corner of the eyes, peeping out from behind a fan or feather, are all in the dictionary of feminine wiles, particularly acquired and practiced in certain South European and South American countries. The language of the eyes accompanied by certain stylized gestures forms the stuff of classical dancing of South and South-East Asia. The Indian style of Kathakali, Bharat Natyam, Odissi and Manipuri dances are characterized by eye movement easily interpreted by the connoisseur.

Looking obliquely or askance reveals a nature which is not very frank. It also suggests unhappiness at the good fortune or happiness of others. But in a young girl, it betokens shyness, genuine or pretended, coquetry, and flirtatiousness.

Frowning brows and worried looks obviously suggest that a person is anxious, over wrought or facing a problem. The habit of frowning leaves deep lines of worry on the forehead or between the eyes. This is why we speak of 'a perpetual frown' or 'wrinkles of worry' spoiling someone's appearance.

Some people have restless eyes. Their eyeballs keep moving from side to side. They keep looking in different directions instead of concentrating on any one object or person. It is a way of avoiding eye-to-eye contact and reveals a shallow and restless nature or a nature not very straight or honest.

12.3 LIPS

A smile on the lips generally says that the heart is at home. A natural, innocent smile can light up the world both for the giver and the receiver. The simple close-mouthed smile conveys happiness. Shyness, amusement and such other likable emotions, then there is the open-lipped smile of greeting and conversation prompted by politeness, friendship, pleasure, interest, excitement. The broader, open-mouthed smile is one of loud laughter, big talk, genuine fun. Spontaneous smiles irradiate the face and are sure to evoke a smiling response, but unfortunately have developed into the professional smile of the doctor, salesman and politician, and the artificial 'Cheesecake' smile of the actress, model and society hostess.

A smile may be cruel, crafty, and vindictive and may chill the blood. If a man smiles between clenched teeth, he is beside himself with anger, stage-villains have of course familiarized us with their devilish laughter, may also frown in concentration. Spiritually inclined or philosophic persons also possess an elevated remote look, uplifted to higher things.

When the mouth is open, lips are open and smiling, and the attitude is pleasant or relaxed, it means that all is right with the world. When lips are pursed, it shows disapproval and displeasure, and when lips are tightly closed, the person has made up his mind not to say or reveal anything, despite the stiffest interrogation. Hence, the idiom 'in tight-lipped silence'. Lips may be bitten or chewed in anger or disappointment or out of nervousness. One may also bite the lips in case of extreme emotion or to hold back tears.

A smile generally parts the teeth, but clenched teeth signify tension and anger, and under extreme emotion they are gnashed or ground together. We too, wet the teeth when tackling a difficult job. Teeth chatter together in extreme cold, or through intense fear accompanied by nervous movements of the hands. A very revealing gesture is the passing of the tongue over the lips to moisten them. This is done when one is dry-mouthed through fear or nervousness, it may be an occasional gesture or repeated rapidly betraying degrees of tension, guilt or falsehood. The tongue may also be gloatingly passed over the lips in easier anticipation. When one is waiting to get ill-gotten gains, or pounce upon and unwary victim, the gesture may be made unconsciously like a spider.

12.4 MOUTH

When the hand goes up suddenly to cover the mouth, it is normally a sign of astonishment. Or it may be that the speaker desires to recall a word or to cut off the flow of speech, realizing that he has said too much. It may also be a gesture of diffidence. More skeptical law-enforcing authorities would take it as a sigh of laying, or as signifying an attempt to conceal information.

The habit of shielding or cupping the mouth while taking confidentially is acquired by person engaged in work of a secret nature, but there are some men and women who wish to demonstrate to the world that they are in possession of vital information of confidential nature, though they may be only wanting to comment on the weather genuine or spurious, it is a gesture meant to exclude others from a 'closed' group.

Sitting with both elbow on the table and both hands interlaced before the mouth is a gesture adopted by one who is following some proceedings carefully, not wishing to commit himself at once, or not willing to talk before his time. He prefers to wait and see.

12.5 HEAD

Involuntary moments of the head, such as the upward, downward and nod of assent, or the negative shaking of the head from side to side, can be very revealing, even when verbal comment is reserved, assent or denial may be signified by different types of motions of the head, in different communities, and if one is not conversant with community or racial gestures, one may read wrong, if is interesting to note that English people expressed surprise by the backward, over-the-shoulder movement of the head which among Indians is a motion of assent, implying 'Yes'.

Bending or bowing the head is usually a sign of agreement and deference to someone's opinion or status. Bowed head and lowered eyes also suggest same or humiliation. The 'cluster' of lowered head, pinching the bridge of the nose and shutting the eyes communicates that the person is thinking deeply and is greatly concerned about the decision to be made. The gesture may be performed when one is alone, but when performed in company, the subject is definitely in a brown study and should be left undisturbed to come out of it.

Evaluation gestures are those associated with thought-fullness, consideration, assessment. The common hand-to-check gesture is one of them. It may denote interest and attention and also deep thought and concern. When the index finger is placed along the check and the other fingers positioned below the mouth, the subject is assuming a critical evaluation cluster.

Forward tilting of the head and body and leaning forward denote interest; sitting back shows indifference or skepticism. Slight tilting or cocking of the head is another sort of evaluation gesture, being the natural position for alertness, curiosity, attention. Sitting or slouch with the head on the hands is, on the other hand, a negative position suggestive of boredom or lack of interest. If a person has absolutely no interest in proceedings, his eyes may droop, or he may even fall asleep.

Women resort to a peculiar tossing movement of the head to show their temper, displeasure, defiance, scorn or contempt. Such women undoubtedly consider themselves superior to the assembled company and adopt a don't care attitude.

12.6 CHIN

The up-tilted chin is a common attitude for the type of woman who tosses her head. It signifies pride, arrogance, disdain. Men too express their arrogant, domineering attitude in this way, sometimes permanently holding the chin at an upward angle, reflecting their general attitude to life and their fellow-men.

Older; mature persons assume a stroking chin position while assessing or judging situation. This gesture can be easily among judges, juries, and members of Boards, Commissioners, or Committees. The stroking chin position also suggests that one has a problem about which one cannot make up one's mind.

Another, 'gesture cluster', evaluative in nature, is sitting with elbow on table, hand covering the mouth and also holding the chin from above. It denotes thinking and assessing without revealing one's feelings. It may also conceal a quiet laugh or a surreptitious yawn of boredom. This is the attitude most common among those who sit on interview boards and among members of committee.

12.7 NOSE

Touching or slightly rubbing the nose with the index finger expresses a feeling of doubt and hesitation, especially when replying to a question. According to some American authorities, this is a gesture of outright rejection or negation. It may be accompanied by other gesture of awkwardness, discomfort such as shuffling the feet, shifting uneasily in a chair, etc. Variations of this doubting gesture are rubbing behind the ear with the index finger, rubbing the brow or the eye. All these gestures suggest that the subject is pondering over the pros and cons of the issue, or weighing up an answer.

The nose, whether up-tilted or held in a normal position, is an index of character. Holding the nose perpetually elevated shows a superiority complex and tendency to treat others with scorn, this gesture may also be accompanied by a downward glance, Characterized by the phrase 'looking down the nose'. When the nose is turned up in the context of a particular situation, it is an indication of dislike, disagreement, rejection. This disdainful attitude is generally associated with girls but may be equally a habit with haughty, 'aristocratic' men.

A slightly quivering nose, as seen in the animal world, is a less obvious signal of alertness, impatience, a desire to start off/ set out immediately. It is also a sign of curiosity, inquisitiveness, keen interest. The detective's nose quivers as he tracks the murderers. An old lady's nose quivers as she gets excited about the latest scandal in the neighbourhood.

A particular sniffing gesture and sound is made by women to show that they have no intention of believing a story, or accepting an explanation, as they know better. They pinch their nostrils superciliously to express skepticism.

12.8 NECK

When the palm is applied to the back of the neck, as if one actually has a pain in the neck, it is as if to say, "This has got me beaten!" and is trying to find a way out of the situation. Such a posture, with the head lowered, is often typical of athletes and sportsmen on the field, pondering over a stoke or throw, or trying to tackle a ticklish situation.

Running a finger round the neck, or getting hot under the collar, is a gesture of acute embarrassment and frustration. Such a person may not be able to react calmly to a situation or keep a cool head. It is also a preliminary step to interrupting a conversation. Women have the habit of unconsciously touching their ears lightly, or playing with their ear-rings, out of nervousness or to attract attention to themselves.

Person advanced in years, and hard of hearing, may make on involuntary movement of cupping the ears, and bending the head in a listening attitude. It is also a confidential gesture like cupping the mouth.

12.9 HAIR

A person who gets flustered, worried, puzzled, may make a ruffing motion through his hair, or scratch the head. Passing a hand over the hair may be sign of exasperation, worry or tension. When the movement is slow, it reveals a thoughtful mood. In women, it may signify vanity or a sense of insecurity When men finger a forelock or frequently brush it off the forehead, they are also feeling at a loss or insecure. It is a way of stalling for time. The symbolical feeling at a loss or insecure. It is a way of stalling for time. The symbolical gesture of tearing the hair is a way of saying that the subject is undergoing tremendous strain on account of sorrow, anger, disappointment, despair.

12.10 SOUND

There are many such gestures that combine certain expressions with sounds. The way we breathe reveals a lot about our emotions. There is the even breath of sleeping 'as sweetly as a child'; the regular normal breathing when things are going right; the holding of the breath at a moment of crisis or suspense, even when a crucial goal is to be scored. Short breaths expelled with an almost snorting/snarling sound denote fury; long sighs may identify the lover, woe-be gone or ecstatic, longer shuddering sighs express grief or bereavement. True to the adage, 'take a deep breath before you speak' a deep breath is generally taken before making an important statement or announcement. 'Eh expelling of breath with a Whew!' sound is an expression of relief that some ordeal is over, some obstacle overcome. It may express admiration at someone's appearance or something special, large, outstanding.

The 'Ugh!' sound, with a wrinkling of the nose and facial muscles, is a sound of disgust and annoyance made when we see something unpleasant, like a frog on our doorstep, or a squashed beetle, or when we refer to something equally distasteful, "Ugh! What a nasty day!"

Another expressive sound—'Task!' signals regret, disgust, annoyance, admonition, and should not be ignored, as it is almost an automatic reaction and very much an index to the mind. A clucking sound made by raising the tongue to the roof of the mouth, and releasing it quickly is associated with self-satisfaction or pleasure. Snapping of the fingers or clapping in admiration may go with it.

Washing softly expresses a variety of feelings. One may whistle out of sheer joy of living, or through fright and apprehension. It is a way of trying to keep up one's courage and build up confidence, by adopting a 'don't care' pose. Whistling is a means of signaling both for legitimate purposes. A crowd disperses on hearing the policeman's whistle, fugitives, law-breakers, revolutionaries, guerilla groups whistle to each other with special notes and tunes that serve as codes and signals. Strangely enough, the mouth may be pursed up to form the sound of a whistle, without actually emitting any notes. It is a habit with some boy/men when they are writing with concentration, or thinking deeply.

Clearing the throat and coughing generally precede singing, giving a talk, making an announcement, etc. It is an attempt to remove the tight, closed-throat feeling that afflicts a novice performer or speaker, but gradually becomes a habit. Deliberate coughing to interrupt, disturb or annoy, conveys boredom and impatience, and also acts as an ironic comment or expression of disbelief.

Humming and hawing is a variation of such throat clearing, signifying hesitation, deliberation or procrastination. It is a way of playing for time. People who 'hum and haw' do not arrive at a decision easily or promptly.

The 'Uh-Huh!' sound with a quizzical lift of the eyebrows is meant to convey a sort of half-hearted agreement, but the speaker wishes to remain non-committed while prepared to listen. 'Ahem!' is a kind of interruption or a way of making one's presence felt 'hm!' is a sound of agreement or of noting a point. It is another way of saying 'Yes'. Some speakers punctuate their words with 'Ah!' or '–Err!' when they shutter and stammer and are unsure of themselves until it become a speech-habit, at time deliberately cultivated or imitated.

12.11 USING OBJECTS

Certain accessories/ornaments/articles of constant use become the 'stage-props', so essential to any action or scene that one feels quite lost without them. One such essential accessory is the pair of spectacles or glasses. In the early years of this century, it was considered fashionable to wear a monocle on a ribbon, and wave it around superciliously when it was not gracing the eye. Elderly dowager ladies held a lorgnette on a long handle and used it to cast intimidating glances on those they disapproved. In our times glasses have become an indispensable and inseparable equipment for gesticulation, being used not only to correct weak eye-sight but also as an necessary to high fashion.

One who deliberately takes off his glasses and cleans the lenses repeatedly is stalling for time and taking the opportunity to consider a question or an option. Another trick to avoid speaking immediately is to take off the glasses and put the ear-piece in the mouth. Teachers as well as speakers from the platform punctuate their talk by gesticulations, holding their spectacles in their hand, in this way, they try to dramatize their talk or drive a point home. As emotional person, or one pretending to be so, may display anger, rejection, despair by taking off his glasses swiftly and throwing them on the table often endangering them. One has to give him time to cool off, or find out how far he is pretending.

Different types of tinted goggles/sunglasses change the appearance of the wearer and are often used as a disguise or camouflage when the wearer wishes to remain undetected: e.g., celebrities, spies, gangsters, secret service men use a wide variety of goggles to conceal their identity. Exotic sunglasses and outsize 'granny glasses' of every shape and hue are a proof of the wearer's ostentatious habits. This is a device to attract attention.

Putting objects in the mouth does not apply only to glasses, but to pens and pencils as well. Writers, poets, students seek inspiration and information in this way. The artist needs a brush not only to paint but to handle, such, manipulate. Short stabbing notions made with the pen and pencil, sometimes held in reverse, suggest advise, accusation, emphasis. When one-stares fixedly at a pen or pencil. While twirling it round, it denotes absorption in a particular train of thought.

12.12 SMOKING

Smoking a pipe offers an opportunity to go through a service of meaningful action such as cleaning, filling, lighting, tapping out a pipe and holding it in different positions in the mouth. Pipe-smoking are generally more patient, mature, and conservative men than cigarette smokers. Their gestures with the pipe are slower and more deliberate, leaving plenty of time to ponder, consider and manoeuvre. Pipe-smokers are supposed to be given to more abstract thinking, like engineers, scientists, technicians but smoking a pipe is also the hallmark of the senior level executive, securely ensconced in his chair.

A pipe is so much a personal equipment that one gets accustomed to holding it between the teeth and speaking, even though it may be stone cold. It becomes a part of a man's thinking process.

Cigar-smoking has also become a status symbol and in certain Latin American countries, it is synonymous with manliness. It is an accepted indication of prosperity, confidence and assurance, associated with a man in his middle years. Unfortunately, for the same reasons, cigar-smoking is associated with the well-to-do law-breakers, the 'godfather' figures of the underworld of crime and patronage. When a cigar-smoker feels confident of his position, he smokes with slow deliberate puffs and handles his cigar with assurance. Rarely a cigar left to smolder in an ashtray, but during moments of stress, a cigar may be allowed to go out, or be bitten through.

A cigar allows even more time for deliberation, as a good cigar has to be selected, tapped at both ends and cut before it is lit. One then waits to see if it has 'caught' properly, or the whole process begins over again. Offering a man a choice cigar is an itself a gesture of camaraderie and cigars are generally handed round at a wedding or a christening, to celebrate a promotion or the satisfactory clinching of a deal.

Cigarette-smoking, in comparison, is associated with younger men and women, given to lighter and more imaginative pursuits. There are a hundred ways in which a cigarette may be held, lit, smoked or put out. The manner of smoking may provide a wonderful study of class distinctions, as smokers range from the sophisticated belle, smoking her Russian or Egyptian cigarette through a jade or amber cigarette holder, to the seedy down-at-heels tramp making do with cigarette stubs picked up here and there. The honest citizens holds his cigarette straight between his lips; the underworld gangster lets it droop from the corner of his mouth.

Smoking becomes so much a part of the mental make-up of some people that they find it impossible to think. Imagine or create without it. Occasional smokers can control their longing for a smoke as much as they can restrain their other desires and actions. The chain-smoker is generally nervous, highly strung, completely dependent on the addicted to the habit. Gay, light-hearted youths who blow out smoke-rings are the extrovert type. Those who inhale slowly prefer to keep things to themselves. Cigarette half-smoked in the ashtray shows that the speaker is deeply absorbed in his occupation/thoughts, or he is keenly interested in what itself that is a sign of tension, but the half-smoked or unsmoked cigarette left to burn itself out, or the cigarette which is angrily crushed in the ashtray, as if the opponent himself is being squashed.

Such gestures and actions are so automatic that one can safely read a person's character and reactions through them. Even when the smoker is absent from the scene, policemen and detectives glean a lot of information and insight from the size of cigarette stubs left unsmoked, scattering of ashes on the carpet, or floor, brand of cigarettes smoked, and tell-tale lipstick mark left on them. It is not difficult for the layman to acquire a similar insight into the nature of cigarette-smokers, or any smoker for that matter.

12.13 DRUGS

Increasing addition to different types of drugs like hashish, cocaine, marijuana, LSD, and to brand medicines and 'pills' producing a drugging effect leaves certain well-recognized symptoms, which also need to be detected. A teacher or employer may have to deal with a young man who is 'high' or 'stoned' under the influence of drugs, and shows alarming behaviour traits.

Parents are the last to accept that their children can be drug-addicts, but there is no getting away from the fact that a majority of young people, particularly belonging to the 15-30 age group, are becoming drug-addicts, the drug-syndrome has caught on today's youth, particularly amongst the student community in urban areas, first out of curiosity and the 'kick' of it and then becoming a habit that results in the worst type of enslavement. The symptomatic behaviour at different stages of addiction may easily be confused with other types arising out of more innocent causes:

1. At the primary stage of addiction, a drug addict may seem gay and bright-eyed, over-energetic and enthusiastic, talking a good deal and too loudly. He may seem to be possessed with a feverish sort of energy which may be mistaken for good health and high spirits, especially if there is appetite.
2. At the second stage, the addict displays a 'leave me alone' attitude, is sullen, moody and morose, seems to prefer his own company and spends long hours playing records or watching TN. Meal times are erratic, and he seems to subsist on snacks. This sort of behaviour may still be explained away as 'growing pains', the onset of adolescence, or the natural expression of a talent that is brilliant but misunderstood.
3. By the time the third stage is reached, there is no doubt that something is very wrong, but the recognition is

already too late. The addict walks around with the blank glassy state of a 'zombie', withdraws into a world of his own, is depressed or hallucinated and almost lost to society. This is final stage when suicidal tendencies manifest themselves as well as the criminal, as the addict has to get his drug by means. The muscles of the face show signs of twitching and the hands are never still. They are either trembling or plucking at something, or the whole body lies inert, as if in a stupor.

Addiction to strong liquor is evident enough when a person shows all the obvious symptoms of extreme intoxication and there can be no doubt about his inebriated condition, but the signs may not be recognizable so easily when he has had a few drinks, but is not totally drunk. In this condition he may be the life and soul of the party and he in a gay, talkative mood, full of high spirits in every sense of the term. The trouble is that his inhibitions have already been relaxed and it is only one step for him to pass from entertaining conversation to embarrassing remarks and off-colour jokes. This man now needs a listener, so he buttonholes the first person he meets and recounts his grievances and airs his complaints against the world, his family-members (e.g., his wife), employers, colleagues and friends. Gradually, his mood becomes more maudlin or sullen and soon assumes the nature of belligerence. He is now ready to knock anyone down, especially if he has fortified himself with a few more drinks. The main point at issue is whether such a half-drunk person is in full possess ion of his senses, and knows what he is saying or doing. Most often he does not, and has forgotten all about it the day after, or if he does, he feels extremely ashamed of himself. Therefore, the tell-tale danger signs should be recognized for what they are, and not much importance or responsibility attached to them.

Question

1. 'Face value broadly affect the personality of an individual.' Do you agree? Discuss some key face values that affect the personality.

13

Personality Depends upon Standing, Walking and Sitting Postures

13.1 INTRODUCTION

We may not immediately realize the impact that certain postures or movements makes on us. But the fact remains that the memory of a sound or a gesture persists with us long after it is heard or seen no more.

A man's total personality may be revealed from his posture and he walk his general stance—though he himself may be quite unaware of it. Some postures may be adopted under emotional stress others become a habit through repeated adoption, for "use both breed habit in a man".

13.2 STANDING

Standing up straight and erect not only gives confidence but embodies a high minded noble attitude embodying desirable qualities. We are, therefore, recommended to "think talk". If we wish to be a good achiever, and not to stoop, slouch, lean, etc. squaring one's shoulders, straightening one's back and looking people straight in the eye is a 'gesture-cluster' conveying determination and self-assurance. It is the mainly stance which helps one to face any adversity, any danger.

One may stand up erect as a gesture of politeness to ladies and deference to superiors, and also to look down on someone in a seated position, to place him at a disadvantage. It is more difficult to 'talk up' to a person than to 'talk down'. When we physically elevate ourselves further and stand on tiptoes, it communicates dominance and superiority and in extreme cases amounts to boastfulness. Children and young people stand on tiptoe with excitement or expectation, almost making dancing motion. “I stood tiptoe upon a little hill.”

The teacher-taught relationship suffers when a formal superior posture is adopted by the teacher speaking or lecturing from a raised platform or podium. The classroom situation is more informal and relaxed in modern pedagogy and such artificial barriers and distinctions have been done away with.

Standing with feet pointed forward is an attitude suggestive of eagerness, alertness, readiness to go forward in a particular direction. It at the end of a meeting or conversation, a person takes up this position with feet pointed towards the door, it is a clear sign that he is anxious to leave. On the other hand, if an employer or someone taking an interview, suddenly rises from a sitting position, at the table, it is a signal that the session interview is over, and the one being granted the interview should leave. Such a standing position may be accompanied by extending of the hand for a parting handshake, or gracefully waving or accompanying the visitor to the door.

13.3 WALKING

A person’s manner of walking depends to a large extent on his physical structure and posture but it has also been found that every individual has not only a distinct style of walking, by which he can be recognized, but that his moods and emotions are also reflected in his movements. When we are happy, we tend to ‘walk on air’, at the other extreme, we slouch dejectedly, gazing at the ground. Active, goal-oriented persons walk ahead with firm, rapid strides, letting the arms swing freely. Those walking with hands in pockets and coats buttoned up to the chin are generally secretive and critical of others the hand-in-pockets attitude, whether standing or walking, has come to be accepted as informal, casual conduct, and is no longer considered to be rule and insolent.

People who are born leaders walk forward briskly, setting the pace, leaving the test to follow. Photographs of political leaders with or without their followers reveal their personal styles, for example, Swami Vivekananda on his ardent pilgrimage of India, Mahatma Gandhi on his historic Dandi March, T.V. viewers at the last Olympics had an opportunity to watch the 'March Past' of Olympic competitors. Despite the regimentation, there was diversity too, revealing certain national traits, e.g. the brisk light step of the Japanese, the free and swinging gait of the Australian team, the informal camaraderie of the Americans.

People who pace up and down for long periods at a stretch are seeking inspiration or some solution to a problem. Nervous pacing back and forth communicates anxiety, or anger, as in the case of a caged tiger. The person is too tense and overwrought to sit down or stand still. Some people cannot make up their minds and arrive at a decision, unless they walk up and down. Hospital waiting-rooms, ante-chambers of offices where crucial decisions are being taken, are excellent spots where such tense pacing is very much in evidence.

Another gesture suggestive of anxiety is shuffling about when standing, and drawing imaginary figures on the ground with the toe. It is also a sign of awkwardness and embarrassment and shy young boys are often found to be reacting in this way. They may also kick a stone about. Kicking at the ground or at an imaginary object is a sign of general irritation or frustration. This is a restrained form of the desire to kick someone. While making this kicking motion, the head is generally lowered and the facial expression is sullen and resentful.

13.4 SITTING

Sitting posture provide an even greater variety. These days one does not mind adopting any sitting posture unless it is at a conference table provided with straight-backed chairs. Designs of modern, futuristic furniture for office or drawing room have changed radically from the rigid upright items of yesterday that did not allow any slackness or relaxation to the free-form chairs of today. In the earlier half of this century there were still certain standards to conform to postures were classified as ladylike (sitting with knees pressed together, feet lightly crossed at the ankles), unladylike (crossed knees or sprawling attitude) or impolite (feel on desk), and these standards were generally accepted. These days one can hardly sit on the 'edge' of a comfortably upholdstered chair; nor is there any way to adopt a ramrod straight position from a tilted swivel chair.

Sitting on the edge of a chair shows a state of tension. It may also mean eagerness and anticipation. Someone why gradually moves forward towards the edge of a chair is willing to co-operate and compromise. This may therefore be interpreted and an action-oriented posture. It suggests that the subject may be on the point of rising from the chair and leaving at the end of the discussion.

The crossed legs position is so common that it does not have much of a special significance, but it has been found that when two negotiators adopt a cross legged position there is generally some argument or confrontation going on. It is interesting to note that while Europeans cross leg over leg, Americans cross legs horizontally, with the ankle of one leg resting on the other knee.

Other typically American gestures are throwing a leg over a chair, sitting with the chair-back serving as a shield, and putting the feet on top of the desk. These are ostensibly all caused comfortable postures which convey that the person is at ease, in a co-operative frame of mind and amenable to suggestion. They may also signify a dominating position and domineering attitude particularly in a superior-subordinate relationship. The man who sits with his leg over the chair-arm or up on the table may be supremely indifferent to what is going on around him, or is deliberately adopting a 'don't care' pose.

When a person is subjected to pressure, tension, anxiety, he automatically adopts a locked ankle position, with a locked hands gesture, it is a way of 'holding oneself in' or try to exercise self-control. The locked-ankle and clenched-hands position shows that the person is trying to hold back something, some strong feeling or emotion. It may relate to the old Army expression "keep your heels locked", i.e., do not disclose anything. Apprehension of some unknown experience like travelling by air, facing police interrogation or under-going medical examination, may cause a person to lock his ankle and sit with hands folded tensely or gripping the arm of his seat/ chair. Candidates appearing for an interview tend to lock their ankles. In such a position, the head may be clenched in the lap or may be gripping a handbag or some such article. Conversely, when people sit with their ankles unlocked and feet apart, they are more at ease and less tense.

13.5 OTHER GESTURES

Male Indians have a peculiar way of showing their fears and tensions by shaking their knees together, as if they were permanently knock-kneed, or by jogging the feet up and down rapidly. It grows into so much of a habit that they cannot think, speak or write without shaking their legs. This rather unattractive habit tends to spoil an otherwise smart appearance or any impression sought to be created.

Anger and frustration may be betrayed by different ways of stamping the foot, walking away with angry clinging of the heels, kicking furniture, etc., although it may not reach the extreme limits of Grimm's little men who dashed his right foot in a range so deep into the carrying on a normal conversation may betray his suppressed anger by drumming with his heel or tapping with his foot. These are signals of impatience too.

Members of an audience/congregation/class tend to fidget in their chairs, repeatedly shift position and shuffle their feet, when they feel bored and tired. People also get fidgety just before recess, tea-break or lunch-break, and express their impatience by shifting position, stretching out their legs, scraping feet, etc.

Drumming or tapping with the feet, keeping time to music, is an involuntary reaction that catches on very fast, as seen at 'Rock concerts', negro 'spiritual' sessions. It is also as much a sign of nervous tension as drumming fingers. Both actions may form a gesture cluster at moments of extreme stress and anxiety.

Straightening one's clothes is another type of fidgeting. Tugging at the waist hand of one's trousers, smoothing out its creases or trying to keep the 'knife-edge' fold, trying and untying shoelaces, are also associated with the decision-making process. It means that a man may be restless because he is too preoccupied with his thoughts.

Wearing the shoe half off, as women sometimes do when they cross their legs or taking them off altogether under a table are other types of fidgeting, but in this case signifying that the wearer is in no hurry and prepared to stay or relax for some time. He or her mood is accommodating.

At informal gathering, people these days do not sit only on the conventional sofas and chair, but on cushions and pouffes, rugs and carpets. It is, therefore, if quite natural to sit with one leg tucked under and adopt a comfortable and relaxed position. Or there is the normal posture of young folk at a party-sitting on the floor with knees loosely against the chest, with the chin sometimes resting on the knees in a listening posture. When alone, one generally ruminates or day dreams in this way.

Hippies, hitch-hikers and men on the road who travel long distances on foot sometimes sit on the floor leaning against a wall, with legs stretched out. While on the subject, it is worth mentioning the slow aimless, 'hippie' style of walking with blank-eyed stare, as if one were coming from nowhere and has nowhere in particular to go to. Their gait is particularly noticeable on crowded pavements with office-goers and shoppers hurrying past.

Questions

1. Analyze the role of standing, walking and sitting in the personality developments.
2. Discuss various other uncommon gestures in personality developments.

14

Personality of the Millennium

14.1 INTRODUCTION

The times are changing and so are the needs of the new/ millennium. There is fierce competition for reaching the top. In any profession you need to be top quality and put your best foot forward to excel. Philip Crosby, the quality guru says, "the executives of the new business environment will have to be a complete personality, smarter and more thorough about dealing with the real world than their 20th century counterpart".

As suggested by Philip, we may like to list important features for the person who can succeed the race in the 21st century. The key characteristics, which need to be developed appropriately, that would help present professionals to become tomorrow's leaders are:

1. **Strategic Awareness:** Earlier if you were doing your job honestly, it could comfortably take you to greater heights. But these days you must be clear with your objective. If the awareness of the strategic route to the final goal is clear you may be the winner at the end of the day.
2. **Adaptability in New Structure and Work Culture:** If you are rigid and not ready to change, you may not be welcome at any important organization. You may be a genius in your own eyes, but an organization wants a team player and adaptability to the new work

culture and the new structure is desired in almost all the organizations.

3. **Ability to Work in International Team:** The world is getting closer and distances between countries are getting smaller with the speed of information technology and globalization of the world economy. If you still like to keep your concept of sticking to your local cult, you will be lagging behind in the race. 'Think global and act local' is the slogan all over the world. We must learn to transform in the global environment.
4. **Language Skills:** Which languages are required to improve your personality may be a very difficult question. But as we can see for ourselves that globalization and for people to meet the international requirement one needs skillful use of the international language such as English. Be more particular to sharpen your language skills in the new millennium.
5. **Basic Understanding of Financial Viability and Its Importance:** All the important work you are doing in any sphere of life has to be financially viable. Anything great but not economically viable shall be summarily rejected. Therefore, you must learn the basic economic lessons. Give a thought about whatever you plan in that perspective in the new millennium.
6. **High Task Orientation:** As the competition is getting fierce and tough, we may be required to be more task-oriented. You cannot leave anything to chance. Make sure everything you have done is as per the plan.
7. **Human Relationship:** For the last few decades the importance of human relationship has come to the fore, but in the new millennium, in the age of knowledge and information, the importance of human relationships will be foremost. The relationship will be the pivotal force for all successful ventures. Therefore, you want to prepare yourself for the new millennium, sharpen your relationship skills.

8. **Self-Reliance:** The new millennium has compelled each and every individual to rely on self-confidence and only a person with self-confidence will win the race.

The Reasons Why a Man Fails

Napoleon Hill has conducted surveys for different kind of persons in different walks of life. Based on a large sample survey and its analysis, he came up with a very interesting list of thirty reasons for failures, which are valid for any person in any country and at any point of time. I will suggest all readers to go through the list of thirty weaknesses. If you overcome and avoid these you need not worry. In this millennium you may be the most effective person with extraordinary personality if you can cope with the following points:

1. Unfavourable hereditary weakness—this is the area where no one can help you but certainly your can always choose other works, where your strength lie.
2. Lack of well-defined purpose of life.
3. Lack of ambition to aim above mediocrity.
4. Insufficient education.
5. Lack of self-discipline.
6. Ill-health.
7. Unfavourable environmental influence on your childhood.
8. Procrastination.
9. Lack of persistence good starter but poor finisher.
10. Negative personality...if you repel people mind it.
11. Control on urge for sex.
12. Lack of well-defined power of decision.
13. One of major six fears.
14. Wrong selection of male in marriage.
15. Over caution.
16. Wrong selection of associates in business.
17. Superstition and prejudice.

18. Wrong selection of a vocation.
19. Lack of concentration on efforts.
20. The habit of indiscriminate spending.
21. Lack of enthusiasm.
22. Intolerance.
23. Intemperance.
24. Inability to co-operate with others.
25. Possession of power, which was not acquired by effort.
26. Intentional dishonesty.
27. Egoism.
28. Lack of capital.
29. Guessing instead of thinking.
30. Any other name of cause, which has caused failure to you in particular.

What is the Indian Way of a Successful Personality?

There are many great personalities in India, but the man who did all the hard work to navigate India into the new millennium of information age is Narayan Murthy, a middle class Indian, who must be the example to be followed by any individual who has dreams to fulfill. He says, "every dream should be given shape and never bother too much for basic needs such as food, shelter and health. Try for something worthwhile even if it seems impossible. Put the interest of the community above your own, you are not sacrificing anything if you are doing this, in a poor community it is difficult to become rich and happy." He has given some very basic tips to transform your personality for the new millennium.

Be Your Own Role Model

Make yourself, your role model: the best model for any person is he himself. The great Gandhian philosophy is to set your own example. Start doing your job honestly, work hard and do not complain about the difficulties, you face. We do not get so many opportunities, if we get any we must not let them go. Murthy says that we need more engineers, doctors, and chartered accountants, but above all we need people with right attitude.

Compare Your with the Best

Good executive quality needs to be compared with the best, the person should not accept the standard, which exists, but benchmark the best in the world. In this, we must not except much from the government. The government may or may not be in a position to provide good number of jobs or remove poverty. It is up to us to make the system more conducive for our own growth.

Share Your Dreams with Others

We can fulfill the dreams of the team if we can inspire others also for a bigger dream. The great names, in the Indian industry such as Kurien, Bhabha, Pitroda and Abdul Kalam are few names that were never bogged down by the circumstances and the limitation of infrastructure.

Mind versus Mindset

Mindset can be the biggest bottleneck. Having good qualities and competence is not sufficient to excel. Having a positive attitude and a right mindset is very critical to achieve success, the numbers told by politician, bureaucrats and businessmen regarding shortage and resource limitation are only to create a sense of scarcity, coming from a weak mind. Most of the East Asia countries like Singapore and Malaysia a few years back had scarce researches, at least we have the basic infrastructure to make the best use of it. There is a continuous struggle between mind and mindset; those who win the battle of mindset will trigger the process of transformation.

Spend Time with Young People, It will Allow You to Think Fresh and Bold

The young generation are oozing with energy and have new and innovative ideas. In any organization which has performed well, the energy of these young people has been channeled in the right direction. The company of young people will never allow you to feel tired.

Questions

1. What are the important features for the person who can succeed the race in the 21st century?

   Or

   What are the key characters which need to be developed appropriately that would help present professionals to become tomorrow's leaders?
2. What are the reasons behind a main's failure?
3. What is the Indian way of a successful personality?

15
Soft Skills

15.1 DEFINING SOFT SKILLS

The technical know-how and the professional knowledge that constitute the basic requirement for appointment to a job are described as hard skills. A degree in surgery is essential to become a surgeon. A degree in architecture is required to become a town planner. The skills acquired while preparing for these degrees are hard skills.

Hard skills are given a lot of weightage at the entry point to a job. But retaining the job and moving upwards in the corporate world are determined by personal attributes like initiative, confidence, commitment, integrity, adaptability, team spirit, etc., along with communication skills, language skills, business etiquette, presentation and negotiation skills, etc. These skills are known as soft skills.

In the U.S.A. and Australia, soft skills are known as world skills. But it would be more appropriate to call them lift skills, for they are indispensable to leading a meaningful and fulfilling life.

15.2 THE IMPORTANCE OF SOFT SKILLS

1. Important for Growth: As suggested above, the initial years of one's career, one's technical abilities get one promising assignments. However, when it comes to growing in an organization, it is soft skills that prove to be the deciding factor. In large organization, in particular, where several candidates with comparable technical expertise are competing for a single promotion, the candidate equipped with better soft skills easily succeeds in overshadowing the others and grabs the higher post.

In one particular instance, just one lapse in business etiquette cost another highly competent official an important promotion. While making a presentation to a gathering which included one lady member, he addressed them as gentlemen. This was construed as an affront to the lady and the official's claims for promotion were set aside.

In another organization, a senior executive, one who would give the best possible solution to any technical problem, was denied promotion because he lacked the ability to carry people along with him.

Companies have now started linking soft skills to their employees appraisals and regard them as an important factor while deciding their compensation packages.

2. Important in Outsourcing Business: Outsourcing is an accepted feature of modern industrial and commercial world. Companies prefer to deal directly with the concerned officials instead of approaching them through the C.E.O. for it saves time and energy. The official's role becomes crucial in such a scenario. Those officials who possess good soft skills and can sustain the contracts their employers have bagged from their clients are naturally given preference over their other colleagues. Since education in India is knowledge-oriented and our education now insist on a mix of technical and soft skills for their fresh employees. It is felt that at least 25 per cent of the mandatory training requirement should be focused on helping them to cultivate soft skills.

15.3 KIND OF SOFT SKILLS

Soft skills can be divided into:

1. Corporate skills,
2. Employability skills, and
3. Growth skills.

1. Corporate Skills: As the name suggests, these skills are mostly needed at higher levels, but acquiring them definitely facilitates climbing up the corporate ladder.

Corporate skills include:

(a) Sensitivity to Political Climate of the Country: As astute reading of the subtle changes taking place in the political firmament gives insights into danger zones to be vigilant about and development opportunities to be grabbed.

(b) Awareness of the changes sweeping the corporate world at large, with special focus on the areas of one's own operations.

(c) Understanding of the functions of financial institutions and other fund-mobilising mechanisms.

(d) Ability to guide, monitor and control organizational operations and behaviour.

(e) Ability to visualize desirable organizational changes and the best time to effect them.

(f) Handling communication channels within the organization, including and effective utilization of the grapevine; information management.

(g) Communication skills, negotiation, persuasion and consensus building skills.

(h) Leadership skills—the ability to take people along, not merely as passive followers but as active and loyal vehicles of the organization's growth.

(i) Defining and projecting the organization's work ethics, evolving the value system that forms the basis of the organization's entire operations.

(j) Maintaining proactive public relations.

2. Employability Skills: Before candidates are handed over the much coveted appointment letter, they have usually to go through a written test, a grueling interview (sometimes more than one) and a group discussion. These evaluating mechanisms have their limitations. Personal qualities like integrity, dependability, commitment are difficult to judge during a brief interaction.

However, it is possible to judge qualities like initiative, confidence, communication skills, team spirit, problem-solving ability, flexibility, positivity and enthusiasm through personal interview and group discussion. Those candidates whose responses reflect these qualities begin their professional career at a much higher level than those who possess only hard skills.

Recently, there has been the case of a candidate who had an M.Tech from I.I.T., Delhi and M.B.A. from I.I.M., Ahmedabad, but who could not get a campus placement in a company of his choice because he was found to be rigid in his attitude and carried an aura of negativity around him. It should be obvious that most of the qualities mentioned above are overlapping or complementary instead of being mutually exclusive. One without good communication skills or without a flexible attitude cannot be a good leader. So, if someone is a good leader, it may be presumed that his communication skills are good. If a person makes a conscious effort to improve one particular skill, several other skills get automatically refined.

3. Growth Skills/Qualities: These are skills, or qualities, difficult to evaluate at the time of the interview but potent enough to shape a professional's career growth graph. They include the following:

(a) **Personal Qualities:**

- Personal health and hygiene, elegance in personal appearance, healthy food habits,
- Qualities like confidence, self-esteem, self-discipline,
- Being organized in personal life; the ability to look forward and plan in advance,
- Time management.

(b) **Interpersonal Skills:**

- Empathising the ability to identify with others and view situations from their perspective,
- Flexibility in approach,
- Respecting difference of opinion and the ability to resolve differences amicably,

- Being a patient listener,
- Having a genuinely caring attitude,
- Having a constructive and outstanding attitude towards other's weaknesses rather than being critical and dismissive,
- Having the ability to work with others as a team,
- Having the ability to guide and support others in order to accomplish a specific good (leadership skills).

(c) **Skills Essential for Corporate Growth and Corporate Culture:**

- The ability to analyse and critically evaluate,
- The ability to priorities,
- The ability to make the optimum use of the resources available,
- Problem-solving an decision-making abilities,
- Creativity—the ability to come out with obsolete ideas to lead the organization towards growth,
- Taking a calculated risk to enhance the performance of the organization,
- Integrity and commitment,
- The ability to assume responsibility, dependability (once a job has been assigned to you, can the boss relax on the assumption that it will be satisfactorily accomplished?),
- Initiative (doing things without needing to be told or persuaded),
- The ability to remain cool under pressure (can you successfully handle the stress that accompanies deadlines and other constraints?),
- Written communication skills, both printed and online written work including preparing reports, writing letters and e-mails,
- Oral communication skills including conducting meetings and holding interviews,

- Multicultural skills (can you understand and relate to people who belong to a different culture perhaps through your knowledge of a second language?).

15.4 HOW TO DEVELOP SOFT SKILLS

Some psychologists believe that soft skills are inherent in a human being and cannot be acquired. This is only partly true. While positive skills can be learnt through a patient and persistent effort, the damaging effects of negative emotions can be minimized through self-discipline. Changing one's personality is a slow process. But it is possible to a certain extent, and the effort and time invested in it do prove to be rewarding. Some useful steps are explained below.

1. Evaluate Yourself: The first step towards changing your personality is to identify your strengths and weaknesses. This can be done with the help of family members, or close friends, or through introspection. If others are evaluating you, request them to be objective and take note of both your positive and negative traits. Besides, you should get at least four to five diverse viewpoints so that you get a fairly accurate and comprehensive assessment. Make a consolidated list of the points and start working to reinforce your strengths and control your weaknesses.

2. Cultivate Elegance: Make a conscious effort to look elegant, not only when you go out but even at home. A regular morning walk, yoga and/or work-out in a gym, and a healthy diet will keep you physically fit. Dress yourself to look dignified and graceful and not flashy and flamboyant. Pay special attention to the accessories. Always were a smile, for there is no dress more elegant than a smile.

3. Imbibe Team Spirit: Team spirit promotes adaptability and cooperativeness, so try to become a part of team activities. Working with others as a team will sharpen your communication skill and help you to overcome such negative qualities as lack of confidence, aloofness, reticence, etc. if you can assume responsibility and muster enough boldness to become the leader of the team, it will work wonders for your personality refinement.

4. Learn to Appreciate: Genuine appreciation of the positive qualities of other people will not only purge you of your negative emotions like egoism, jealousy and malice but also broaden your outlook and help you transcend yourself. It will also endear you to your colleagues and earn you their adoration.

5. Manage Your Emotions Intelligently: If you are unable to rid yourself of your negative emotions completely, at least keep them in check. How often have we landed into an embarrassing situation because of a fit of fury that we could not control or a sarcastic statement that though we sincerely regret, we cannot retract? Such situations can be avoided by a sensible management of negative emotions. For example, even anger has a place in life. If we can channelize our anger and direct it to the right person, at the right time, in the right quantity, it can become an effective tool in our hands. So, use anger like a master and do not allow yourself to become its slave. Another emotion that you need to keep in check is tension: do not get tensed up at the slightest provocation.

6. Learn the Art of Time Management: If you are able to plan your activities, it will save you a great deal of time and wasteful effort. It will give you sufficient time for further planning and reduce the incidence of stressful situations.

7. Learn to Relax: Remaining cool and relaxed all the time will bring a glow and radiance on your face, and make your personality attractive. You should relax, with yoga, music, a chat with the spouse, a tete-a-tete with a close friend, by reading a good book, or by sitting in meditation.

Question

1. Briefly comment on the following statement:
   - (a) Hard skills can get you a job, but it is your soft skills that will help you keep it.
   - (b) Soft skills are not inherent, they are acquired.
   - (c) Good health and a relaxed mind are basic to acquiring soft skills.
   - (d) How do you distinguish soft skills from hard skills?

(e) Discuss the various kinds of soft skills.

(f) Suggest some strategies to improve one's soft skills.

Stimulate Yourself

1. Study the career graph of two of your seniors. Compare and contrast both their professional qualifications and their soft skills. Find out how the one with better soft skills has fared in life. Do you find any close relationship between their career graph and their soft skills?
2. Analyse your personality. Identity the soft skills you lack. Have you ever suffered because of your weaknesses? How can you develop the soft skills you lack?

16

R.S.V.P. Formula for Outstanding Success

Personality development is of very much importance to us all from many angles. We live in a Dynamic World where we cannot keep a static position. We have to keep on growing, till last breath of our life. We have to drive best satisfaction in our personal and community life on physical, mental and spiritual levels. We have to do our best, to better our own selves and the world. Personality Development is on a micro level where we take an individual as a unit, and help him or her to grow up together on a macro level, we come to Human Resources Development. It is a matter of great pleasure and it is also a very healthy sign for us all, that very many institutions in the private sector and also government departments have started paying much attention to the subject of Human Resources Development.

For this we must follow R.S.V.P. formula for outstanding success. What is R.S.V.P.?

Read (R)

I must read—I must widen my reading horizons to learn the secrets which will make my life easier. It will ensure my success in every field of human endeavor. How else but by deep reading can I receive the truth which come from the Natural Laws?

But if I only read on surface, I cannot really learn anything of permanent value. I did not learn my lessons in school by merely reading them in the same way that I read the daily papers. Therefore, I must....

Study (S)

I must study those things which I read. I must do more than merely apply my eyes to the printed page. I must apply myself, my mind, my ideas, my thoughts to the substance of the words I read. By doing this, I will begin to make divine powers grow within me. That power comes from understanding and to build up that deep understanding I must study and get myself ready. All great people in the past studied and prepared themselves for higher achievements in their lives. I must do that—namely to study in great depth.

Once I am successful in building up that power—I will be required to apply it in my real life situations. I will strive to develop clear outlines or blueprints of when, where and how to apply the new powers generated within me. For this I will have to....

Visualise (V)

I must cultivate the capacity to visualize in concrete form, everything I read and study. I must learn to take a mental or written suggestion and be able to project like a motion picture on the hidden screen of my mind's eye. I must really see those suggestions, those plans, those goals, in solid form in my mind's eye. Then and then only I can successfully attain the same in reality.

Visualization is far more than mere imagination. It is always more complete, more detailed. In short, it has the effect of adding the potential of reality to the unsatisfying dream that is imagination.

The man who creates a new and important invention often starts with mere imagination of dream. But, as his mind ponders on the IDEA, he begins to visualize with an even increasing exactness of details of the same.

He begins to 'see' his invention almost as though it were physically present in front of him. This I must do. It is not easy at first. But by constant practice I will find out way to turn my dreams into realities. I can reach very high levels of achievement if I....

Perform (P)

The manner in which I perform my various talks in my work areas and in my hobby areas will shape my future personality development, I promise to myself and other that 'I will do my best' in all my undertakings.

Abraham Lincoln rightly said: "I am not bound to win—but I am bound to do my best. I will work on that suggested line. I will do my best to improve my performance day by day, hour by hour, minute by minute. And I am humbly sure that by the help of 'His' grace ultimate success will be mine."

Questions

1. What do you understand by the term, R.S.V.P.? Discuss the role of R and S in Personality Development.
2. Discuss the role of "P" in personality development.

17

Start and Continue Strong Action Line

17.1 INTRODUCTION

Personality Development is not such an adventure, which you can undertake successfully while resting in your "Easy Chair" only. You will have to make determined efforts to translate your good thoughts—your cherished plans and goals in real achievement of your life.

Many people possess excellent knowledge of their plus (+) points and minus (–) points, but they do not take any worthwhile steps—either to overcome their weakness or using their strong points in a profitable manner. For example, some people have a fine 'knack' to make new friends—help worthy projects—make their life sublime—but they do not take suitable steps to do many things of which they are capable of.

You are in a position to do 1001 good things in your life, but if you do not act on them—the result will not be there. I feel this is enough for the background against which I am building up this chapter.

In the following areas, START taking vigorous actions. Do not postpone the START. It is to be done NOW only, otherwise it will be too late—it will be NEVER.

In any worthwhile achievements of our human life, STARTING is very much important. Start vigorously and continue your strong action line. Brick by brick—Brick by Brick you will have to build up your future career. By God's Grace your achievements will be praiseworthy.

17.2 FIRST IMPROVE YOUR PHYSICAL HEALTH

Lokmanya Tilak very rightly said that if you want to do any good thing in life—you must possess sound body. In sound body only resides sound mind.

If your body is weak—and if your mind is strong there will be an imbalance between them—between your mind and body.

George Bernard Shaw said:

> If you have good health, use it well. That is meant for good use. Do not hoard it or like old mind, it is liable to get sour and go bad.

So in the matter of health—you will work on twin objectives. First, you will keep your body in 'ship-shape condition and you will enjoy good health which you have acquired as a result of your efforts. Read some good health book and follow its recommendations.

You may also read some healthy sex-book and get necessary knowledge. Some 25-30 years back young people were very much shy to ask the books which dealt with sex and health. Now a good change has come over. Young people are encouraged to read healthy sex-books written by doctors and other competent authorities in the field. Know your body well. Know your mind well. Understand body signals. Understand mind signals and live on scientific lines.

17.3 DEVELOP SOCIAL GRACE

It is very important quality be to developed by all of us. It is the ability to feel at home in any social setting. If you possess it, you are never overcrowd by people. You know how to deal with your fellow beings. Some authors term this quality as Social Sense. By virtue of this quality you are acquainted with their weaknesses and specialities. It is similar to tact. A tactful man knows how to listen to others and when to keep his mouth shut altogether. They know how to handle men and situations completely.

Tact and social grace are possessed only by the man who takes the trouble to learn all he can about his fellow-men who is interested in them and rubs-shoulders freely with them. They are to be learnt from Real Situations—Books tell us the need to do that—and we have to find out ways to acquire such knowledge—such experiences—to make us successful.

For this end in view—strike a balance in your life—between EXTROVERT PERSONALITY and INTROVERT PERSONALITY, BE AN AMBIVERT. The extrovert is a person whose interest turns outwards. His attempts are directed towards the external world. You will find that good teachers, doctors, lawyers, administrators, sportsmen, actors are extrovert by nature. The introvert is the individual whose interest turns inwards and his efforts by nature. The introvert is the individual whose interest turns inwards and his efforts are directed towards enrichment of inner life. Extroverts are DO-ERS and Introverts are BE-ERS. The Extrovert's chief qualities are a strong desire for activity and overpowering of ruling attitude. He is cool and composed, he is not passionate. He does not contemplate deeply on life and problems intimately connected with individuals and groups. Because most of his attention is given to outside world, his inner life suffers. It is with a view to stifle the demands of his inner life—that he throws himself into more and more of activity, he tries to adjust his ideas to the reality that exists about him.

He reacts quickly to the influences of his environment. Since his whole aim in life is to adjust himself to its demands, he fits into the scheme of things harmoniously. His ideas are the ideas of most people. So such extrovert people become leaders of masses. They know MASS PSYCHOLOGY well, they are able to take best advantages of other people and situations which change from time to time. They are able to be more successful in acquiring good wealth, good positions and good life partners.

Extrovert person is a practical person. A good salesman knows his customers well. In the same manner he knows about the qualities of other people and try to make them happy. So he is eager to please with a ready laugh. For these and many other similar reasons akin to be mentioned and this point—his behaviour and personality are more approved by common people—then those of introvert people. Extroversion brings him into the public eye. He is admired more.

The introvert's qualities, on the other hand, are having a lack of absence of outside activity. Such person is of a 'Reserved' type. He sits more in a quiet place and does the work. When he is free, he broods over life and its problem.

He does more of the foundation work for other people, for society and human beings at large. He is like a dreamer. He moves ahead of his time and contemplates deeply as what should be done. His work never produces quick results. He fades out in background. He does not get enough payments for services rendered by him. So, for obvious reasons, he is not duly recognized by other in the society.

He sticks fast to his values. He finds it very much difficult to make compromises with other people—and situations. He is very passionate. Once he is provoked, he will not tolerate any injustice or any nonsense thing. He fights tooth and nail. He has the courage to follow his conviction. Writers, painters, music composers, artistes, philosophers, etc., are of introvert type.

Introvert person is not much of a 'Vocal Type' person. Such a person keep his feeling to himself as a consequence of which he suffers silently the pains and scars of his life.

Generally speaking, his qualities are not popular with general mass of people. Very frequently they are misunderstood by other people who live on surface of common existence.

An introvert creates his own private world and withdraws himself in that. He is unable to adjust efficiently to the realities of practical world. In many cases such people have been recognized by others after their death.

We can cover many points in this discussion. I request you to think on this topic leisurely and conduct group discussion. You must attend the Speaking and Personality Development classes, we should have discussed such topics in great detail. We should have shared knowledge with each other.

So let us sum up this topic, strike a balance between introvert and extrovert personality to go up in life. Develop your lifestyle gradually step by step. For doing that, your attitudes are of much importance. Tight attitude in our life, help us to develop our abilities in fine manners.

Some of our abilities are received by us through our inheritance from our parents and our grandparents. It is quite natural that with passage of time, all things of past, all the things done by our forefathers cannot be kept intact by us. Moreover, some things of past have outlived their utility so we have to discard them. So we have to take a sensible approach in this area. Let us keep our past good traditions with open minds. We may be called upon to modify some of them in modern times, let us do that. Such open minds will contribute much to develop our own lifestyle in a flexible manner.

Say, for example, in the past, people were very much against contracting loans and debts. In modern age, to acquire a house in big cities, to send children to college for higher education, to enable them to marry and settle down in their life, big funds are required.

Middle-class and lower middle class people have to take long-term loans and liquidate them in smaller regular instalments. When people borrow money they should first conduct frank search in their own life. It would not be wise to take loan from others, for unproductive purpose. While contracting loans we must ensure ourselves that we will have enough and regular source of income to pay such loans. Let us not imitate lifestyles of our rich neighbours. Let us not borrow money to keep up false pre-tenses. Otherwise, we shall cripple our own lifestyles. So let us think well before entering into debt-Traps. This is applicable for individuals and also for the nation. Reflect well on this topic.

If you have the cheerful temperament, which enable you to realize all your potentialities to make a success of your life you deserve our warm compliments. Continue in your own style. Keep notes of success and achievement of yours in different areas of life. Review them once in a week and explore the possibilities and opportunities to add new entries in our note-book. Do keep such note-books. They will help you to go up.

But if, on the contrary, you are sluggish, or you lack self-control, or if you are 'moody' or suffer from regular and frequent phrases of depression and cheerlessness, you should do something about it. You will make your WILL POWER strong. You will have more honest self-talks in having deep probe in your personality make-up. Try to find out your weak points and proceed to overcome them.

SMILE MORE, SMILE BIG. Smile as many times you can during the day even when you are alone, recall some joke or recall some pleasant experiences and smile pleasantly.

Gradually you will be able to smile effortlessly. A ready smile is an important asset in your personality. It is like a flag which indicates the friendly, open and unbiased approach. Broad smiles will help you to solve your problems without tension. SMILE will help you to drive away your gloom. When you are in a joyful and auspicious company of smiling people negotiations will be smooth. There will be absence of hostility. Competition will not humiliate you, or pull you down.

This is nicely explain in poetic way—LAUGH AND WORLD LAUGHS WITH YOU—keep this thing permanently fixed up in your mind. CULTIVATE 'YOUR' APPITUDE in your relations with others. Reduce the size of 'I', 'MY', 'MINE' make them as small as you can. Be more humble. By making yourself humble—you will be able to win the hearts of others.

Make 'You', 'Your', etc. More capital—more big in size. Use more EMPATHY in your dealings with others. Understand their needs—understand their desires—understand their dreams and help them to fulfill them, FIND THE NEEDS AND FILL THEM WELL.

By doing this, you will not be nervous, you will not be let down by others, if you think of giving more services to your fellow-men than working for your own benefits and rewards.

Incidentally you will have better personality; if you are less concerned about yourself and your personality then you are about getting useful things done for others' benefits. You should be optimistic—out and out optimistic—even in most trying situations to build up your personality very strongly—very effectively.

An optimist radiates good cheer. People are attracted to him by this sunny disposition. His lifestyle is sound. Many people with a bad lifestyle are not able to keep pretence of being optimists for a long time. They are exposed quickly and other people do not trust them.

Pessimism is a characteristic of person who has made up his mind never to be taken unawares by any important events. He is extra-cautious in taking any decision in his life. He doubts and doubts much. So his self-development, his personality development is much stifled.

BE ENTHUSIASTIC. Give yourself joyfully over to the adventure of living. If you do this, you will never feel dull or bored. You will never have time to feel sorry for your life—for your works. Your complaint will be that you do not have enough time to do many nice things—which you like to do. You will live much 'Qualitative life'.

Please do not like grumblers or cynics. Have faith in life and abiding cheerfulness. Keep yourself in cheerful mood—and people will extend your warm welcome at any time, at any place.

Questions

1. Which are the efforts that help in translating good thoughts into achievements of life?
2. What does George Bernard Shaw say about good health?
3. How you can make a balance between Extrovert Personality and Introvert Personality?

18

Communication

18.1 MEANING

Communication is the process of sharing facts, ideas or emotions between two or more persons.

> Communication means an exchange of facts, ideas, opinions, information or emotions by two or more persons.
>
> —*Newman and Summer*

> Communication is the intercourse by words, letter or message, intercourse of thoughts or opinions. It is the act of making one's ideas and opinions known to others.
>
> —*Fred. G. Meyar*

> Communication is the process of passing information and understanding from one person to another.
>
> —*Keith Davis*

> Communication is the sum of all the things one person does when he wants to create understanding in the mind of another. It is a bridge of meaning. It involves a systematic and continuous process of telling, listening and understanding.

18.2 NATURE OF COMMUNICATION

1. Communication is required in all managerial functions. However, it is an integral part of the directing process; and assumes greater significance at the directing stage.

2. Communication is a function of every manager. Hence, it is a pervasive managerial function.

3. Communication is a continuous process throughout the organizational life.

4. Communication is a two-way process. This emphasizes on the feedback aspect of communication i.e., the sender of the message must get the necessary response (or reaction) of the recipient of the communication.

5. On the basis of system and nature, communication is bifurcated into two major categories: (i) Formal communication, and (ii) Informal communication.

6. On the basis of expression (or channels or methods), communication might be, oral or written.

18.3 IMPORTANCE OF COMMUNICATION

1. **Growth in the Size of Organization:** Most of the organizations nowadays are growing larger and larger in size. The people working in these organizations may be spread over different states of a country or over different countries. Keeping in touch with them, sending across directions and getting feedback will be possible only when communication lines are kept working effectively.

2. **Growth of Trade Unions:** Over the last so many decades trade unions have been growing strong. No management can be successful without taking the trade unions into confidence. Only through effective communication can a meaningful relationship be built between the management and the workers.

3. **Growing Importance of Human Relations:** Workers in an organization are not like machines. They have their own hopes and aspirations. Management has to recognize them above all as sensitive human beings and work towards a spirit of integration with them.

4. **Public Relations:** Every organization has a social responsibility, specially towards the customers, government, suppliers and the public at large. Communication with them is the only way an organization can projected a proper image of itself.

5. Advances in Behavioural Sciences: Modern management is deeply influenced by exciting discoveries made in behavioural sciences like Psychology, Sociology, Transactional Analysis, etc. all of them throw light on subtle aspects of human nature and help in developing a positive attitude towards life and building up meaningful relationship. And this is possible only through communication.

6. Technological Advancements: The world is changing very fast, owing to scientific and technological advancements. These advancements deeply affect not only methods of work but also the composition of groups. In such a situation proper communication between superiors and subordinates becomes very necessary.

18.4 PROCESS OF COMMUNICATION

The communication process involves the sender, transmission of a message through a selected channel and the receiver. Although the process of communication is more than the sum total of these elements, understanding them can help explain what happens when one person tries to express an idea to others.

18.4.1 Sender

The process of communication begins with a sender, the person who transmits a message. The branch manager explaining new product lines to the sales force, a computer programmer explaining a new program to a co-worker, accountant giving financial report to its superior are all senders of communication.

18.4.2 Message

A message is any signal that triggers the response of a receiver. Message could be verbal (written or spoken) or non-verbal (such as appearance, body language, silence, sounds, yawns, sighs etc.).

Encoding

The sender must choose certain words or non-verbal methods to send an international message. This activity is called encoding. While encoding a message, one needs to consider what contents to include, how the receiver will interpret it and how it may affect one's relationship. A simple "thankful" message will be relatively easy. In contrast, to inform 200 employees of a bad news about salary cut or bid on engineering plants to construct a ₹ 50 crore industrial building will require much more complicated, carefully planned message.

18.4.3 Channel

How will you send your message? Should it be sent via an electronic word processing system to be read on the receiver's screen or through the printed word or through graphic symbol on paper, or via the medium of sound? Briefly, should one write or speak?

The choice of channel or medium (written or oral) is influenced by the inter-relationships between the sender and the receiver. It also depends upon the urgency of the message being sent. Besides, one may consider factors such as importance, number of receivers, costs and amount of information.

Generally, it has been observed that if the message requires an immediate answer, an oral channel may be the better choice. But if the message contains complicated details and figures or if its subject requires filing for future reference, a written communication is necessary. Furthermore, whether your message receiver is inside or outside your organization affects your choice of the medium. For internal communication, written media may be memos, reports, bullets, job descriptions, poster, employee manuals or even electronic bulletin boards. Oral communication may be staff meeting reports, face to face discussion, speeches, audio tapes, telephone chats, teleconferences or even videotapes. Another oral channel, though unplanned by the sender, is the 'grapevine' through which news and rumours often travel quickly.

External written communication media may be letters, reports, proposals, telegrams, faces, electronic mails, telexes, postcards, contracts, ads, brochures, catalogues, news releases etc., you may communication orally face-to-face, by telephone, or by speeches in sole or in panel situations personally before groups or via teleconferences, videoconferences or TV.

18.4.4 Receiver

A receiver is any person who notices and attaches some meaning to a message. In the best circumstances, a message reaches its intended receiver with no problems. In the confusing and imperfect world of business, however, several problems can occur. The message may never get to receiver. It might be sent but buried under a mountain of files on the recipient's desk. If the message is oral, the listener might forget it. Even worse, a message intended for one receiver might be intercepted by someone else or your colleague may take your friendly joke in an offensive manner. Similarly, your 'boss' suggestion may be taken to be an order for you for example, a competitor might see a copy of your correspondence to a customer.

18.4.5 Decoding

Even if the message reaches intact to its intended receiver, there is no guarantee that it will be understood as the sender intended it to be. The receiver must still decode it attaching meaning to the words or symbols, it may be noted that decoding is not always accurate. It depends upon individual experiences. The problem is that all of us do not have identical experiences with the subject or symbols chosen by the sender. Even within India, attitudes, abilities, opinions, communication skills and cultural customs vary. And if the communication is between people of two different countries, say India and Japan, the problem increases. There are greater chances of misinterpretation; personal biases may intervene, as each receiver tries to perceive the intended meaning of the sender's idea in his or her own receptor mechanism.

18.4.6 Feedback

Ultimately, the receiver reacts or responds to the communication sent by the sender. The response could be based on clear interpretation of the symbols sent or it could be based on misunderstanding or misinterpretation of the symbols sent. Whatever the response of a receiver to a sender is, it is called feedback. Some feedback is non-verbal smiles, sighs, nods and so on. Sometimes it is oral, as when you react to a colleague's ideas with questions or times it is oral, as when you react to a colleague's ideas with questions or comments. Feedback can also be a feedback. Failure to answer a letter or to return a phone call can suggest how the non-communicative person feels about the sender. Feedback is an important component of the communication process, because ultimately the success of failure of the communication is decided by the feedback we get.

18.5 FORMAL AND INFORMAL COMMUNICATION

18.5.1 Formal Communication

Formal communication is designed by the management. It is an official communication which takes plane through the line of authority or chain of command. The basic purpose of designing such communication is to connect various sub-systems of organization and coordinating their functioning for achieving organizational goals. Such communication is official and part of formal organization which operates through formal relationship of superior and subordinate. According to the direction of communication it may be of the following types:

1. Downward
2. Upward
3. Horizontal or Lateral
4. Diagonal or Crosswise.

1. Downward Communication: Communication in the place, flows downwards. That is why, traditionally this direction has been highlighted or emphasized. It is based on the assumption that the people working at higher levels have the authority to communicate to the people working at lower levels. This direction of communication strengthens the authoritarian structure of the organization. This is also called Down Stream Communication.

Limitations of Downward Communication

(a) **Distortion/Dilution:** Quite often the communication originating at the highest level gets distorted or diluted on the way to the lower levels. Sometime the messages may get lost. It has to ensured that the receiver fully understands the purport/instructions/directions coming from above. This requires an efficient feedback system.

(b) **Delay:** Another drawback of downward communication is that often it becomes time-consuming. The more the levels the greater the chances to delay. That is why sometimes managers choose to send their messages directly to the person concerned.

(c) **Filtering:** Sometimes managers may withhold some valuable information from the employees. In such a situation the employees becomes frustrated, confused and powerless. This may spoil the employer-employee relationship.

2. **Upward Communication:** The function of upward communication is to send information, suggestions, complaints and grievances of the lower level workers to the managers above. It is, therefore, more participative in nature. It was not encouraged in the past, but modern managers encourage upward communication. This is direct result of increasing democratization. This is also called up stream communication.

Limitations of Upward Communication

(a) **Psychological:** Certain problems, primarily of psychological nature, may come up in upward communication.

(b) **Hierarchical:** Many managers do not like to be 'told' by their junior. They may not be patient enough to listen to them or may even suppress the message sent to them from below. In such a situation the employees may feel let down.

Ways to Overcome the Limitations—Ombudsperson

In order to tide over such problems an ombudsperson plays an important role. The concept of Ombudsman or Ombudsperson was first used in Sweden to go into the complaints of lower level employees against government officials or agencies. Now a number of companies in many countries have established positions for persons to investigate employees, complaints and grievances. An Ombudsperson, therefore, effectively mediates between the employers and the employees and smoothens upward communication.

1. Lateral or Horizontal Communication: The type of communication can be seen taking place between persons operating at the same level or working under the same executive. Functional managers operating at the same level, in different departments, through their communication, present a good example of lateral communication, present a good example of lateral communication. The main use of this dimension of communication is to maintain coordination and review activities assigned to various subordinates. Occasions for lateral communication arise during committee meetings or conferences in which all members of the group, mostly peers or equals, interact. The best example of lateral communication can be seen in the interaction between production and marketing departments.

2. Diagonal or Crosswise Communication: Diagonal or crosswise communication takes place when people working at the same level interact with those working at a higher or lower-level of organizational hierarchy and across the boundaries of their reporting relationships.

Advantages of Diagonal Communication

(a) **Coordination:** The crosswise communication serves the important purpose of coordination through information meetings, formal conferences, lunch hour meetings, general notice etc.

(b) **Practicable:** As we know not all communication takes place strictly on the lines of organizational hierarchy, i.e., downward or upwards.

(c) **Morale Boosting:** By providing opportunities to lower level workers to interact with managers in informal meetings it gives their morale a boost and further commitment to the organization. More and more organizations are now encouraging crosswise communication and building up bonhomie.

Limitations of Diagonal Communication

(a) **Fear of Infringement:** The superior may feel it an infringement that his subordinate has been given undue importance and that he has been by-passed.

(b) **Resistance to Compliance:** The superior may not implement the suggestion as he has not been consulted.

(c) **Anarchy:** The lack of accepted procedures may lead to internal anarchy and external animosity.

18.5.2 Informal Communication

Informal communication is considered a part of functioning of informal organization. In such communication, information is transmitted and exchanged among the employees through their personal and social relations. Such communication occurs beyond the line of authority between the employees having no direct reporting relationship. Informal communication is considered necessary for satisfying social needs of the employees because through such communication they get socialized and make social interactions. Through informal communication they share experience and make exchange of information on personal matters as well as organizational matters which are related to them. Such communication has not been designed and planned by the management but even then it operates in a formal organization and is also known as 'Grapevine'. It is because it has no set boundaries rather it may move in any direction. It flows around water coolers, canteens, lunch-rooms and other places wherever the people get together in a group. Through such communication, oral, and unofficial, information is circulated among the employees. For example, keep it with you only, 'nothing is official about it' or 'it is in between you and me only' are various modes of informal communication.

Table 181: Distinction between Formal and Informal Communication

Formal Communication	Informal Communication
The chain of command and relationship of superior and subordinate is a base of formal communication.	Personal and social relationship developed among employee provide base for it.
Only official matters are communicated through it.	It communicates both as well as non-official matters.

Formal Communication	Informal Communication
It is slow moving because it has to go through chain of command.	It is very fast because it moves around social and personal relations.
Formal communication network is deliberately designed as a part of formal structure of organization.	It arises automatically and is a part of informal group organization.
Its objective is to secure smooth functioning of organization.	It provides social satisfaction to the employees.
Organization bears its cost.	No cost is involved in it.
It has set boundaries, mechanism and channels.	It has no definite structure, directions and boundaries.

Verbal Communication

The word 'verbal' means connected with words and the use of words. Human beings are the only species gifted with the use of words that makes a language. As has been stated previously, the process of communication involved the use of a common set of symbols between the sender and the recipient. Words are the most accurate and powerful sets of symbols. That is why it is observed that all serious or formal communication is in words. And the words may be spoken or written. Spoken communication or the communication employing speech is known as oral communication.

Verbal Communication—Oral

As speech comes before writing it is worthwhile to take up oral communication before written communication. Man learns to speak much before writing. In the same way, in an organization people speak much more, and much before writing. There are a number of occasions, both formal and informal when the people speak before committing themselves in writing. In fact, speech, or oral use of language, acts as the first binding factor between one person and another. That is also the reason why communication becomes conversational in nature.

Advantages of Oral Communication

1. The first and foremost advantage of oral communication is that it provides immediate feedback to the participants in the communication event. While engaged in talk with somebody we can ask for clarification or further elaboration, justification, etc.

2. Oral communication is time saving.

3. By drawing the people together oral communication builds up a healthy climate in the organization. It brings the superiors and the subordinates nearer.

4. Oral communication, just sounding personal, becomes an effective tool of persuasion. Everybody knows the importance of persuasion in business.

5. Oral communication is not only time-saving, it is also very economical. It saves the money spent on stationary in an organization.

6. Oral communication also provides the speaker opportunity to correct himself and make himself clear by changing his voice, tone, pitch, etc.

7. In oral communication the speaker enjoys the advantage of understanding the groups he is addressing. He can immediately understand the group's reaction and arrive at a satisfactory conclusion.

Limitations of Oral Communication

1. Oral communication may not always be time saving. Sometimes a happens that meetings go on and on for a long time without arriving at any satisfactory conclusion.

2. Oral messages cannot always be retained in the listener's memory. The speaker himself may always not recall what he verbally said or meant.

3. In the absence of record, oral messages do not have legal validity.

4. If the speaker has not carefully organized his thought oral message may lead to misunderstanding.

5. The length of the message may pose a problem. If the message is long it is not always suitable for oral communication.

6. It becomes difficult to fix responsibility for anything going wrong or for any mistake in oral communication.

Verbal Communication—Written

After discussing oral communication it is worthwhile to discuss the nature and importance of written communication.

While oral communication comes naturally and spontaneously to man, written communication requires a lot of effort. By its very nature, writing is a result that speech comes first and writing comes afterwards. In all languages of the world writing appeared ages after speaking. History of civilization shows us different stages through which the formation of letters of the alphabet of any language has passed. But one thing is clear, whatever has been written, unless destroyed, has become permanent. Words spoken are, however, likely to be forgotten. That is why written communication is indispensable.

Characteristics of Written Communication

1. Written communication is a creative activity that requires a lot of imagination and effort to arrive at the finished product. While oral communication is spontaneous. Written communication is based on conscious effort. Let us take the example of a report that we want to present. We first of all have to collect all the necessary information, arrange it in a logical order and write them out very carefully. We have to be careful at every step. That is not always the case with spoken messages or other forms of oral communication. Letters and reports, nicely produced, reflect the image of the organization. The more creative and imaginative the writers the brighter the image of the company.

2. Another important characteristic of written communication is the time factor that is involved in it. Oral message, in a face-to-face situation or through telephone reach the receiver immediately and the feedback almost always comes immediately. This is not the case with written communication. The sender has to plan out his message, viz., a letter or report carefully and encode it with great care. Then he sends it to the person for whom it is meant. The receiver takes his own time in decoding it. Then he gives it a careful thought or filters it through his mind and plans out his reaction to it. Sending back the reply or his comments on it will take some time. So it is to be kept in mind that written communication is a time consuming activity.

3. Thirdly, it is to be noted that written communication has fewer cycles than oral or face-to-face communication. Oral

communication is a multiple cycle event. Oral messages get immediate response that leads very often to further exchange of words. This is not possible in written communication. Mostly it is a one-cycle event.

Importance of written communication: Written communication is so important that it is not possible to think of a business organization without it. The working of any organization depends to a large extent on the exchange of letters, reports, etc. there are various reasons for it. And the most important reason is that face-to-face communication is not always possible because the workers of an organization may be spread over widely through geographical distances. We have, therefore, to depend on exchange of letters. Modern technological distances have not decreased the importance of letters. Modes of transmission have changed. But written communication remains as important as ever.

Advantages of Written Communication

1. It provides us records, references etc., on which important decisions rest.

2. It builds up the legal defences of the organization through records, letters, instructions, etc.

3. It promotes uniformity of policy and procedure and build up proper guidelines for the working of the organization.

4. It builds up the image of the company.

5. It makes for accuracy and dependability (Oral communication may be changed or interpreted in different ways. But in written communication the message/information is stated very clearly or unambiguously).

6. It is permanent.

7. Responsibility can be easily assigned (One may go back on the spoken words. But not so on the statement in black and white).

Limitations of Written Communication

1. It builds up unmanageable clutter of papers and files. It costs a lot to the organizations.

2. It is time consuming, Immediate feedback is not possible.

3. It is costly in terms of money and man-hours.

4. It becomes effective in the hands of people who are poor in expression.

5. Absence of immediate clarification.

In conclusion, we can say that written communication remains the backbone of an organization; whatever be its disadvantages or limitations. Almost all formal communication is in writing.

Barriers to Communication

Communication is the lifeline of all business. Anything going wrong in it may cost the organization dear. Managers often complain that one of their greatest problems is communication breakdown. Specialists have made serious studies of it and have isolated certain factors that cause this problem. It is worthwhile having a look at these causes of communication breakdown.

Noise

Noise is the first and foremost barrier to communication. It means "interference that occurs in a signal and prevents you from hearing sounds properly". In a factory, for example, the continuous noise made by machines makes oral communication difficult. In the same way some technical problem in a public address system or a static in a telephone or television cable will distort the sound signal and affect communication. Adverse weather conditions or some fault in the ultramodern telecommunication systems may also spoil the effect.

Noise does not mean only this. It also encompasses many other factors that may exist at the end of sender as well as that of the receiver. The sender may resort to ambiguous or confusing signals. The receiver may mess up the message owing to inattention or may spoil decoding because of wrong or unexpected interpretation. The receiver's prejudices may also come in the way of his understanding the message in the right spirit. We must therefore keep in mind that communication is always likely to be spoilt by 'noise' that stands for so many things.

Lack of Planning

Communication is not a casual affair. Unfortunately many people take it lightly. The result is that the message to be sent across may not be carefully planned. There are innumerable examples of people who would give an ill planned, long-winding lecture while a short presentation with tables or graphs would be sufficient. Such an event would turn into one of miscommunication or malcommunication. In the same way some people may not care to choose a suitable time and place that are so necessary for effective communication.

Semantic Problems

Semantics is the systematic study of meaning. That is why the problems arising from expression or transmission of meaning in communication are called semantic problems. Oral or written communication is based on words. And words, limited in number, may be used in unlimited ways. The meaning is in the mind of the sender and also in that of the receiver. But it is not always necessary for the meaning in the mind of the sender to be the same as in the mind or receiver, must, therefore, depends on how the sender encodes his message. The sender has to take care that the receiver does not misconstrue his message. The sender has to take care that the receiver does not misconstrue his message, and gets the intended meaning. Quite often it does not happen in this way. That leads to semantic problems. It can be ensured only if we aim at clarity, simplicity and brevity so that the receiver gets the intended meaning.

Cultural Barriers

Cultural differences often come up as communication barriers. We have to be especially careful in this regard as of now we have to operate in international environment. The same category of words, phrases, symbols, actions, colours mean different things to people of different countries or different cultural background. For example, in the United States people love to be called by their first names while in Britain, and to a large extent also in India, people like to be addressed by their last name. In the North American States a sign of 'O' made with the forefinger and thumb stands for 'OK' while in the Southern States it is construed as obscenity.

Wrong Assumption

Quite often we act on assumptions, without caring to seek clarification for them. We should make all possible efforts to maintain our goodwill and not act impulsively on assumption. If, for example, a customer writes to us that he would like to visit our office or factory without telling us that he would like to be picked up and we assume that he will manage to come on his own, it may lead to loss of goodwill. So it is necessary to be circumspect in such matters.

Socio-Psychological Barriers

The attitudes and opinions, place in society and status-consciousness arising from one's position in the hierarchical structure of the organization, one's relations with peers, seniors, juniors and family background—all these deeply affect one's ability to communicate both as a sender and receiver. Status consciousness is widely known to be a serious communication barrier in organizations. It leads to psychological distancing which further leads to breakdown of communication or miscommunication. Often it is seen that a man's high up in an organization builds up a wall around himself. This restricts participation of the less powerful in decision-making. In the same way one's family background formulates one's attitude and communication skills.

Emotions

Emotions plays a very important role in our life. Both encoding and decoding of message are influenced by our emotions. A message received when we are emotionally worked up will have a different meaning for us than when we are clam and composed. Anger is the worst emotion and enemy of communication.

Selective Perception

Most of the factors cited above lead to selective perception. It means that the receivers selectively see and hear depending upon their needs, background, motivations, experience and other personal characteristics. While decoding the message, most of the receivers protect their own interests and expectations into process of communication leading to a particular kind of feedback that may become a communication problem.

Filtering

Filtering means that the sender of a message manipulates information in such a way that it will be seen more favourably by the receiver. A manager, for example, like to tell his boss what he feels or what his boss wants to hear. In this process, he is filtering information. The net result is that the man at the top never gets objective information. In the same way, the people at the lower levels condense and synthesise information so as to get maximum benefits for themselves. They hold back to ignore some important part of information. The more vertical levels in the organization, the more chances are for filtering. This is a very frequently occurring communication problem.

Information Overload

Unchecked inflow of information very often becomes another barrier to communication. It may stifle the senior executive or bore and frustrate him. When people are bogged down with too much information they are likely to make errors. They may also delay processing or responding to information/message atleast for some time. And delay may become a habit, causing serious communication problems. People may also become selective in their response, and selectively is not communication-friendly. On the other hand, it is a communication problem.

Poor Retention

As a corollary to the problem mentioned above it is worth noting that people are also likely to forget messages reaching them. Therefrom, arises the necessity to repeat the message and use more than one medium to communication the same message.

Poor Listening

Poor listening may lead to serious communication problems. Too, many people are interested in talking, and mostly talking about themselves. They are so much involved with themselves that they do not have patience to listen. The result is that they are not interested in the speaker whose words go waste. Everybody knows that the importance of listening, but very few actually practice patient, active and empathic listening. That is why so many communication problems crop up. Poor listening accounts for incomplete information and also poor retention. One may simply not get the desired result if this keeps on happening.

Goal Conflicts

Very often clashes of the goals of various units and sub-units of an organization lead to communication breakdowns. Communication should serve as a conflict-reduction exercise. But the goal conflicts act as communication reduction mechanisms. Different units internalize their own goals, and that leads to the splitting or bifurcation of interests in the organization. When people start competing for the fulfilment of their narrow interest communication suffers.

Offensive Style of Communication

It is quite obvious that offensive style of communication lads to communication breakdown. It is a rather sensitive point. If a manager sends a message in such a way that the workers/juniors become defensive and their relations get strained and communication suffers. Hence, it is absolutely necessary for the management to adopt a persuasive style of communication.

Insufficient Period for Adjustment

It is a well-known fact that people respond to change in different ways. They take their own time to adjust to any news or proposal for change. While the purpose of communication is to effect change it should be kept in mind that the employees whose duties, shifts, etc. are going to be change should be given sufficient time. Only then the communication will be effective.

Loss by Transmission

Communication often suffers or gets diluted when messages pass on from person to person in a series of transmissions. They get diluted on the way. Special care has to be taken that the intended message reaches the person concerned.

Tips for Effective Communication or 7cs.

Once we know the barriers to effective communication we must know the guidelines for effective communication. Anxiety associated with communication is known as communication apprehension, such anxiety tends to be influenced by one's self-concept. Besides apprehension, communication concept can be impaired via bypassing in discrimination.

Clarity of Purpose

In the first place we must be clear about what we want to communicate. This requires careful planning. Somebody has very aptly said, "the major mistake in communication is to believe that it happens". It should be kept in mind that all communication is a result of thinking in advance and planning out what has to be conveyed to whom, in what way and when. No meaningful communication takes place off hand or at random.

Cater to the Head and Heart

Emotional involvement is every bit as important as information when it comes to attracting an audience and motivating listeners to change. An emotional response will increase the time and energy a listener spends thinking about the message. Furthermore the decisions that are reached logically are strengthened if the decision is also emotionally rewarding. The focus should be on the needs of the receiver.

Sharing of Activity

Effective communication is the responsibility of all persons in the organization. They may be at any level—managerial or non-managerial. All of them have to work towards a common goal. It means, therefore, all of them, in different ways, have a share in the process of communication. That is why managers are advised to consult with others whenever necessary. A useful practice is to remember the heading 'For Action' and 'For Information' when communications are being planned.

Use of Symbols

It has been repeatedly said that communication is carried through a mutually understood set of symbols. It means that both encoding and decoding should be done through symbols that are familiar to the sender and the receiver. That is why managers, and especially the specialist staff, are advised to avoid using highly technical vocabulary or jargon that is understood only within a strictly limited group. They should remember that beyond their technical vocabulary there is a commonly understood language that does not create any communication problem.

Focusing on the Needs of the Receiver

Whenever we communicate we must keep in mind the needs of the receiver of the message or information. It should be our effort to see that whatever message or information we send across must be of value to the receiver. This awareness on our part will make him more receptive.

Use of Feedback

A renowned authority on organization behaviour says, "use feedback". Communication is complete only when the message is understood by the receiver. We can never know whether he has understood the message unless we get the feedback. Many communication problems arise because of misunderstandings and inaccuracies. We can avoid these problems by asking questions, requesting a reply to our letter, and encouraging the receiver to give his reactions to the message.

Listening

Communication cannot be effective unless, the receiver listens with due attentions or participatively. It further shows that communication is a joint responsibility of both the sender and the receiver. Participative listening is an essential condition of effective communication.

Controlling of Emotions

It is rather sad to note that we do not always communicate in a fully rational manner. Our reasoning is often clouded by negative feelings or emotions. The result is that all kinds of misunderstandings come up due the emotion-loaded encoding of the message or misinterpretation of the incoming message at the level of decoding. That is why modern management experts advise us to exercise self-control. Emotions, especially negative emotions can simply disturb communication.

Politeness of Manners

In communications, tone of voice, the choice of language and the congruency of logical connection between what is said and how it is said influence the reaction of the receiver. That is why managers are nowadays advised to avoid authoritarianism or in other words, to exercise authority with grace. Politeness begets politeness and encourages participative communication involving people at all levels. Truly effective communication is based on politeness and finesse.

Elimination of Noise

It has been noted in the preceding chapter that noise is the first and foremost enemy of communication. Every possible effort must be made to eliminate the element of noise that distorts communication at the transmission stage. Anything going wrong with the sound equipment or any disturbance in the transmission line is bound to spoil communication.

Clarification of Assumptions

No effective communications can be based on assumptions. Every effort must be made to clarity assumptions and have a clear, positive picture of the receiver or our message. In the same way the receiver also must get rid of all assumptions about the sender.

Avoidance of Ambiguities

Connotations and ambiguities lead to semantic problems. The sender of the message should be careful to see that the receiver does not have to go beyond the text of the message. It is, therefore, advisable to use explicit words and expressions. And words having double meaning should also be avoided.

Socio-psychological Background of Communicators

All effective communicators take care to understand the socio-psychological background of the receivers of their messages. The golden rule is 'First understand, then be understood'.

Completeness of Message

An effective message is a complete message. The receiver should not be left guessing. It may lead to misunderstanding. A complete message carries all necessary facts and figures.

Conciseness of Expression

Completeness does not mean inclusion of unnecessary details or diversions. An effective message is concise and crisp. For this purpose the sender must be clearheaded and properly focused in his vision.

Cordial Body Language

This point is especially important for face-to-face oral communication. We must be careful to see that we maintain proper posture including confidence and politeness, eye contact and, as far as possible pleasing gestures. And positive body language is based on positive feelings.

Commands Attention

By demonstrating how relevant the message is for the receiver and taking him realize its usefulness by shoeing that it is compatible with listeners 'beliefs the communication can be effective'. Attention is very necessary to ensure that all the relevant details are included in correct and clear manner.

Questions

1. Define the term 'communication' and trace its origin.
2. How is communication a social activity?
3. Why is communication so important to an organization? How does it relate the organization to the outside world?
4. Explain the process of communication with examples.
5. Why is downward communication regarded so important? What are the limitations?
6. Write a short note on the importance of upward communication.
7. What can managers do to facilitate the free flow of information?

8. Write a note on the importance and functions of "Ombudsman".
9. What is informal communication? What is the difference between formal and informal communication?
10. What do you mean by the word 'verbal'? Why is verbal communication regarded as serious?
11. Write a note on the importance of oral communication.
12. What are the limitations of oral communications?
13. Write a note on the characteristics of written communication.
14. Write in your own words the advantages and limitations of written communication.
15. Why is written communication indispensable to an organization?
16. Write short notes on the following:
    (a) Filtering
    (b) Information overload
    (c) Goal conflict
    (d) Status consciousness
    (e) Emotions and communication
17. Show how offensive style is the greatest barrier to communication.
18. Write a note on the socio-psychological barriers to communication.
19. How does culture affect communication?
20. Discuss the statement, "First understand, then be understood".
21. Discuss the importance of the following in effective communication.
    (a) Politeness
    (b) Clarity
    (c) Feedback
    (d) Completeness

19

How to Write an Impressive Resume?

19.1 MEANING OF RESUME

Resume is a piece of paper, which goes to prospective employer before you can reach there. It is a document that tells about you to the employer/consultant. A resume must reflect your personality in a holistic manner. We must know what must be covered in a resume and the information which may be avoided, what is the optimum size of a resume, what should be the font size, etc.

The objective of preparing a well-written resume is to get the attention of the employer at the first place. In fiercely fought competition, it must have a different approach. These days, many employers, make first level selection by screening the resumes. This stage is not in control of your other abilities as the resume is the source of information for the HR consultant. Therefore, even if you have any edge over others, you may lose the race in the very beginning if the resume does not have the right presentation.

The resume must have the following:

1. The Size of Resume: The resume should have an optimum size of not more than two A4 size papers. The size must be enough to have the information required for the post you have applied for. The experience and other details must not be exhaustive. Resumes written in more than two pages are a waste as consultants hardly have the time to read the extra pages and the annexure you have attached to it.

2. The Font in the Resume: The font in the MS-Word format should be New Time Roman in 12 size. The other artistic fonts used for the resume do not go well with the employer. It shows unprofessional presentation and attitude. The resume should be structured such that it also indicates your personality.

3. Tell the Facts, do not Exaggerate: The person who will scrutinize your CV is experienced and must have seen several hundred such CVs prior to this. You are fooling yourself, if you hide some information or exaggerate your achievements. It is very easy on the part of an experienced consultant to assess the facts.

4. Tailor Make Your CV: In most cases people prepare the CV once, get it laser printed and send copies to vacant positions which appear on the net/newspapers. But just imagine if someone serves you rice and sambar for breakfast even if he has a choice of idli to eat. The ingredients of rice and idli may be the same but they fit in the different requirements at different times of the day. Similarly, if a company is looking for a particular post, you need to present yourself as per the company needs.

5. Synopsis of Your Suitability: We all cover the academic qualifications, extra-curricular activities, experiences, hobbies, etc. in our CVs. But what can separate the men from boys is the clearly spelled synopsis of what makes you suitable for the post. The synopsis has to be covered in a brief paragraph stating your strength, which can fulfill the requirement of the "post you have applied for".

6. Covering Letter: The covering letter is required to be polite, referring to the source of information about the vacant position. The letter must not have the details of your bio-data as they are not recorded in offices. You must not give too much emphasis on your need of the job, rather the way the company would benefit from your service to the organization.

Decoding the Advertisement Requirements

It is important to know the requirements of the vacant position in the company. The companies generally use some of the common jargons, which convey certain messages. We need to understand these message prior to taking up the assignment.

Some of the HR consultants have very aptly said that, the job advertisement conceals as much as they reveal. When you are scanning an advertisement you will find some of the jargon, such as dynamic and persons who can take initiative, flexible, etc. let us find out what these jargon should mean to an applicant.

The first thing a person must do after seeing the advertisement is to visit the website of the company, contact through the telephone number, get the information you feel necessary to understand the job profile. Let us find out the actual meaning of few of the jargons commonly used.

1. Need to Take Initiative: In such a situation, the company may need a person who will need little support to execute the project. He is required to have the urge and fire in his belly. The person needed for such positions must be energetic, opportunity-grabbing and raring to go. You must have the drive to take an initiative on your own accord.

2. Proven Track Record: In such cases people are interested to see the work achievement in terms of facts and actual figures. Nobody generally is interested to know the name of the project or products you have dealt with, they may be interested to see what you did there.

3. Need a Sense of Humour: Gone are the days when people used to expect an officer to be reserved, tight-lipped and talk only business. With the trend changing fast, an executive is required to behave in a more sensible way and can share lighter moments with his team. The working environment is supposed to be enjoyable. Of course, he is not required to be cracking, jokes but he certainly should not be grim-faced.

4. Quick Learner: In the fast world of today one does not have much time to learn on the job. He is required to be sufficiently capable to start within a fortnight. He cannot expect that the company will provide him long duration in-house training before assigning the job.

5. Dynamic Individual: As minute division of labour has been done away with, companies are trying to seek people who can change positions in their jobs pretty fast. Most of the MNCs do need such people. Therefore the dynamics of the individual must match the dynamics of the company.

6. Demanding Environment: The policy of the new generation companies is very simple, keep less people and pay them better. If they are motivated they can take up more responsibility. It is always better to have few motivational individuals rather than a host of lazy, unmotivated workers. Therefore if a company is looking for a demanding environment, the company is indicating no fixed working hours and the person may have to play more than one role.

7. Play a Key Role: In such cases you are supposed to be the person who will lead the team and will be responsible for its failure or success. Your leadership qualities and the ability to get work done will be the requirement of the job.

8. A Promising Future: When the company is not too sure of its future they may use these kinds of jargons. The companies must have clear strategies and goals, which they want to achieve. Anything very unclear and vague can be attractive but not always good. The experience of the best of the brains losing a few of their best years in dot.coms is still fresh in our memory.

9. Fresh Culture and Exciting Strategy: In traditional Indian society where every change takes a long period to implement, positive change in our work culture is always welcome. But do not forget that structural reforms in UK were completing in two years whereas we, after ten years of reforms, have crossed very few hurdles.

10. Attractive Salary and Benefit Packages: The company is not so sure about what the right salary will be. They would like to judge an individual on a case-to-case basis and will take a decision based on the suitability of the candidate.

Common Pitfalls in Writing a CV

There are many things a person must avoid when writing a CV. Let us try to find out what these irritants are:

1. Keep your resume error free, both in terms of language and facts. The errors in your CV may a consultant think that if you are so careless with your CV, how can you be careful about the job?
2. Give only the relevant information about yourself. Do not write everything about your life. Nobody is interested in your personal background.
3. Uncomfortable zones must not be touched upon in a CV, similarly the glorious events in your life may not sound so glorious to the recruiter.
4. Irritants such as failure in exam, marriage or business may be left to be discussed during the interview. They should not form a part of the CV.
5. Never give wrong information.
6. Do not beat around the bush. Irrelevant information can frustrate the attempt of a recruiter to find a CV amongst a heap of CVs. Try to convince the recruiter with relevant information only.
7. Avoid flamboyant and flowery language. The sections in your CV telling about who I am, what are my strengths, where I would like to be in ten years. Should not give the impression that the applicant is boastful of himself.
8. Do not send your photograph unless it is specifically asked for.
9. Do not touch upon unnecessary details such as reasons for leaving your job, the details of the perks and other facilities you get in your present job, etc. these, if required, might be discussed during the interview.
10. Never send a poor quality photocopied CV, this can only give an impression that you are applying to a lot of places.
11. Family achievements and family background will unnecessarily waste precious space of your CV.

Questions

1. What points should be covered in a Resume? Explain in detail.

Or

Resume is a document that tells about you to the employer/consultant. Explain.

2. Jargon means dynamic and persons who can take initiative, flexible, etc. What there Jargons should means to an applicant.
3. There are many things a person must avoid when writing a CV. Explain in detail.

20

Interview

The word 'interview' may be defined as a conversation between two parties that is structured and prepared to achieve a purpose involving the exchange of information. The use of word 'parties' has a special significance. In most of the interviews there is a single interviewer and a single interviewee, but it is possible that an individual may be interviewed by a group; a group by an individual or a group by another group. The second important word in this definition is 'purpose' which means that at least one of the parties, engaging in the conversation has a goal in mind. Ronald B. Adhler and Jeane Marquardt Elmburst define interview as "a two-party conversation in which at least one person has a specific, serious purpose". The other important words are 'structured and prepared' which imply that the interview has been preplanned to atleast some extent in terms of form and content. The difference between conversation and interview is that whereas conversation is more informal, casual and spontaneous, an interview is formal, serious and structured. In conversation both parties speak equally but in interview the interviewee speaks more and the interviewer asks more.

LETTERS OF INTERVIEW, APPOINTMENT, CONFIRMATION LEAVE, PROMOTION, TRANSFER, RESIGNATION AND TERMINATION OR DISMISSAL

A letter asking the person, seeking employment, to appear in person before the prospective employee on the appointed day, date, time and place, is called the letter of an interview.

On receipt of the applications for job from the candidates, the prospective employer screens the applications and those persons who are found most suitable in respect of qualifications, experience, etc., are called to appear for an interview. They are requested to come in person and discuss with the appointing authority about their work, experience, etc., before finalizing appointment in the organization. The main purpose of calling a candidate for an interview is that the prospective employer could judge for himself whether the candidate, who has applied for a job, is fit for selection for the post or assignment or not. It is only after the interview that the appointment is finally decided upon by the prospective employer.

ESSENTIALS FOR DRAFTING A GOOD INTERVIEW LETTER

For drafting a good interview letter, the following points, should be remembered:

1. Give a reference to the application for job advertised by the prospective employer.
2. Mention the exact day, date, time and place of interview.
3. State whether the candidate, appearing for an interview, is required to produce his/her original certificates, testimonials, etc.
4. State clearly whether or not the applicant would be paid any conveyance charges for appearing for the interview.

EXAMPLE 1

Specimen Letter Calling a Candidate for an Interview

A.B.C. Company Limited
5-Parliament Street, New Delhi.

Ref.No. ABCL/STF. Apptt./2009 2nd July, 2009

Miss Usha Rani
1/6519 Azad Gali
Rohtas Nagar,
Shahdara, Delhi–110032

Madam

With reference to your application dated.................for the post of a Steno Typist, you are advised to appear for an interview on Monday, the 16th July, 2009 at 11.00 A.M. at the above address.

Please bring all your original certificates/testimonials at the time of interview. Please note that no conveyance charges would be paid to you for this.

Your faithfully,
Sd/-
Personal Manager

EXAMPLE 2

An Interview Letter for the Post of a Bank Manager

Young Bank of India
H.O. Mount Road, Chennai

Ref. No. CO/PD/STF/120/2009 5th July, 2009

Shri/Smt./Miss......................
....
....
....

Dear Sir/Madam,

Ref.: Your Application for the post of Senior Manager in our Bank

We refer to your application dated................on the above subject. Kindly call on us for a personal interview on 24th July, 2009 at 3.00 P.M. at our Head Office.

You are advised to bring with you the original certificates/ testimonials along with complete details of your present emoluments duly authenticated by a Competent Authority.

Please note that you will be paid first-class Train/Bus by shortest route on production of tickets/receipt.

Thanking you,

Your faithfully,

General Manager

EXAMPLE 3

Calling for a Second Interview

Dear Sir/Madam,

With reference to your application dated...........for the post of a private Secretary in our organization and subsequent interview on.......you are advised to call on us personally on ......at........P.M. for a second interview with our Chairman and Managing Director at the above-mentioned address and to have formal discussion before release of your appointment letter.

Please note that you will be paid second-class Train/Bus fare by the shortest route on production of ticket/receipt.

Yours faithfully,

General Manager

Types of Interviews

Interviews may be classified into eight categories:

1. Employment Interviews
2. Orientation Interviews
3. Counseling Interviews
4. Performance Appraisal Interviews
5. Grievance Interviews
6. Correctional Interviews
7. Exit Interviews
8. Information Gathering Interviews.

1. Employment Interviews: The purpose of a typical employment interview is to evaluate an interviewer who is applying for a post in the organization. The applicant may be an outsider who has applied for a post in the organization and is thinking of joining it. He may be a current employee who is seeking a transfer to another position or city within the organization. In such an interview, the interviewer attempts to learn about the applicant's educational qualification, his past experience, his personal goals, his knowledge and his achievements in similar type of work. However, the applicant too, has a purpose. His purpose is to evaluate the position of the organization, its potential as a satisfying place to work. While the interviewer asks questions to the interviewee, he also observes his behaviour, his interest in the job, his maturity and communication abilities. Although it is very difficult to assess the real potential of the applicant in the interview lasting a few minutes only, yet it is vital to get as much relevant information as possible from the interview both in terms of the facts and in terms of interviewee's attitude and behaviour. The different types of interview used in an organization are given in Table 20.1:

Table 20.1: Types of Interviews

Types of Interviews	Purposes
Employment interviews	Selecting new employees for the organization or selecting current employees for transfers within the organization.
Orientation interviews	Familiarizing new employees with the organization.
Counseling interviews	Helping employees with the career, personal, or job-related problems.
Performance appraisal interviews	Evaluating the employee's job performance.
Grievance interviews	Hearing and responding to employee complaints.
Correctional interviews	Instructing employees to change behaviour if the employee consider unsatisfactory.
Exit interviews	Gathering information from the providing help to an employee who is leaving the organization.
Information-gathering interviews	Collecting work-related information from persons within or outside the organization.

Source: Dalmer Fisher, *Communication in Organization*, Jaico Publishing House, Mumbai, 1999, p. 455.

Regarding the role of the applicant in 'Employment Interviews', he must make a thorough self-analysis, in order to be able to respond fully to questions on topics such as personal strengths, weaknesses, accomplishments, failures, goals, abilities and reasons for being interested in the job. He should also be prepared to ask such questions about the organization and the job as opportunities for advancement, support for part time education, etc.

2. Orientation Interviews: The purpose of orientation interviews is to acquaint the new employee with his job and with the organization. It is also to establish a positive relationship between the employer and the employee. It is said that the first impression is the last impression. The initial attitudes and perceptions formed in this interview strongly influence the employee's motivation and morale on the job. They also give a lasting impression of employee's personality on the employer.

> In this type of interview it is always the interviewer who plays the important role, therefore he must make ample preparation for the purpose. He must provide to the interviewee a copy of job description: he must give instructions relating to parking, insurance and other benefit programmes, information on company policies, office space and devices such as computers, calculators and telephones equipments. He must also introduce the culture of the organization; its traditions, values, etc. He must introduce the employees to people who will assist him in his training and further orientation. He must also give to the employee initial specific tasks to perform. This is a not all. The manager conducting such an interview must provide information that the employee needs at the same time clearly stating performance expectations from him.

3. Counseling Interviews: Normally a counselling interview is initiated by the manager of an organization to address a problem that needs attention, but sometimes such as interview may be sought by an employee to discuss a problem. In a counselling interview, it is not always the counsellor counselling a subordinate, alternatively is superior may seek help and guidance from a subordinate. The problem that is discussed may be job-related or some personal or family problem which may affect work performance.

4. Performance Appraisal Interviews: Performance appraisal interviews are conducted with several purpose, one of them is to appraise the work performance of an employee. These are also conducted to recognize the accomplishments of an employee; to give him a clear picture of his performance, to discuss needs for improvement and to induce the employee to improve his job performance. Whereas some of the organizations hold such appraisal interviews periodically, yearly or half-yearly and some organization hold them whenever the need is apparent.

> Performance appraisal interviews have a great impact on the employee's reaction to the organization. If he is praised highly for his work he may become emotional and happy and resolve to work still harder for the organization which evaluates his hard work. But if the achievements of the employee compare unfavourably with the targets set before him at the time of his appointment, the interview may prove an eye opener for him. However, if the employee does not agree with the assessment, such an interview give him an opportunity to voice his disagreement most effectively. He can express a desire to help the manager by supply him the facts he might not have known or understood about the performance.

5. Grievance Interviews: A grievance interview gives an opportunity to the employee to bring a complaint to the management voicing his grievance with the functioning of the organization. The interview is less formal at the preliminary stage and most grievances are resolved at the time of the interview.

> There are certain difficulties that come in his way of such interviews. When an employee appears before his boss, he may not be able to express himself fully and clearly due to the exalted status of the later. The other difficulty comes when the interview becomes a test of strength between the two parties. In such an interview both the employer and the employee should try to establish a climate of open ways. Only then can the interview provide an opportunity for counselling and resolving the grievance. The approach of the employer should be clinical or curative rather than 'legalistic' and punitive.

6. Correctional Interviews: A correctional interview is conducted to take corrective action or disciplinary measures against an employee who has violated standards of conduct or disrupted organizational cooperation or who has seriously failed to meet job performance requirements. It is very difficult to conduct such an interview because the employee and the employer both are likely to be on the defensive. Another difficulty in such an interview comes because most of the employers or managers do not want to reprimand employees for fear of counteraction or for the sake of personal relations.

Correctional interviews should be conducted when both the parties are calm. If a mediator or some representative of the employee or some union leader is also allowed to attend the interview along with the employee, it might prove useful. Presuming that he is guilty, the manager in such an interview should not accuse the employee openly. If he doubts what the corrective measure can be, he should not state it openly. The employee should be given opportunity to express his feelings frankly.

7. Exit Interviews: Such an interview is usually conducted by some personal specialist of the organization to find out why an employee has decided to leave the organization. It is possible that in such an interview the personal specialist may learn the things the employee would not want to tell the manager. He may reveal problems which the manager and the organization must solve.

> Exist interviews prove unproductive if the employee choose the remain silent and does not tell sincerely the reasons of leaving. It is also possible that the employee may be thinking of returning to the organization. In such a case he would not criticize the organization. It will be more useful if, in such an interview, the interviewee is told that the matters discussed in the interview will be treated as strictly confidential.

8. Information Gathering Interviews: The main purpose of information gathering interviews is to gain information for further decisions and actions. Such interviews may occur between peers, between superiors and subordinates or between organization members and outside persons.

One popular form of information gathering interview is survey interview which is conducted to collect data from a number of people. That data are analysed and interpreted to determine future action. Manufacturers and employees conduct such type of interviews for improving and adapting their products to consumer's expectations. Whereas most of the information interviews are formally planned a chance meeting with a person may present an opportunity for seeking information. In all such interviews, whether planned or spontaneous, the interviewer has to be more effective and he should try to put the interviewee at ease and to establish rapport. If the interview is planned, the interview should formulate a list question to be asked in order to cover all desired topics.

STAGING AND CONDUCTING EFFECTING INTERVIEWS

Planning the Interviews

Although many people think that interviewing is a very simple activity, yet the fact remains that it is a very difficult task which should be handled skillfully and for this purpose adequate preparation must be made. Preparation for the interview includes strategy, content, managing the setting, environment, time and even seating arrangement.

1. Content: First of all the interviewer should plan the content of the interview. He should establish the purpose of the interview, learn about the key areas to be discussed, anticipate the psychological climate and determine the structure of the interview. Once the purpose of the interview has been determined, the interviewer should prepare a list of questions to be asked in the interview. If he is going to conduct an employment interview, he should verify material on job application and study it thoroughly. The interviewer must also inform the interviewee about the organization.

2. Resume: The second step for the interviewer is to be fully conversant with the resume of the candidate before he conducts the interview, if the interviewer knows something about the candidate and addresses him with his name, he creates a better impression. Moreover, if the interviewer is thoroughly prepared, he can ask better question. The thorough preparation becomes still more important in correctional interviews where the interviewer has to support the critique of the interviewee with factual evidence. The next important thing in the preparation for the staging of the interview is the mental conditioning of the interviewer and the interviewee. Both of them should have faith in each other and they should leave aside the prejudices that they may be having. This mental conditioning plays a very significant role in grievance interviews and correctional interviews.

3. Strategy: Another important thing is the structure of the interview which should be decided beforehand. In a directive strategy the interviewer controls the pacing and the subjects that the interview will cover. It is useful for acquiring large amount of detailed information. In such a strategy a questionnaire is prepared and questions are asked from that. But in a non-directive strategy, the interviewee controls the topics and pacing of the interview and the interviewer assumes the role of emphatic, non-judgemental listener. This strategy is more useful in counselling interviews.

4. Environment: Apart from these essential preparatory things, the environment, the timing and the seating arrangement, play an important role and they must be given due attention in the preparation of the interview. The interview may be staged in the office of the executive or in the cafeteria near the office but there should be an environment of informality and open expression. Privacy and freedom from interruption are important for the interview's continuity.

5. Timing of Interview: The interviewer should decide the time for the interview considering his business and engagements. Of course, it will be according to the mood and motivation of the interviewer. Some like to hold such interviews in the evening while others feel more at ease in the early. However, the day of the week should also be decided by the interviewer. Some like to hold such interviews in Sundays while other like Monday or some other day for reasons best known to them.

6. Seating Arrangements: Regarding the seating arrangement, physical distance between the interviewer and the interviewee is important. Some people feel uncomfortable sitting nose to nose in an interview. A distance of about five feet is considered quite comfortable in a two person interview, but this distance may vary depending upon the type of interview. In information gathering interviews, this distance can be less than five feet. But in correctional and appraisal interviews, where the manager wishes to main psychological distance, he may sit across the table from the subordinate. There can be no hard and fast rule for seating arrangement because different interviewees react differently to different seating arrangements.

CONDUCTING THE INTERVIEW

1. Opening of Interview: Opening is the most important part of the interview. Its purpose is to set the tone for the interview and to motivate the interviewer and the interviewee to communicate freely and accurately. On the one hand, it establishes the rapport, while on the other hand it explains the purpose of the interview.

2. Building Positive Relationship: The interviewer should build a positive relationship with the interviewee. The traditional approach involves greeting the interviewee graciously and having a small talk about weather, family matter, etc. but the modern approach is slightly different. If the interviewer observes tension of the interviewee, he may use a few words of encouragement and show genuine concern. But this rapport making stage should not take much time so that the time for the actual interview is not curtailed.

3. Explain the purpose of Interview: Once the rapport has been built, the purpose of the interview should be explained clearly. Even though both the parties know it very well yet the interviewer should state the interview goal, is meaning etc. This kind of orientation reduces the anxiety of interviewee, it also avoids misunderstanding.

4. A word about the Type of Question to be Asked: The information which the interviewer wants to gather from the interviewee will determine the type of questions to be asked. Even then, the basic choice for the interviewer in framing questions is whether question will be open or closed. Open questions are broad in nature and they allow enough freedom to the interviewee to respond. The answer to such questions needs to be more than a few words and it amply reflects the interviewee's power of speech, command over language and way of expression. Questions like, "Tell me about yourself". "What are your view about the current political scene?" "How do you feel the problem developed?" contain enough scope to reflect the personality of the interviewee.

Closed Question on the other hand, restrict the interviewee's response to a specific topic. Questions like, "how long have you worked there?" "Which training courses have you passed?" "Why have you decided to leave the company?" and "What did you do when the supervisor abused you?" Elicit specific kind of information the interviewer desire. Whereas the closed questions save time and provide answers easy to record, open questions explore the attitude and feelings behind factual answers.

INFORMATION GATHERING INTERVIEWS

Planning the Interview

The interviewer should:

1. Define the purpose of the goal to be achieved through the interview.
2. Identify the person to be interviewed and exclude the persons who will not be of much help to him in the information gathering process.
3. Analyse their social, economic, educational and cultural background.
4. Know interviewee's personal prejudices and presumptions.
5. Prepare a questionnaire or list or questions to be asked.

6. Decide the time and location of interview. If possible, get an early appointment for the interview.
7. Dress up properly before going for the interview.

CONDUCTING THE INTERVIEW

During conducting of the

1. First greet the other person in interviewee's cultural numbers and introduce himself.
2. Explain the reason for conducting the interview.
3. Explain the interviewee the information needed by him.
4. Tell him the time duration, it will take.
5. Ensure that his responses will be kept confidential, if the situation demands so.
6. Motivate and pursue him for cooperation.
7. Ask question directly; if he hesitates, indirect way can be used.
8. Give ample time to the interviewee to explain him.
9. Never interrupt him, but listen him emphatically.
10. Thank him at the end for his sincere cooperation.

SELECTION INTERVIEW

Selection interviews are held to find most suitable candidates for the job, as an interviewer, following points must be considered for selection interviews:

PLANNING INTERVIEWS

1. Screen the application forms and call only suitable candidates.
2. Call the candidates through letters in advance. In the letter, mention clearly the venue, date, time and required documents.
3. Make proper seating arrangement for the candidates in waiting room as well as for the selection committee in the office.
4. Keep the interview room separate from other business activities. Any type of disturbance should be avoided.

5. Prepare classified information about various candidates and give its copies to all the members of the committee.
6. Decide before hand the question to be asked by various specialists of different areas.
7. Prepare the list of candidates, showing sequence in which they will be called. Such list should be exhibited in the waiting room.

Conducting Interview

1. Welcome the candidate and respond to his greetings.
2. Initiate the dialogue between yourself and the interviewee.
3. Make the candidate feel at ease by asking very common question about his name, academic qualification, the reason for preferring the organization, etc.
4. Encourage the candidate to express more by responding through facial expressions, eyes and nods of the head.
5. Listen attentively.
6. Respect the sentiments of the other person, even if you do not agree with him.
7. Accept for the time being what the candidate says than criticizing in destructive way or showing surprise.
8. Make full enquiry about the interviewee's knowledge, experience, motives and habits.
9. Give equal attention to the verbal as well as non-verbal expressions of the interviews.
10. Use simple language so that the interviewee can understand him.
11. Thank the interviewee at the end and wish him best of luck.

Interviewee's Preparation for the Interview

The interviewee should prepare himself for the interview. He should:

1. Know the organization and nature of job before hand.

2. Know his habits and hobbies and think over them thoroughly.
3. Anticipate the possible questions related with job and subject, and prepare them thoroughly. Ponder over them, how to express them to interviewers?
4. Prepare a file where all required documents like interview letter, certificates, etc., are arranged.
5. Dress suitably to look decent.
6. Arrive for the interview before time, so that you can rest and relax there for some time.
7. Regain confidence before entering the interview room.

Interviewee's Conduct During Interview

1. Greet the interview board with polite wish.
2. Sit in natural way when asked to sit.
3. Pay attention to the question asked by interviewer and respond them naturally by consciously.
4. Be honest in answering question. If you do not know, admit it politely.
5. Answer in brief and to the point.
6. Be positive in your approach, express enthusiasm for the organization and the job, and demonstrate that you are really interested to serve.
7. Avoid shifting of seats, biting finger nails, playing with paper weight, adjusting knot of necktie, etc. that shows your nervousness and anxiety.
8. Never annoy or offend the interviewer.
9. Control your negative emotions and impulses.
10. Tell in frank and polite manner about the previous job without criticizing previous employer and colleagues.
11. Avoid looking funny or too serious.
12. Thank the interviewers at the end and move out of the interview room in confident manner.

Table 20.2: The Communication behaviours of Successful Interviewees.

Behaviour	Unsuccessful Interviewees	Successful Interviewees
Statements about the position.	Had only vague ideas of what they wanted to do; changed "ideal job" up to six times during the interview.	Specific and consistent about what they wanted; were able to tell, why they wanted the position.
Use of company name.	Rarely use the company name.	Referred to the company by name four times as often as unsuccessful interviewees.
Knowledge about company.	Made it clear that they were using the interview to learn about the company and what it offered.	Made it clear that they had researched the company; referred to specific brochures, journals or people who had given them information.
Level of interest, enthusiasm.	Responded, neutrally, to interviewer's statements: "OK", "I see", Indicated reservations about company or location.	Expressed approval of information provided by the Interviewer non-verbally. That's great Explicated desire to work for this particular company.
Non-verbal behaviour.	Made little eye contact, smiled infrequently.	Made eye contact after smiled.
Picking up on interviewer's cues.	Give vague or negative answers even when a positive answer was clearly desired ("How are your math skills?").	Answered positively and cues confidently and backed up the claim with a specific example of "problem-solving" or "toughness".
Response to topic shift by interviewer.	Resisted topic shift.	Accepted topic shift.
Use of industry terms and technical jargon.	Used almost to technical jargon.	Used technical jargon: "point of purchase display", "NCR charge", two column "approach", Direct "mail".
Use of specifics in answers.	Gave short answers in 10 words or less, sometimes only one word; did not elaborate. Gave general responses: "fairly well".	Supported claims with specific personal experiences, comparisons, statistics, statements of teachers and employers.
Questions asked by interviewee.	Asked a small number of general question.	Asked specific question based on knowledge of the industry and the company. Personalized question: "what would my duties be?"

Behaviour	Unsuccessful Interviewees	Successful Interviewees
Control of time and topics.	Interviewee talked 37% of the interview time; initiated 36% of the comments.	Interviewee talked 55% of the total time. Initially subjects 56% of the time.

Source: Based on research reported by Lois J. Einhorn, "an Inner View of the Job Interview: An Investigation of Successful Communicative Education (30 July 1981), 217-18; and Robert W. Elder and Michael M. Harris, eds., the Employment. Interview Handbook (Thousand Oaks. CA: Sage, 1999), 300, 303, 327-28.

APPRAISAL INTERVIEWS

An executive can a subordinate and tell him his shortcomings and the ways to improve them. But this style is unfair and unproductive if the executive's evaluation is incorrect. Despite its disadvantage, this style is suitable when employees are inexperienced or of lower status or are too loyal identified with the management.

Best is the conduct appraisal interviews. In these interviews the employee is given a chance to explain the cause of his performance. After listening to the subordinate, the executive evaluates the summaries of the interview, by telling him how to improve. With this, chances of misunderstanding are reduced.

Better than this way is to appraise the performance and solve the problems collectively. Both executive and employee review the situation and decide about the future course of action.

To make the appraisal interview effective:

1. Both interviewer and interviewee should meet in synergetic environment.
2. Shortcomings should be pointed in constructive manner.
3. Free and frank discussion should be there.
4. Future course of action should be decided collectively, as in case of win-win situation of negotiation.

Appointment

A letter signed by the employer and issued to a candidate, instructing him to join duties/service at a certain salary and stating other terms and conditions of the job, is called an Appointment Letter. It is also called a letter of 'offer' because it contains an offer of the job from the employer to the candidate. The offer may or may not be accepted. If the offer is accepted, all the terms and conditions mentioned in the letter are to be followed by the person who accepts the offer.

In most of the organizations, after the written test and an interview, a final decision about selection of a candidate is taken by the employer. If the candidate is found most suitable for the job, the letter of appointment or offer is issued to him on receipt of which the candidate may join the service.

Nowadays, an Appointment Letter is more formal and brief. It is drafter very carefully in order to avoid any complications in future.

Essential for Drafting

While drafting an Appointment Letter, the following points should be remembered:

1. Give a reference to the application of candidate, written test and subsequent interview for the post applied for.
2. Express pleasure in appointing the candidate for the post.
3. Mention whether the appointment is on temporary basis or on probation. Write the period also.
4. State the details of salary giving grade, allowances, requisites or other benefits attached to the post.
5. Mention the date, time and place of reporting for duty by the candidate. Also mention the last date of joining the service.
6. Give clearly the other terms and conditions or formalities which are to be completed by the candidate before joining the service, like medical examination or obtaining a medical certificate or depositing cash security etc.
7. Make a mention of the conduct rules to be followed by a candidate.
8. Advise the candidate to convey his written acceptance to the letter of offer or appointment.

EXAMPLE 1

An Appointment on Probation

MODERN INSTITUTE
Punjabi Bagh, New Delhi.

Ref. No. MI/Gen./120/2009 Dated: ....

Miss Poonam Verma
15/16, Old Rajinder Nagar
New Delhi-110060

Sub: Appointment for the Post of a Stenographer.

Madam,

This has a reference to your application dated.......and subsequent interview for the above post.

The Management is pleased to appoint you for the post of Stenographer on a consolidated salary of ₹ 7,500 per month.

Please note that you will be on probation for a period of six months and during this period one month's notice or salary in lieu thereof is to be paid by either side if you wish to leave the organization on any ground or the Management is not satisfied with your work and conduct. After the probation period, a notice or salary in lieu thereof shall be extended to three months.

You will have to abide by all the rules and regulation of the institute, a copy of which is enclosed.

Please sign and return the office copy of this letter as have accepted the appointment and the terms and conditions.

Your faithfully,

Director

Encl: As above

EXAMPLE 2

An Appointment of a Clerk in the Bank

YOUNG BANK OF INDIA
H.O.: Parliament Street, New Delhi.

Ref. No. YBI/STF/4320 Dated :................

Shri/Smt/Miss.................

....

....

Dear Sir/Madam,

With reference to your Application dated...............for appointment in the Bank. We are happy to inform you that you have been selected in the service of the Bank as a Clerk-cum-Typist on the following terms and conditions:

1. Your monthly substantive salary will be ₹..............p.m. plus usual allowances admissible according to the Award/ Settlement.

2. You will be on probation for a period of six months. Your services are, however, liable to be terminated in the sole discretion of the Bank even before the expiry of the probation period, without assigning any reason but with one month's notice or on payment of a month's pay and allowances in lieu thereof.

3. You shall report for duty to the manage, Loan Department at the Head Office at your own expenses on or before............ failing which the offer of appointment will be deemed to be cancelled.

4. You are required to produce a clean discharge certificate from your last employers at the time of joining.

5. You are required to produce before joining the Bank the following:

(a) Educational certificates, the original, and satisfactory proof of your age.

(b) A medical certificate from a Registered Medical Practitioner not below the rank of M.B.B.S., testifying that you are in a fit state of health and strong enough to perform the strenuous duties required by a Bank Employee.

(c) Four Copies of your photograph of passport size on joining the bank at your own cost.

(d) To execute on Bank's Standard Service Agreement, Identity Form and Secrecy Pledge, at your own cost.

(e) You will give us the names of two respectable persons (not related to you preferably known to the Bank with their addresses, to whom reference about your reliability, trustworthiness and good character can be made).

(f) The bank shall have the right to allot any duties to you for which you may be considered competent, and have the right to transfer you to any office of the Bank or to send you to any other place, where the business of the Bank may need your services.

(g) You will be governed by the Rules of the Bank in force from time to time in all matters including salary, leave, travelling allowances and other rights and privileges admissible under the regulations applicable to Bank Employee.

(h) The appointment shall be cancelled in case all the above formalities are not completed within 10 days from the date hereof.

(i) You will be required to deposit a cash security of ₹ 1,000 (Rupees one thousand only) before joining the Bank (as Cashier/Godown-Keeper).

(j) You will attain typing/computer speed of 40 words per minute within five months from the date of your joining Bank service failing which your service will be terminated.

Your faithfully,

Chief Personnel Manager.

I..................Son/Daughter of Shri..............hereby acknowledge receipt of your letter of appointment and accept the offer on the terms and conditions mentioned therein.

Signature : ....

Date : ....

Confirmation in Service

Any letter which is written by an Employer and addressed to the Employee intimating that he/she is confirmed or made permanent in service, is called the Letter of Confirmation in service.

Generally, the appointments are made on probation at first. The period of probation (which we may call as a trial period also) caries from three months, six months to a year or two years, depending upon the rules and regulations framed by an organization. The probation period is kept in order to adjudge the person appointed in service, with regard to satisfactory work output and his/her conduct during this period. Besides, the employee also gains sufficient speed and efficiency of work. On successful completion of probation period, a letter of confirmation of service is generally issued by the employer. The probation period may also be extended if the work and conduct of an employee are not found satisfactory.

When an employee is confirmed in service, he becomes entitled to many benefits like provident fund, medical facility, leave, gratuity, etc.

Essentials for Drafting

While drafting a Letter of Confirmation in service by the employer, the following points should be kept in mind:

1. Express pleasure while addressing the letter to the employee.
2. Write the name of employee, post held, data of joining and the date from which confirmation will be effective.
3. The number or nature of any resolution passed by the management may also be quoted.

4. Express the hope that the employee would show good progress and efficiency in future.
5. The confirmation letter should be brief and to the point. Not many details should be included in that letter.

EXAMPLE 1

Confirming an Employee in Bank's Service

YOUNG BANK OF INDIA LTD.
(Regd. Office: Parliament Street, New Delhi)

Ref. No. YBIL/STF/Est.
Shri/Smt/Miss..................Clerk/Typist
C/o Office
....
....

Dear Sir/Madam,

Ref: Your confirmation in Bank's service.

We have the pleasure to inform you that you have been confirmed in service after satisfactory probation period of six months with effect from ....(date).

Your faithfully,
Establishment (Manager)

EXAMPLE 2

Another Letter—Confirmation in Service

Mr.........................
....
....

Dear Sir,

Ref.: Confirmation of services.

I am pleased to convey to you the Board's Resolution confirming your services in the ....department.

You will now be drawing your salary in the grade of ₹ ....

You are also entitled to the usual benefits of the provident fund of the company and other benefits of leave, medical and leave travel concession as admissible to the other confirmed staff of the company.

I am sure that you will show good progress and efficiency and make a rewarding career in the company.

Your faithfully,
Establishment (Manager)

Leave

An application for leave is a letter written by an employee addressed to an employer or immediate boss requesting the grant of leave for a certain period. Mostly the format of an application for leave is printed or cyclostyled in every organization.

However, a separate letter may be addressed to the employer or the officer concerned in the organization.

The following types of leave may be granted to be employee:

1. Casual leave
2. Privilege or earned leave
3. Sick or medical leave
4. Special or extraordinary leave.

Please note that though availing of leave is a privilege of an employee, granting of leave is a discretion of the management. At time, depending upon the exigencies, the management may also refuse the leave to an employee.

Generally, 8 days casual leave are allowed to an employee during a period of one year; one month's EARNED PRIVILEGE leave is allowed on completion of 11 months continuous service and the SICK or MEDICAL LEAVE is allowed depending upon the hospitalization of the employee.

Usually the intimation for availing leave by an employee is given in advance by making an application on the prescribed form or as per the specimen given.

EXAMPLE 3

Leave Application (Specimen)

Sir,

As I have an urgent work at home, kingly allow me two days casual leave w.e.f. ....to.................

Thanking you.

Your faithfully,

Sir,

Kindly excuse my absence for one day i.e., on...............as I have an urgent piece of work at home.

Your faithfully,

Sir,

As I have to go to hospital for a medical check-up, kindly allow me one day's casual leave for today.

Thanking you.

Your faithfully,

N.B. For availing the privilege or earned leave, generally one month's notice is required. Hence, the application for privilege or earned leave should be made at least one month in advance by giving valid reason for availing the long leave.

EXAMPLE 4

Printed form of
Application for Leave

The Manager
XYZ Institute, New Delhi.

Sir,

Kindly grant me leave for...........days, from.................
to................for the following reasons:

....

....

The address given by me is correct and all communications will be deemed to have been received by me. In case, I will overstay or absent without prior sanction for eight days, my service will be deemed as terminated, without any notice. If I have to extend my leave on medical grounds, I will send a Medical Certificate or if for other reasons, obtain prior sanction for leave. Submission of application for leave will not mean that leave has been granted.

Address during the leave period..
....
Date ....
Name ....
Recommended....................................
Signature..

FOR OFFICE USE ONLY

ENTITLEMENT:

Casual...............................sanctioned...................days leave.

Earned...................................Casual/Earned/Without Pay.

Leave entered in the..

Leave Records folio..

Secretary

Signature

Promotion

Where an employee works well and to the entire satisfaction of his Superiors, he/she may be given chance to work on a high post or scale in the same organization. Nowadays, the promotions are made on the basis of qualifications, experience and a written test or an interview. The past service record is also taken into consideration. On getting promotion, the employee is entitled for higher emoluments, powers and also higher benefits in many respects. When the promotion is given in the same organization, usually a letter of promotion is issued to the employee by the competent authority.

While drafting a Letter of Promotion, the following points should be kept in view:

1. The letter should be addressed to the employee considered for promotion by name and his present designation.
2. There should be an expression of pleasure while informing about the promotion.
3. The date from which the higher post or scale is applicable should be clarified.
4. The new or higher/grade of pay and the details of other benefits etc., should be incorporated in the letter.
5. The addressee should be asked for an acknowledgement of letter.

EXAMPLE 5

Letter of Promotion

INDIA INTERNATIONAL LTD.

Regd. Office: Parliament Street, New Delhi.

No. .... Dated.....................

Shri S.K. Gupta
Stenographer
Central Accounts Department
New Delhi.

Dear Shri Gupta,

I have the pleasure to inform you that you have been promoted as Senior Private Secretary to the Personnel Manager of our organization. You will take charge of the new assignment from 15th of July, 2005. You will report for duty to the personal manager on the above date.

Your scale of pay in the new cadre will be ₹ 6950-30-7200 and your basic salary from 15th of July, 2005 has been fixed at ₹ 6950 p.m. in the new scale of pay. You will also be entitled to other allowances and perks available under the new grade. The other conditions of service will remain unchanged.

Please acknowledge receipt.

Yours faithfully,
(XYZ)
Secretary

Transfer

A transfer involves change of place of working of an employee in an organization. The transfer from one place to another may be in the same post or it may be on promotion. Usually, at the time of appointment, there is a clause in the Appointment Letter, that an employee may be transferred to any place in India, depending upon the exigencies, at the discretion of the management. Though the transfers are generally not welcomed by the employees, the Management has to effect transfers for so many reasons and as a policy of administration. For officers or executives, the transfers are a must and after every three or four years period, they are shifted from one office or place to another. There is a gradation for places also—'A' class city, 'B' class city or 'C' class city. The allowances and other perks are also different for different places. On transfer to the new place of posting, the emoluments are changed automatically. There are places like hill stations, the emoluments are changed automatically. There are places like hill station, where some extra allowances are also paid to the employees. In order to effect the transfer of staff from one place to another, a letter is prepared which we call as a letter for transfer.

1. The letter is prepared and a "Memo" or as an 'Office Order'.
2. It is addressed in the personal name of the employee concerned with designation.
3. The name of the new place of posting is mentioned together with the data from which the transfer is effective.
4. It may also be mentioned whether any joining period is allowed and if the employee is entitled for any travelling expenses on transfer.
5. An intimation about the employee's relieving the existing post/office is also given in the letter.
6. The employee is instructed to report for duty at the new place immediately or within a stipulated period.

EXAMPLE 6

Letter of Transfer

No. .... Date........................

MEMORANDUM

It has been decided to transfer Shri A.B. Singh, presently working as a Steno-typist at our Janpath Office, New Delhi to Faridabad office with immediate effect.

He should, therefore, be relieved immediately with instructions to report for duty to the manager, Faridabad Office. His salary for the month of July, 2009 will be drawn at Faridabad. He may avail the joining period afterwards.

Personnel Manager

Shri A.B. Singh
Steno-typist
Janpath Office
New Delhi.

CC to:

1. The Manager, Janpath Office, New Delhi. He should arrange to relieve Mr. A.B. Singh immediately with instructions to report for further duty at Faridabad.

His personal file, leave record etc., should also be sent to Faridabad office.

2. The Manager, Faridabad Office for information. He should report the date of joining of Mr. Singh to our office.

Resignation

When an employee desires to leave the post/service due to some reason, a letter addressed to the employer or immediate boss in this behalf is called the letter of Resignation.

1. Dissatisfaction from the present post and/or the organization.
2. Promotion or better prospects elsewhere.
3. Transfer to an outside place not liked by the employee.
4. Any unavoidable circumstance like enmity or difference of opinion with colleagues or seniors, bad health, sickness or under medical advice, etc.

Essentials for Drafting a Letter of Resignation

While drafting a letter of resignation, utmost care should be taken because a letter of resignation serves as a notice to leave the service and during that period, the employer may also try to take some revenge from the employee like delay in relieving etc. Hence, the following points should be remembered while drafting a letter of resignation:

1. So far as possible, the exact reason of resigning should not be mentioned in the letter. Instead, the words like "Due to unavoidable circumstances" or "Due to circumstances beyond my control" be used.
2. The letter should be addressed to the immediate boss under whom the employee is serving or to the competent authority of the organization.
3. The name of the post last held should be given.
4. The period of notice as per rules be mentioned.
5. The date on which the person should be relieved be mentioned. If there is no date of relieving from duty, mention that you should be relieved on the last date of the notice.

6. There should be an expressed of thanks to colleagues and seniors of the organization for the co-operation extended by them during the service period. Note that in no case the dissatisfaction about the organization be mentioned in the resignation letter, otherwise there may be a problem in getting you relieved from the duty.

EXAMPLE 7

Letter of Resignation

New Delhi

Dated: 1st July 2009

The Secretary
Adarsh College Society
Chitragupta Road
New Delhi

Sir,

It is to inform you that due to unavoidable circumstances, I cannot continue in the service of your college as a Lecturer in Commerce. I, therefore, submit my resignation from this post.

This may be treated as 3 months' notice as per the rules and I should be relieved from the duty on or before 1-10-2009.

I thank to all of my colleagues and superiors who have been co-operating with me for all the time.

Yours faithfully,
Sd/-
(XYZ)
Lecturer in Commerce

Termination/Retrenchment and Dismissal

A termination refers to discontinuance of service of an employee by the employer. It is also called 'Retrenchment'. The termination or retrenchment of service of an employee can be done from the Employer's side, either on expiry of contract or during the probation period, if the employee's work and conduct are not found satisfactory or after taking the disciplinary action against an employee. In case of termination, there may be a clear discharge from service and the employee is entitled for all the benefits as on retirement.

Dismissal generally refers to a qualified quit of service of an employee. The services of an employee working in an organization may either be terminated or dismissed, depending upon the discretion of Management.

However, for drafting a letter of Termination or Dismissal, the following points should be remembered:

1. The letter should be addressed to an employee by name with the designation last held.
2. A reference may be given to the contract of service or any action, taken against the employee.
3. The date from which the order is, effective, should be clearly mentioned.
4. The letter may be written either as Office Memo or as an Office Order.

EXAMPLE 8

Termination/Dismissal of an Employee

No. .... Dated:........................

OFFICE ORDER

In term of clause No.............. of Service Regulations, it has been decided to terminate/dismiss the service of Shri/ Miss.........................., now serving as .... (designation) at ....Office, with effect from the date of service of this Office Order on him/her.

In accordance with the above referred Regulations, he/she will be paid 3 months' emoluments in lieu of notice.

Sd/-

Designation of
Competent authority

Shri/Miss...
....(Designation)
....(Office).

Questions

1. What is interview? What are the various type of interviews?
2. How information gathering interview is conducted? What are the points that interview or and interviewee should consider for information gathering interview?
3. What should be the behaviours of interviewees during interview?
4. What are the points that interviewer should keep in mind while staging and conducting interview?
5. What is a letter of appointment? What precautions are taken while drafting it?
6. Draft a letter on behalf of M/s. A.B. Fertiliser & Co., Post Box No. 500, Mumbai-1, asking a candidate to appear for an interview for the post of a Private Secretary.
7. Suppose you are the Chief Personnel Manager of M/s. Management India Ltd. Connaught Place, New Delhi; draft a letter calling a candidate for an interview in reply to his application for job.
8. On behalf of M/s. Simla Trading Corporation Ltd., Asaf Ali Road, New Delhi, draft a letter of appointment for Miss Ranjana Verma, appointment as Steno-Typist from 1st of next month.
9. Mr. Avinash Kapoor has been appointed as Accounts Assistant in your Organization. Draft a letter of appointment to be issued to him.
10. Miss Jyoti has been confirmed in service as a Private Secretary. Draft a suitable letter of confirming her in the service.
11. Draft a letter transferring the Accounts Officer of your organization from your Chandni Chowk, Delhi Office to Ghaziabad (U.P.) Office.
12. Mr. D.S. Sharma working as a Senior Accountant in your organization, wants to resign. Draft a suitable letter of resignation.

21

Speeches and Presentations

21.1 INTRODUCTION

Speeches and Presentations are indispensable part of business communication. Every business executives and employees have to make formal as well as informal speeches. Executives have to make speeches at company meetings, seminars, conferences, etc. Sales employees have to make hundreds of mini presentations to persuade the potential customers to buy. The chairman of the company has to deliver speech at the annual general meeting of the company. As one progresses in his career presentational speaking skills that involve selling ideas, assume greater importance than technical training. Their effectiveness and success depends upon their ability to sell their ideas. Speeches and presentations involve the same fundamental principles of oral communication and provide the advantage of influencing people with enthusiasm and apparent confidence which written document cannot.

But compared with presentations, speeches are more formal and are delivered more on formal occasions; presentations are usually short and less formal. These are delivered with demonstrations of audio-visual aids followed by answers to questions from the audience.

21.2 SPEECHES

Characteristics of a Good Speech

> Talking and eloquence are not the same; to speak and to tell are two things.
>
> —*Ben Jonson*

A good speech must possess the following characteristics:

1. The first and foremost requisite of a good speech is clarity. The speaker should be clear in his ideas and he should have a good command over language, in which he is speaking, to express his ideas clearly so that they are instantly understood by the listeners.
2. The second requisite of a good speech is its length. It shall neither be too brief nor too long. If the speech is too long, it will fail to sustain the interest of audience for a long time. If it is too brief it may end even before it exercises a hold over the attention of the listeners. Here the speaker should follow the principal of 'The Golden Mean'. He should express his ideas in a lucid manner talking most relevantly to the topic. He should concentrate on the elaboration of a few selected points of the issue.
3. The third characteristics of a good speech is that it should be informative an illuminating so that the audience can gain something from it. If the speaker is repetitive and dwells at length on the points already known to the listeners, he will simply bore the audience who will turn a deaf ear to whatever is being spoken.
4. A good speech should be interesting and it should appeal not only to the minds of the listeners but also to their hearts. If the speaker marks an appeal to the emotions of the listeners he can easily win their heart over to his side, and if the speech appeals to the head also, it will have the most desired effect.
5. The next requisite of a good speech is that it should be tuned to the wavelength of the audience. For example, if the speaker is delivering the speech to the management trainers or managers, technical terms of management can be used frequently. But, when the speech is being delivered in the annual meeting of shareholders the use of such technical terms should be carefully avoided.
6. A good speech should not be too formal that the personal touch is lost. It is the personal touch in the

speech that establishes a rapport between the speaker and the listeners. If this personal touch is missing the speech will easily go off the heads of the listeners who will keep gaping at the speaker.

7. A good speech should convey concrete facts rather than vague or abstract ideas. As already stated, a speaker should convey briefly and clearly his ideas to the listeners. If he himself is vague and tries to convey abstract ideas, he will fail to sustain the interest of the listeners who are more easily drawn to concrete, tangible facts. According to Dale Carnegie, "A modern audience, regardless of whether it is fifteen people at a business conference or a thousand people under chat and in the same general manner that he would employ in speaking to one of them in conversation."

A good speaker should speak with such intensified and exacted naturalness that his hearers never even dream that he has been trained. They are so much lost in the naturalness of the manner that they are conscious only the manner.

21.2.1 How to Make an Effective Speech?

Speaking involves no art, all of us do speaking day in and day out but the speaking which compels listening, the speaking which leaves an impression on others is definitely a difficult art requiring conscious efforts and deliberate planning. To make a speech effective the first requisite is the desire to excel, the desire to impress, the desire to win. Delivery of a good speech involves two steps: (1) The preparation for the speech, (2) The delivery of the speech.

21.2.2 Preparation for the Speech

Preparation involves organizing the thoughts which lie scattered in the mind. Once Winston Churchil was having a stroll in the lawn, sipping his morning tea, when his wife addressed him lovingly, "are you thinking of what to say in the senate meeting today"? Churchil quietly answered, "I am thinking of what not to say at the meeting?" Preparation for the speech involves not only organization of relevant thoughts but also careful selection of thoughts. The speaker must exclude irrelevant thoughts from the draft of the speech. It will be still more useful if the speaker jots down the points to be touched in the speech and arranges them in a logical order. The next step for the speakers is to decide upon the language them in a logical order. The next step for the speakers is to decide upon the language in which he is to express his thoughts. He should prepare the whole speech before hand. "A well-prepared speech is already nine-tenth delivered" remarks Dale Carnegie in his book, how to develop self-confidence and influence people by public speaking. Lee Lacocca adds with emphasis to it, "Speech requires a lot of preparation. There is just no way around it—you have to do your homework. A speaker may be very well informed, but if he has not thought out exactly what he wants to say today to his audience, he has no business taking up other people's valuable time."

A speech cannot be cooked like a meal just a few minutes before its delivery. It must stem and grow out of the head and heart of the speaker. For this the speaker must collect, organize, analyse the facts to be present in the light of the purpose to be achieved. The famous speech of Antony in Julius Caesar of Shakespeare was a well-planned speech which made such a profound appeal to the hearts of the listeners that they rose to mutiny against the conspirators.

21.2.3 Delivery of the Speech

The second step is the delivery of the speech. Once the preparation has been made, the opening of the speech is very important. The speaker must appeal to the hearts as well as heads of the listeners and create interest in their minds. He may open the topic with a striking quotation, he must emphasize how the topic affects the vital interests of the audience. The speaker should put his heart into the speech. It should look as if the speech is flowing not out of the mind of the speaker but out of his heart. He should vary the pitch of his voice according to the point to be emphasized. He may flow up and down the scale from high to low and back again but during all this he must maintain eye conduct with the audience. An important point to be discussed is the length of the speech. The speech should neither be too long now too short. The speaker should consider sympathetically the time that the listeners have been sitting through and he should not over tax their patience. The optimum time for a speech can be from ten minutes to half an hour depending upon the occasion and the purpose of the speech.

The ending of the speech is not less important. Closing of a speech is the most strategic part and should be carefully made. Towards the close, the speaker must summarize, restate and outline briefly the main points of the speech. The closing may be with a befitting verse, a biblical quotation or a relevant joke but it must reflect the profundity and earnestness of the speaker.

21.2.4 Guidelines for Delivering Speech

In the start of the speech

The opening of the talk is highly important. The speaker has to create interest in the minds of the audience. After formally addressing them, he can gain the immediate attention of his audience by:

1. Raising a question.
2. Narrating a related interesting story.
3. Opening with a striking quotation.
4. Telling how the topic affects the vital interests of the audience.
5. Highlighting the shocking facts.

21.2.5 During Speech

1. One should put one's heart into the talk. It should look as if speech is not flowing out of the mind but also out of the heart of speaker.
2. Stress the important words.
3. Vary the pitch of voice flowing up and down the scale from high to low and back again.
4. Establish and maintain eye contact with the audience.
5. Speak loudly enough to be heard.

At the End of the Speech

The close of a speech, being most strategic part, should be made carefully and in accordance with planning in advance. Dale Carnegie suggests the following seven ways of closing:

1. Summarizing, restating, outlining briefly the main points you have covered.
2. Appealing for action.
3. Paying the audience sincere compliment.
4. Raising a laugh.
5. Quoting a fitting verse of poetry.
6. Using a biblical quotation.
7. Building up a climax.

As the speech flows from the speaker, it is much imperative that the speaker should be profound thinker, enthusiastic, earnest, honest and balanced.

Speeches to Motivate

> If I want to succeed in guiding a human being towards a given goal, I must find him where he is and start right there. To help a person. I must of course, understand more than he does, but above all I must understand what he understands.
>
> —*Soren Kier Kegaard*

Business executives have to make speeches to motivate different subordinates for high performance and productivity. These motivational speeches are planned in the same way as other speeches are planned, but the only difference is that of purpose. Other speeches may aim at informing the audience or building goodwill, but motivational speeches him at motivating the individuals.

21.3 WHAT IS MOTIVATION OF THE EMPLOYEES?

Before delivering motivation speeches, executives have to identify the motivation of the employees. Motives are the inner urges of an individual that channelize him to work. Each individual has urge to work and management has to transform these urges and drives in realization of organizational objectives.

Psychologists like Maslow hold that man is motivated by his needs that may vary from basic needs like food, shelter, hunger and thirst to self-actualization.

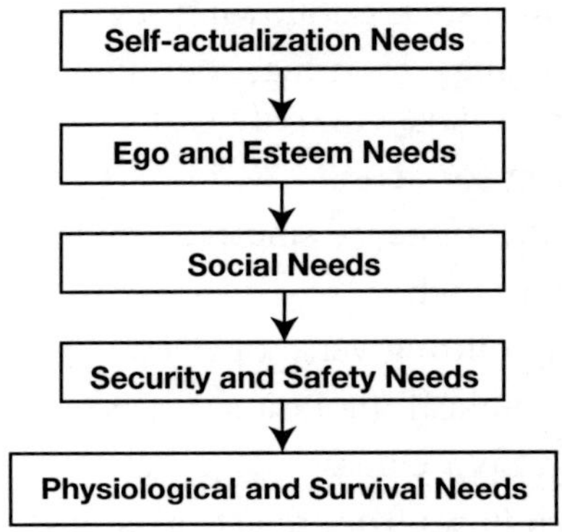

Fig. 16.1: Five Categories of Human Needs

Accordingly to Maslow, human needs can be classified into these five categories:

1. Physiological and survival needs include the basic needs for food, water, sleep, sex and other physiological requirements.
2. Safety and security needs include the desire for physical protection of property, job security, etc.
3. Social needs include the desire for affiliation and affection, sense of belonging, emotional needs for love and friendship, etc.
4. Ego and esteem, needs include the desire for self-respect, self-esteem, etc.
5. Self-actualization needs include the desire for self-fulfilment and self-realization i.e., need to become everything that one is capable of becoming.

According to Maslow, human needs move in ascending order from lowest to the highest. Once one set of needs is satisfied, this minds of need ceases to be a motivator. These needs are interdependent, each higher set of needs emerges when the lower set has been completely or reasonably satisfied. Most of people have a higher satisfaction at lower level than at the higher need levels. Accordingly 85 per cent, safety needs 70 per cent, belonging needs 50 per cent, egoistic needs 40 per cent and self-fulfilment needs 10 per cent.

Executives have to identify at which level most of their employees are living. Besides Maslow's dominating theory of motivation, there are many theories of motivation that provide useful insight for motivating people. But it is well established that economic and psychic rewards are established $E = mc^2$ (in his famous theory of relativity), Ken Blanchard advocates that enthusiasm equals mission times cash and congratulation. To him both cash and congratulations are important. But cash comes first. You have to feed a person's material needs food and clothing, before you can feed his or her spirit with congratulations.

Once "cash" aspect of workers' needs is satisfied, "congratulation" should be taken care with motivational speeches.

21.4 PLANNING AND DELIVERING MOTIVATIONAL SPEECHES

21.4.1 Planning

Before delivering motivational speeches, executives should analyse the level of needs at which majority of employees are living. Usually lower level employees want hike in wages, job security, education for their children and housing facilities. Higher level of executives, whose lower level needs are fulfilled, want to learn and excel more. Therefore, while delivering speech each type of audience needs should be considered.

Then collect the relevant literature and information like how the profits have gone up and how waves/salaries have gone up, what company has contributed in housing facilities, learning opportunities, etc.

If possible, write the speech in advance or think about the main points which are to be highlighted. Pick up catchy words or sentences like quotes and fit them in the speech.

21.4.2 Delivering Speech

While delivering speech, following points should be considered:

1. Be careful about the body language. Always see the audience face to face.
2. Vary the pitch of voice flowering up and down the scale from high to low and back again. Speak loudly enough to be heard.
3. Use catchy words or quotations with extra stress.
4. Appeal to the audience for action.

(a) A speech by the secretary of a firm to announce the resignation of a director

Ladies and Gentlemen,

It is with a feeling of regret that I announce that Mr. G.S. Virdi will not be able to continue his association with us as the director of the company. Since he is going to U.K. on a government, he has been forced to resign all his directorships including ours.

Mr. Virdi is an authority on taxation and company law. He has been on the Board of Directors of a number of reputed organizations and has gleaned rich experience of handling company affairs. His advice has always been helpful to us in farming our policies. If our firm enjoys an enviable position in the business world today, much of the credit for it goes to Mr. Virdi.

On behalf of the Board of Directors, shareholders and members of the organization, I express our sense of appreciation and gratefulness to Mr. Virdi's association with us. I hope, when he returns from U.K. he will renew his relationship with us.

(b) A condolence speech to pay homage to a departed soul

Ladies and Gentlemen,

It is extremely painful to think that R.N. Sharma, one of our dearest colleagues is no longer with us. It was only yesterday in the evening that he bade us farewell. He looked so cheerful that non of us realized he was going to leave us forever. He has a severe heart attack and before any medical help could be provided, he breathed his last.

Mr. Sharma has been with us for the last twenty years as sales manager. He was a dedicated worker, who impressed one and all with his sincerity, honesty and sociable nature. He was an optimistic person who carried the light of hope and joy wherever he went. He was very popular with his colleagues who held him in high esteem.

Mr. Sharma's death is very tragic because he left behind his aged mother, his wife and two school daughters. While we offer heartfelt condolence, and pay homage to the departed soul, we pray to God to give strength to the members of his family to bear this irreparable loss. May God grant peace to his soul.

(c) A brief speech by the Chairman of a Company announcing the transfer-cum-promotion of a branch manager

It gives me great pleasure to announce that Mr. M.K. Soni, branch manager is hereby promoted to the post of area manager and transferred to Chandigarh with immediate effect. He will join the new office in the first week of April 2005.

Mr. Soni, as you know, as an eminent person who has earned a name for himself by virtue of his integrity and sincerity in the Commercial world. As branch manager at Karnal, he performed his duty very efficiently to the full satisfaction of the company. In recognition of his hard work tenacity of purpose, keen insight and enterprising ability, we have decided to promote him to the post of area manager. We hope that in his new assignment, he will leave no stone unturned to take the company to still greater heights of glory.

(d) A brief speech bidding farewell to a colleague who has reached the age of superannuation

Ladies and Gentlemen,

We have assembled here this evening to bid a hearty farewell to Mr. V.S. Seth who is retiring today after rendering a meritorious service of twenty-one years to the company.

Mr. Seth joined our company at a mature age of thirty-six when he had already put in fifteen years of service as branch manager for Pepsys. In recognition of his excellent work he was invited to join as a branch manager with much better prospect. During his stay with us he performed his duties with utmost sincerity, hard-work and dynamism. He endeared himself to one and all with him affable nature, his bland and shave talk. His dynamism and his optimistic outlook to life impressed all. Words fail to express our affection and regards for Mr. Seth who has been a genuine friend and guide for us all.

We wish Mr. Seth, his wife and all other members of the family God's choicest blessings. May God bless Mr. Seth with good health, prosperity and abiding peace of mind.

We shall always cherish the memory of Mr. Seth's ennobling company.

21.5 PRESENTATIONS

Business executives have to make number of oral presentations on different occasions like training employees, introducing new product, etc. Making effective presentation involves developing a strategy that fits the audience and purpose having good content, and organizing material.

21.5.1 Purpose of Presentations

Oral presentations have the following three basic purposes.

1. To inform
2. To persuade
3. To build goodwill

1. To Inform: The basic purpose of presentation is to inform or teach the audience regarding new schemes, new proposals, or new products, etc. training presentations basically aim at informing the new entrants about the organizational policies and procedures. Sales presentations are made to inform the audience about the features of the product that benefit the readers.

2. To Persuade: Presentations have another distinctive purpose of persuading the audience to act or to believe in certain ways. For example, sales presentations are made to persuade the buyers to buy the product.

3. To Build Goodwill: Still another purpose of presentations is to entertain the audience. Therefore, at the end or during presentation, jokes are cut to entertain the audience.

21.5.2 Kinds of Presentations

There are basically three kinds of presentations:

1. Monologue presentations
2. Guided discussions
3. Sales presentations.

1. Monologue Presentations: In monologue presentations, the speaker speaks without interruption and at the end, answers the questions of the audience. The speaker plans the presentation in advance by collecting the relevant literature and anticipating audience's demand. This kind of presentation is most used in classroom situations. But it leads the audience to get bored. Therefore, good delivery skill is needed to retain the attention of the audience and to make it more interesting.

2. Guided Discussions: In the guided discussion, the speaker presents the question or issues that both speaker and audience have agreed in advance, and acts as facilitator to help the audience with the expert knowledge. This type of presentation is very useful when the audience has knowledge of the subject. Here the speaker has to supplement with his specialized knowledge. Compared with monologue presentation, guided discussions have following advantages:

(a) More audience response
(b) More detailed analysis
(c) More commitment to the result.

But this kind of presentation involves more time.

3. Sales Presentations: A sales presentation is made to convince the audience for buying the products or services or accepting the new idea. In sales presentation, the speaker to the audience, asks question that raise their curiosity for the product, overcome their negative assumptions regarding product and finally gains their commitment to buy the product or service.

21.6 FACTORY AFFECTING PRESENTATIONS

Following factors affect the effectiveness of the presentation:

Audience Analysis

If the speaker has analysed the audience in proper way before presentation, his presentation will be more effective. On the other hand, poor or improper audience analysis leads to ineffective presentation. The style of the presentation is largely dependent upon the type and size of the audience. If audience is large, presentation should be more formal whereas informal presentation can work in small audience.

Communication Environment

Communication environment effects the effectiveness of the presentation. Much of the audience notices the physical things surrounding the speaker, the stage, lighting arrangement, background, etc. proper arrangement of these things can enhance the impact of the presentation. If there is noise in the surrounding environment, it detracts the audience from listening and consequently leaves unhealthy message.

Personal Appearance

Personal appearance of the speaker has great impact on the audience. Well dressed up person can deliver good presentation. Therefore, the speaker should wear neat and take time to check his appearance just before starting presentation.

Use of Visuals

Visual can enhance the professional image of the presentation. Different research studies demonstrate that presenters using latest visual techniques are perceived as better-prepared, more persuasive, more credit and more interesting than speakers who do not use visuals. But visuals work only if the technology on which they depend works well. Therefore, presenter should check the equipment in advance before presenting.

Opening and Closing of Presentation

The beginning and closing of a presentation are the emphasis. Those presenters who can open the presentation with interesting remarks which are likely to create more interest and enthusiasm for listening the presentation. On the other hand, presenters with poor opening are likely to leave the audience bored. Similarly, the ending of the presentation has profound impact on the audience. Endings, with vivid and positive pictures are more likely to have profound impact on the audience.

21.7 ORGANIZATION OF PRESENTATION

Clearly in presentation is essential that comes with proper organization of the information. Organizing the information in proper manner can make the message more understandable, keep the audience happy and boost the image of the speaker. Proper organization of presentation enhances the effectiveness of presentation. On the other hand, improper organization of the presentation will not influence the audience. Improper organization of presentation is reflected as follow:

Taking too long time to get to the post inclusion of irrelevant material:

1. Leaving out necessary information.
2. Mixing up of ideas. To overcome these problems, presentation can be organized in one of the four standard patterns.
   (a) **Chronological:** It starts with past, moves to the present and ends by looking ahead.
   (b) **Problem-causes-solution:** It explains the symptoms of the problem, identifies its causes and suggests the remedial measures.
   (c) **Excluding Alternatives:** It shows the symptoms of the problem, suggests possible solutions, explains the reasons why these do not work and ends the discussion with a solution that will work.
   (d) **Pro-Con:** It explain the advantages and disadvantages of problem(s).

Language and Words

The quality of presentation is affected by the language and words. To make the audience understand the message, the speaker has to talk in the language known to the audience. To enhance the impact of presentation, he should choose the catchy words that appeal to the heart and emotions of the audience. If the language spoken by presenter is different from audience's language, and words used are stereotyped, it is likely to have least impact on the audience.

Quality of Voice

Quality of voice of the presenter affects the effectiveness of the presentation.

The vivid voice is likely to have greater impact upon the audience whereas monotonous voice will not influence the audience.

Body Language

The effectiveness of the presentation is also affected by the body language of the speaker. A speaker having eye contact with audience is likely to impress more than a speaker reading out the handouts. A speaker who looked more at the audience is judge as better informed, more experienced, more honest and friendliest than speaker who delivers the speech with less eye contact. With eye contact members of audience feel that speaker is talking to them.

Similarly, confidently moving speakers are likely to have more impact than nervous speakers. To calm one's nervousness, one should be well-prepared, take several deep breaths, relax one's muscles, pause and look at the audience and use body energy in strong gestures and movement.

Answering Questions

The effectiveness of presentation is also affected by presenter's skill in handling questions asked at the end of presentation. A speaker who answers the audience's questions and handles hostile questions with tact is likely to influence the audience more. On the other hand, a speaker who answer rudely will leave negative impact upon the audience.

Giving Effective Presentation

Giving effective presentation involves developing readers benefits, overcoming objections, closing research, analyzing data and designing slides. Like speeches, these presentations, are based upon the principles of oral communication. Every successful and effective presentation requires:

1. Strategy
2. Structure
3. Support
4. Speech

Strategy of Presentation

The strategy of presentation involves:

1. Deciding the general as well as specific purpose of the presentation. The general purpose may be to inform, to persuade, to entertain or to make rapports with the public at large. The specific purpose of speech is targeted at specific audience to be influenced.
2. Deciding the possible results expected from the audience.
3. Knowing and analyzing the audience, their economic and social status, their demographic characteristics, their cultural background and their personal preferences.
4. Deciding the time, location and the manner they are to be influenced.

Structure of Presentation

Before delivering speech the person should organize his ideas properly. In any presentation (a) first "what is to be told" is told, (b) then it is told and (c) at the end "what has been told" is told. The outline of the presentation is as follows:

Introduction

Attention gaining statement

The main theme.

Body

....

....

....

....

Conclusion

1. Review
2. Closing statement

For structuring the presentation the speaker should:

1. Gather material in the light of the theme of the presentation from libraries, company files, interviews with knowledgeable persons, formal or informal survey, etc.

2. Organize the facts and insights into main points and sub-points in the body of the presentation. For this, it should be ensured that:

(a) Presentation is not lengthy.
(b) Main points should be stated with claims based on trials and tests conducted by national or international laboratories.
(c) The points should be presented in logical sequence.

3. Decide how to capture the listener's attention and purse him to listen.

Attention can be captured by:

(a) Asking a question.
(b) Telling a story.
(c) Making a starting statement.
(d) Quoting some authority.

4. Plan the conclusion in advance. The conclusion makes the review of what has been said.

5. Decide what has to be said at the end to appeal for action.

Support

Supporting material is vital for making the presentation effective. It clarifies to speaker's ideas, makes the presentation more illuminating as well as interesting and leaves relatively permanent impact on the mind of listeners. The visual aids like diagrams, charts, tables or pictures that make points more quickly and clearly that words, are to be used through supporting material. These supporting materials are as follows:

1. White Boards: White boards are easy and economical means of presenting the information. But they are not portable, therefore, they can be used at permanent place. Moreover, writing on black board consumes time.

2. Handouts: Handouts provide a permanent record of the ideas presented not reduces listener's need to take notes. These handouts should be circulated at the end of the presentation. This is done to avoid any distraction of attention of the audience.

3. Flip Charts: Flip Charts consists of a large paid of papers, revealing various visual presentations attached to an easel. These charts are easy not economical to use. Moreover these are portable. But they are difficult to prepare and are relatively fragile as they become shabby after being handled to presentation. For making flip charts effective,

(a) The easel should be placed away from direct light otherwise the reflection will make it difficult to read.

(b) While writing on these charts, letters should be magnified to at least four time than normal so that they are readable.

(c) There should be use of more than one colour.

4. Overhead Projector (OHP): Overhead Projector casts an image of the transparencies on a screen. Transparencies are frequently used visual aids especially when audience is large. With sketch pens or colour pencils, matter can be written on them. The better way is to write in block letters or drew graphs etc., to computer and have their print (either through Photostat machine or laser printing) on transparencies.

Transparencies are effective means of projecting graph charts or data on the scene, which are visible to the large audience. Presented matter can be erased and transparencies can be reused for new presentations or they can be stored for future use.

To make it more effective,

(a) Pay attention to the focusing,

(b) Show transparencies only when they are discussed,

(c) Use paper or cardboard to cover the parts yet to be discussed.

(d) Face the audience as you speak.

5. 35 mm Slider: 35 mm slider like OHP transparencies cast an image, but they have different uses and properties. They are used to show an actual photographic image in the dark room. With developments of new software program, it is easy to transfer computer generated visuals into slides. Of course, slide have better impact and attraction than OHP transparencies, but they are expensive to use. To make their use more effective:

(a) use soft cloth to clean the dust on lens.

(b) use a remote control device with a long cord.

(c) talk to the audience, not to the screen.

(d) be prepared to hold the attention of audience without slides even if the power fails.

6. LCD Projectors: LCD projectors are several steps ahead of conventional OHPs. These projectors are more compact and more powerful and can be directly presentations. With the effective use of computer graphics, colourful pictures and detailed graphs, textual information can be made more rich and attractive. This LCD projector has wide application and suitability for all sided groups but its initial investment cost is very high.

7. Videotapes: Videotapes are very informative and attention grabbing presentational supports. They are best for illustrating the persons in action and presenting living image of the situation. To make it effective, it is essential that they should be edited with proper narration and musical accomplishments. One of the most obvious drawbacks of videotapes is that they are highly expensive. Every business house cannot generate its own. But they can be brought from professionals.

Speech

The last part of presentation is delivering speech, which can be:

1. Manuscript that involves reading word for word from a prepared matter.

2. Memorized that involves reciting word for word from memory.
3. Extemporaneous which is planned with broad ideas but not written or memorized.
4. Impromptu which is unexpected, sudden and on the spot.

Of these speeches, extemporaneous speech is the most effective as it is more spontaneous and enthusiastic. But one should also be ever ready to deliver important presentation by predicting what can be asked for presentation. How to respond to the situation by accepting the challenge without any apology.

Good delivery of presentation or speech involves caring about number of factors which include visuals, verbal and vocal.

Visual Elements

1. Dress up effectively to look smart.
2. Be confident and authoritative in your book.
3. Establish and maintain eye contact while delivering the speech.
4. Avoid looking at the notes.
5. Stand upright.
6. Do not try to close the presentation in hurry.
7. Move out confidently after presentation.

Verbal Elements

1. Use exact words and pronunciation.
2. Keep most sentences short.
3. Use active voice.
4. Address your listeners directly.
5. Avoid emphasizing mistakes.

Vocal Elements

1. Speak in enthusiastic and vivid voice.
2. Speak loudly to be heard, neither soft nor shouting.
3. Be more alert and aware of your voice.

Questions

1. Explain the characteristics of a good speech.
2. Explain how to make an effective speech.
3. Design various speeches.
4. Explain how presentation differ from speeches.
5. Discuss various types of presentations.
6. Which factors affect the presentation? Explain in detail.
7. Every successful and effective presentation requires 4 S. Explain this statement.

22

Speaking and Listening

22.1 PRONUNCIATION

Good Pronunciation shows how sophisticated you are and what background you come from. The best ways of learning it are: (1) exposure to native speakers, (2) listening to BBC news, and (3) turning to dictionary again and again. However, the following tips will help:

Suffixes (end-additions to words)

Suffix	Example	Correct Pronunciation
Able	Acceptable, fashionable, workable	U as in 'us' Ubl (not abl)
Age	Breakage, postage, drainage	I as in 'ij' (not aj)
Ative	Illustrative, qualitative, quantitative	Utiv (not ativ)
Cracy	Democracy, autocracy, aristocracy	Krusi (not Kracy)
Ment	Government, Development, Management	Munt (not ment)
Gamy	Monogamy, Bigamy, Polygamy	Gumi (notgeme)
Gram	Telegram, monogram, diagram	E as in 'ten' germ (not graam)
Graph	Autograph, telegraph, photograph	Gref (not graaf)
Logy	Psycology, Sociology, Biology	Luji (not lojee)

Prefixes (beginning-additions to words)

Prefix	Example	Correct Pronunciation
Mal	Maladjusted.zmal nutrition, malcontent	Mel (not Maal)
Trans	Transform, translate, transplant	Trens (not trans)

I have not used phonetic symbols to indicate correct pronunciation.

Silent Letters

Sometimes some letters in a word are not pronounced. They are called silent letters. They spoil pronunciation. Here are some patent examples.

Adjust	U-just	Not Ad-just
Adverb	A as in 'at' Ad-veb	Not Ad-verb
Forehead	O as in 'on' For-id	Not Fore-hed
Ghost	O as in 'home' Cost	Not Ghost
Heir	Aur (as air)	Not Haur
Thumb	Thum	Not Thumb
Tomb	Toom	Not Tomb
Vehicle	Vee-ikl	Not ve-heekl
Waistcoat	O as in 'home' Ways-kot	Not wayst-kot
Wednesday	Wenz-di	Not wed-nes-day

Noun-Verb Problem

Some word have one pronunciation as nouns and another as verbs; as,

Acent (N)	Ek-sunt	Accent (V)	Ek-sent
Contest (N)	O as in 'on' con-test	Contest (V)	Cun-test
Converse (N)	O as in 'on' con-vus	Converse (V)	Cun-vus
Convert	O as in 'on' con-vut	Convert (V)	Cun-vut
Decrease (N)	Ee as in 'trees' 'see' dee-krees	Decrease (V)	di-drees
Export (N)	O as in 'on' eks-pot	Export (V)	Iks-pot
Progress (N)	O as in 'home' pro-gres	Progress (V)	Pru-gres
Project (N)	O as in 'on' pro-jekt	Project (V)	Pru-jekt
Rebel (N)	Rebl	Rebel (V)	Ri-bel
Refund (N)	Ree-fund	Refund (V)	Ri-fund

S and Z Problem

Never Pronounce s for z and z for s. Note the following:

Advise (N)	Ud-vasis	Advice (V)	Ud-caaiz
Cabs	Kebz	Cease	Sees
Disease	di-zeez	Oo as in 'Boot' Loose	Loss
Lose	Oo as in 'Boot' Looz	Scissors	Si-zuz
Use (N)	Oo as in 'Boot' Yoos	Use(V)	Yooz

Stress Problem

Stress is the extra force, used in speaking, on a syllable. Syllable is a word or a part of word spoken at a stretch; as uninformed of three syllables. If we stress the wrong syllable, the pronunciation is spoilt. Here are some examples:

Ability	Ubi-luti	Not aybi-litee
Admission	Ud-mi-shun	Not ed-mee-shun
Cadet	Ku-det	Not ke-dut
Calamity	Kulemuti	Not ke-lum-ity
Cassette	Ku-set	Not-ke-sit
Equality	O as in 'on' Ikwo-luti	Not eekwo-litee
Hedonism	Hee-dun-izum	Not hi-don-izm
Necessity	Ni-ses-uti	Not ne-sis-ity
Pedestrian	Pi-des-trian	Not pe-dis-triun
Preposition	Pre-pu-zi-shun	Not pri-po-zee-shun

100 Most Mispronounced Words

Some word have one pronunciation as nouns and another as verbs; as,

Absent (Adj.)	Eb-sunt	A as in 'At' Not Ab-sent
Absent (V)	Ub-sent	Not Ab-sent
Adjective	A as in 'At' A-jik-tiv	Not Ad-jek-tiv
Amateur Amu-tur	A as in 'At' Not Amay-tiur	

End-r pronounced before vowel, as in 'Car is': not oribiybced before consonant, as in 'Car' was/Pronounce the end-r when it is followed by a word beginning with a vowel; s is 'Car is'. Do not pronounce the end-r when it is followed by consonant; as in Carwas.

Among	Umung	A as in 'At' not Among
Ass	Es	Not Aas
Bona fide	O as in 'Home' Bona-faidi	Not Bonaa-faid
Bicycle	Bai-sikl	Not Bai-sikul
Bigamy	Bi-gumi	Not Bai-gemee
Brochure	O as in 'Home' Shyore as 'sure' Bro-shyor	Not Bro-shur
Bulletin	Oo as in 'Book' Boo-lutin	Not Boo-letin

Among	Umung	A as in 'At' not Among
Career	Ku-riur	Not Ke-riur
Carier	Ke-riur	Not Ku-riur
Clerk	As in 'bazaar' Klaark	Not klurk
Comb	O as in 'Home' Kom	Not komb
Democracy	O as in 'on' Di-mo-krisi	Not De-mo-kresee
Development	Di-ve-lup-munt	Not Duv-lup-ment
Dilemma	Di-lemu	Not Dai-lema
Divorce	O as in 'on' Di-vos	Not Dai-vors
Elastic	Iles-tik	Not Ilaas-tik
Enclosure	O as in 'Home' In-klo-zur	Not En-klo-zur
Era	Leru	Not Eraa
Excuse	Kyoo like 'Queue' iKs-kyoos	Not Eks-Kyoos
Exist	Ig-zist	Not Eg-zist
Fiance	Fi-aan-say	Not Fi-en-see
Fiancee	Fi-aan-say	Not Fi-en-see
Forlorn	O as in 'on' Fu-lon	Not For-lorn
Fury	Fyoo like 'Few' Fyoouri	Not Fyooree
Gaiety	Gay-uti	Not Gay-tee
Garage	Ge-raaz	Not Ge-rayz
Government	Gu-vun-munt	Not Gu-varn-ment
Grammar	Gre-mur	Not Graa-mur
Hereditary	Hi-re-duti	Not He-ree-di-turi
Heredity	Hi-re-duti	Not H-ree-dity
History	His-turi	Not His-tree
Hyperbole	Hai-pu-buli	Not Hai-pir-bol
Indigestion	In-di-zes-chun	Not In-dai-ge-shun
Inefficient	In-ifi-shunt	Not In-efee-ciunt
Infamous	In-fu-mus	Not In-fa-mus
Iron	Ai-un	Not Ai-run
Is	Iz	Not Is
Jakal	Jeki	Not Je-kol
jeopardize	Je-pu-daiz	Not Jio-paar-diaz
Jeopardy	Je-pu-di	Not Jio-paar-dee
Kangaroo	Oo as 'boot' Ken-gu-roo	Not Kun-gaa-roo
Kerosene	Kuru-seen	Not Kero-seen
Knoll	O as in 'No' nol	O as in 'on' not nol
Later	Lay-tur	Not Le-tur

Among	Umung	A as in 'At' not Among
Latter	Le-tur	And Lay-tur
Leopard	Le-pud	Not Lio-paard
Lieutenant	Lef-ten-unt	Not Lyoo-tee-nent
Mass	Mes	Not Mass
Mattress	Me-triss	Not Met-tres
Moustache	Mus-taash	Not Moos-tesh
Mythology	Tho as in; 'Thought' Mi-tho-lugi	Not Mai-tho-lugi
Necessarily	Nesus-er-uli	Not Nese-su-ri-lee
Necessary	Nesus-ri	Not Nese-ruee
Necessity	Nises-uti	Not Nese-sitee
Nuance	Oo as in 'New' Nyoo-aans	Not Noo-aans
Obey	Ubay	Not O-bay
Obtain	A as in 'Main' Ub-tan	Not Ob-tan
Onion	Uniun	Not Oniun
Opera	O as in 'on' Op-ru	Not Ope-raa
Police	Pu-less	Not Po-less
Precis	Prey-see	Not Pre-sis
Prefix	Free-fix	Not Pre-sis
Preposition	Prep-uzi-shun	Not Pre-po-zee-shun
Quorum	O as in 'Not' Kwo-rum	Not Ko-rum
Sample	Saampl	Not Sempt
Sew	O as in 'Home' So	Not Soo, nor like 'Few'
Sieve	Siv	Not Seev
Swan	O as in 'on' Swon	Not Swaan
Syllabus	Si-lu-bus	Not Si-lay-bus
Synonym	Si-nu-nim	Not si-no-nim
The	Thu before consonant Thee before vowel	Not thu or Thee Indiscriminately
Theory	Th as in 'Though' Thi-uri	Not Thi-ori
Thermos	O as in 'on' Thu-mos	Not Thur-mus
Thesaurus	O s in 'on' Thi-so-rus	Not The-so-rus
Through	Thu-ru	Not Tho-ro
Tortoise	O as in 'on' To-tus	Not Tor-to-is
Tournament	Oo as in 'Book' Toou-nu-munt	Not Toor-naa-ment
Ultimate	Ulti-mut	Not Ulti-mayt
Villain	Vi-lun	Not Vi-layn
Visa	Vee-zu	Not Veesa

Among	Umung	A as in 'At' not Among
Vitamin	Vi-tu-min	Not Vi-te-min
Vocabulary	Byoolikeue Vu-kebyoo-luri	Not Vokeboo-luri
Vouchsafe	Oo as a; 'Book'; ch of 'Chin' Yaayooch-sayf	Not Vaaoo-shayf
Waistcoat	O as in 'Home' Ways-cot	Not Wayst-cot
Was	O as in 'on' Wos, when Stressed O as in 'on' Wos, Wus, when unstressed	Never Waas
What	O as in 'Hot' Wot	Not Waat
Were	War, like 'Fur'	Not wayur
Womb Woom	Oo as in 'Boot'	Not Woomb
Xylophone	O as in 'Home' Zailu-for	Not Zilo-fon
Yesterday	Yes-tu-day	Not Yus-tur-day
Zebra	Zebru	Not Zebra
Zero	O as in 'Home' Ziuro	Not Zeero
Zoology	First o like 'home' second of like 'on' zo-ol-ugi	Not Zoo-logee

Ticklish Words

Chic	Sheek	Not Chik
Connoisseur	O is in 'on' Konu-zur	Not Konoi-siur
Dilsettante	Dili-ten-ti	Not Dile-ten-tee
Facetious	Fu-See-shus	Not Fayee-ti-us
Kaleidoscope	O as in 'Home' Ku-laidu-skop	Not Ke-leedo-skop
Liaison	Li-ayzn	Not Lai-sun
Mannequin	Muni-kin	Not Menee-kwin
Onomatopoeta	First O.like 'on'; Second o like 'Home' one-metu-peeru	Not One-meto-poiaa
Rhinoceros	O as in 'o' Rai-no-surus	Not Rino-cerus
Suite	Sweet	Not Soot

Salutations and Manners

1. Say 'Good Morning' when you meet someone in the morning, and 'Good Afternoon' when you meet after 12 Noon and 'Good Evening' when you meet in the evening.

2. Say 'Good Day' when you part early in the day and 'Good Night' when you part in the evening. 'Good Bye' can be said at any time of the parting.
3. Say 'Thank you' when someone does you some favour or when you accept something; as 'Thank you for the compliment'.
4. Say 'No, Thank you' when you refuse something; as 'No, thank you, I don't take tea.'
5. Say 'Sorry' to apologize; as, 'Sorry, I have not done the homework.'
6. Say 'Sorry' when you did not understood or hear; as, 'Sorry, could you say that again?'
7. Say 'Please' to ask for something; as, 'Could you please lend me your pen?'
8. Say 'Please' to your equals or inferiors, and 'kindly' to your superiors; as, (to your teacher); 'Kindly forgive me.'
9. Say 'Excuse me' if you want to go past somebody; as, 'Excuse me, may I reach the window?'
10. Say 'Excuse Me' also when you want to attract attention; as, 'Excuse me, could I know you name?'

To use these polite words brings you no credit; but not to use them may hurt others.

23
Understanding Human Behaviour

Human being are the creatures on earth who are governed by logic and the sense of pride and vanity. They are also governed by their whims and desires. As such, you cannot take work from people at the fun-point. Those days have gone when the rule of thumb was prevailing and people were asked to work even against their whims and desires. In the present-day-world, even the beggar does not tolerate the unwarranted preachings of donors. The things have changed and we have to have better understanding of human behaviour under the present context. What is needed in the present time is the love to humanity and the tactfulness to handle all situations in such a manner that there is the least resentment, bitterness, revengefulness, etc. the time has come when we have to be very watchful, careful and thoughtful and consistent for the sake of growth and development. We have to be quite practical.

Besides the above, we find in the human-world that all the people are not alike. Some people are arrogant without any power of tolerance whereas the others are submissive and peaceful with a lot of patience and forebearness. Some are coward whereas the others are brave and stout. Some are friendly whereas the others are not having the socializing nature. Like this, all the persons are not alike and that they have different nature and temperament. Why it is so? The answer to this question lies in knowing the various factors governing psychology of people.

23.1 FACTORS INFLUENCING PSYCHOLOGY OF PEOPLE

The human-psychology is mostly governed by the following factors:

1. Hereditary Character: When a person takes birth in a family he or she gains most of the family traditions from grandfather, grandmother; parents, i.e., mother and father. The blood-cells remain in the child and while he or she grows, the hereditary characters remain in the personality. The daughter of a singer would have a lot of singing qualities derived from mother. It has been found that the ward of an actor would also become an actor. The son of a doctor would become a doctor. Even though it is not cent per cent true yet it happens in majority of cases. So, hereditary characters play in important role in development one's own personality.

2. Family Atmosphere: The psychology of a person may also be affected by the environment of a family. Some families are well-disciplined, highly cultured and well-educated. While their children remain in the family, they learn all those things and then act accordingly for the whole of their family. On the other hand, there may be families where they do not have system or care for the children. In that case, the grown-ups remain the same like spoilt one, indisciplined and rude.

3. Education: The educational background plays an important role in the personality development. In the initial stage, a child goes to school and thereafter joins the College or University. Where the education is not proper or untidy, the child is not able to develop well and thereafter misses the track. One more thing, a shallow knowledge is always dangerous. So, one has to gain complete knowledge by education. It is also observed that well-educated persons behave differently than the illiterate ones. The behaviour of an illiterate person is totally different than the literate one. The more we read, the smaller cells of our brain are broadened and we gain more confidence and power to think and act.

4. Surroundings and Friend Circle: The surroundings and the friend circle also play as important role in the personality development. When a person passes most of the day and night time in the company of friends or with the persons living around the residence or office, all that happens there makes a man to behave accordingly. That is why, most of the people like to live at places which are advanced and developed ones so that people enjoy the company of sobre persons and get better guidance.

5. Incentives: Most of the people change their behaviour or way of working based on incentives available for hard-working or no incentive despite overwork. When a person knows that he or she is going to be rewarded for better work, the results would be better. The incentive may be in the form of promotion or financial gain or any other. The fact remains that everyone in the modern days likes to work for incentive.

6. Incident or Accident: Quite a few people change their behaviour on the happening of some incident or accident when their behaviour abruptly changes towards others. A ruthless dacoit might become a saint or an innocent person might become a dangerous robber. Any of contingent forces might lead to change the behaviour though undesired or even against the wishes.

7. Experience: The human behaviour changes as per the experiences gained by a person. When person gains experience of something, it is natural that the things which give sad experience those are avoided and the favourites are repeated. We Find a lot of difference in the behaviour of a fresher or inexperienced one as compared to the experienced person. In business, the experience has more weightage.

On knowing the aforesaid factors, we may have a better understanding of the human behaviour particularly in the business world. We should know well how to deal with the people differently under different circumstances. The top priority should be given to knowing their familiarizing with the person with whom we are to deal with. There should be total effectiveness and impressiveness in our behaviour towards others.

23.2 GENERAL RULES

For dealing with Human Psychology:

1. Always try to attract the other people to you so that you have an opportunity to deal with them effectively. The other people must feel that it is worth talking to you. For the purpose of attracting others, you should develop your personality in such a manner that yours is one of the most attracting personality. This can be done through personal grooming, neat and clean dress, good physical appearance as well as sobre habits, etiquettes and manners. Just as we say, respect is commanded and not demanded, in the same way you should respect people to earn your own respect. Try to build up your image amongst others that they would like to talk to you, not haste you. Your behaviour should be friendly and business-like.
2. When the people approach you or call on you personally, you should give them a warm welcome and attend them properly. Let the others say what they want to say. You should be a patient listener. Never speak in between till you are required to speak.
3. There may be matters for your favour and in others you may not have to favour but go against. Normally, people are happy when they get positive reply but feel bad when they get negative reply from you. It is important for you to keep balance in both the cases. If you have to say 'Yes', please do it instantly. When you have to say 'No', that should also be conveyed decently and courteously. You should never be rude to others while saying 'No'.
4. Secrecy is very important. Keep the matters confidential till you are required to disclose.
5. Your communication is required to be proper, efficient and complete in all possible manner. Most of the problems arise due to communication gap.
6. For proper handling of people, it is necessary that one should have canvasing and convincing powers. The former involves salesman qualities or marketing abilities like arousing interest, creating desire, stimulating

action, etc., whereas the latter may be achieved by through all-around knowledge and experience. The people who come to you must go well-satisfied so that they come again and like to talk to you.

Questions

1. Discuss different factors which influence psychology of people.
2. Discuss some of the general rules which are considered important for dealing with human psychology.

24 What do People Expect from You

What do people expect from you and how should you behave? Different people have different expectations from you. It actually depends upon the position you hold the official world. Many times, you hold a key-position and only those people approach you who have the same kind of work from you. If you are in educational line, only the people who have works connected with education come to you. If you are in the administration, the people know your powers and authority and they come to you for that type of work. The modern people are more wise and intelligent. They may not be interested in wasting your time as well as their own time. However, we have made an attempt to discuss in the following points the expectations of people in your official position and that how should you respond to that.

24.1 WHAT THE PEOPLE EXPECT FROM YOU?

1. Don't lie. It wastes my time and your. I'm sure to catch you in the end and that is the wrong end.

2. Watch your work, not the clock.

3. Dishonesty is never an accident.

4. Mind your own business and, in time, you will have a business of your own to mind.

5. Don't do anything here that hurts your self-respect.

24.2 THE BEST WAY FOR YOU TO DO IS

1. Make and leave a good impression over the people with whom you deal with on behalf of your employers or superiors.

2. Show and prove your worth for the benefit of employers and the Organization for which you are working. It is better you become the loyal right-hand of your boss by becoming indispensable.

3. When the boss or employer has relied upon you, you should not shake the confidence of your employers. Be honest and hard-working.

4. Keep the house always in order so that you do not waste time in retrieving the information required by your boss or employer.

5. Try to adopt the manner and style in which you are required to work for the benefit of your Organization.

24.3 WHAT THE COLLEAGUES EXPECT FROM YOU?

The work is always a co-operative effort. You equal of colleagues in the same department or other divisions holding the same rank, many have certain expectations from you. They may feel as under:

1. You should work with the same spirit as your other equals are doing. They may not tolerate your going ahead, rather they always try to pull your legs and try to show to higher ups that themselves are much better than you.
2. The colleagues might need your friendly treatment and mixing attitude. A sort of moral support of yours might be needed.
3. Healthy completion between the equals might be expected from the top management for better productivity. The individual efforts may be appreciated or depreciated and the top management may adopt pick and choose policy on the basis of individual performance.
4. It is expected that if an individual amongst the equals given excellent performance, the others might follow suit. If something bad is done, the other might take a lesson therefrom.

24.4 THE BEST WAY FOR YOU IS

1. Always show and try to utilize you special talents for the benefit of your Organization for securing better and quick promotions.

2. Never allow any interference from your equals but you should try to improve your skills and efficiency by taking lesson from those who are really doing better than you.

3. Never criticize others rather you should try to prove that you are doing the best which no one else could do. Taking credit for pointing out other's mistakes and without showing your individual performance may not give you any benefit in the long-run. Your superior know everything and may not care for your criticism.

24.5 WHAT YOUR SUBORDINATES EXPECT?

1. The subordinates always aspire for a pat of hand on them. They are poor and might need all sorts of support from your including financial support, writing the application or filling in their forms or recommendations in official matter, etc.

2. The subordinates may not tolerate your harsh treatment and may express their resentment for causing any harm by you to their self-respect. They have the least tolerance power.

3. They are mostly busy in gossip and chit-chats here and there and may expect you not to disclose the matters to the higher bosses or sometimes they might need you to convey their sentiments to the higher-ups.

4. The subordinates may help you to know many confidential matters which they come to know by working for the big bosses while disclosing the credentials, they might need your assurance not to disclose the confidential and might relay upon you for this.

24.6 THE BEST WAY FOR YOU IS

1. Always speak to them mildly and to the point. Scold them but with a pat of hands on them.

2. Do not try to develop personal relations with your subordinates and also not indulge in their gossiping, etc., try

to keep and maintain a distance to maintain your dignity and honour.

3. Help your subordinates as much as you can and also give them the best piece of your advice for their betterment and improvement.

4. Keep your constant watch on them and check them frequently to desist them for doing wrong things.

Expectations of Your Customers, Suppliers, Debtors and Creditors

These persons have business relationships with you. Most of the businesses are based on trust, good faith and mutual understanding between each other.

Following expectations of these persons from you are as:

1. Showing promptness in attending to their matters in general. Any delay creates annoyance and financial losses.
2. The business promises or commitments are required to be honoured on time, otherwise it disturbs the business dealings.
3. Maintaining complete records of business events as a documentary evidence or reference for any time in future.
4. Canvassing and convincing qualities are necessarily required in a businessman for making progress in business. These are the prerequisites for a successful businessman. One has to be good guide, friend and a master of business secrets.

However, in respect of business dealings, you must remember the followings:

1. You should be well smart, impressive, knowledgeable and competent to deal with all sorts of people you come across with differential treatment depending upon requirements and exigencies of business.
2. Business ethics and norms must be followed under all circumstances. These consist of your high morale,

tolerance power, treating the policy etc. All these may be adopted as bread and butter.

3. The word given to anyone once, has to be honoured what may come otherwise it hurts the business and progress cannot be achieved.
4. The powers of judgement and quick decision-making are a must for the businessman so as to allow him to assume the risk. Risk is profit and profit is risk.

Questions

1. Underline different expectations from your colleagues from you.
2. What are the common expectations from customers?

25

Time Management

'Art is long and time is fleeting' is the proverb which holds true in the modern day. The workload has increased to such an extent that time catching has really become the greatest problems of the days. The vast field of work has got to be adjusted to the limited time. How to adjust the unlimited work to limited time, is the problem of 'time management'. In literal terms, time management is the process of getting the work done on time. In other words, the problems of 'time' management is how to adjust your time schedule in such a way that neither your time is wasted nor do you waste the time of others, 'Time' is valuable. 'Time' is money. No one has got the time and everything has got to be accomplished on time, otherwise the wastage and futility. Hence, the importance of 'time management'. Whatever may be your business or profession, you need to adjust your time efficiently in such as yourself, for your family, friends and for your business or official work also. The time schedule has to be followed in a way that you are able to adjust all your requirements and that you do not lose but gain. You may not miss any opportunity also. Always remember that 'Time' once gone, never comes back.

A Time-conscious person never gets defeated in life. One has not to face desperation or dissatisfaction in life. On the other hand, the careless people not worried about time, may always remain in doldrums and unconfident. In our day-to-day life, we have seen that, people mostly like the persons who are punctual and time-conscious. It adds many points to a person's personality. Once the schedule of time is disturbed, it has large repercussion. You do not miss one but one hundred. That is the impact of not managing the 'time'.

You must know that 'Nature' is very much time-conscious, there is always a fixed time of 'Nature' when the rainfall is to take place, when snowfall is to take place when winter is to come or when the summer is to start. We have twenty-four hours in a day and 365 days in a year. There is no change in that 365-66 days. What we mean by this? The meaning is that when the 'Nature' has a fixed time-schedule for everything, how the human-beings could pull on without fixed timing. Once the time-schedule of 'Nature' is disturbed the man has to face all sorts of atrocities of 'Nature'—The tremors, the earthquake, the floods, the drought, etc. We, as human-beings, are always living and growing in the lap of 'Nature'. So, like 'Nature' we should always be time-conscious, working on time, sleeping on time, eating on time and playing on time. Any change in time-schedule might make us restless and worthless. We must understand the utility the time that save ourselves from any sort of trouble and inconvenience.

25.1 UNDERSTAND THE UTILITY OF TIME

For time management, we may remember the following:

1. Prepare Your Own Time—schedule as to what to do and when: Fix up your own timings for working, sleeping, rest and recuperation, meetings with people, attending to family members, studying, playing, etc. It would help in maintaining your daily routine. Avoid working when you are to sleep. Avoid sleeping when you are to work. Don't mix work and play together. If you stick to your time-schedule, you would be happy and cheerful otherwise feel disturbed all the time that create in mind.

2. Fix-up Priorities of Work: What to do first and what afterwards. When you are over-burdened with work, it is always useful to fix-up the priority. The most important work involving your interest is required to be attended on time. In case you feel that you have lesser time at your disposal, you may avoid the avoidable work for the time-being and re-schedule your other timings.

3. Any Change in Your Time—Schedule has to be closely watched and weighed upon: In case you feel that the change is possible and may not affect your best interest, then do it otherwise you should not try to change the time already fixed-up in advance.

4. Always Keep Some Time for Yourself: When you may feel free. It always better to give rest to your mind after the work. The leisure time may be utilized for preparing your plans, regaining your energies and creating fertility of your brains.

5. Always Keep Informed and be Informed Whenever there is Some Change in your Time-schedule: It saves your precious time as well as the time of others. The others also do not feel bad of it. In case you become late somewhere, leave the message to the other person so that he or she might not lose any opportunity or might not suffer any lose. It is a part of human courtesy also. The 'courtesy' begets courtesy. There should not be any communication gap.

6. When You are Unable to Reach on Time: Due to some mishappening or occurrence of any untoward incident, etc., you may apologies later when you find time to meet next or if you have any means of communication, you should communicate the information at your earliest. It keeps healthy atmosphere and good human-relations. These days, we have many facilities commonly available for all the time like the mobile phones with SMS facilities, etc. So there should be no problem in communication.

7. The Time Management May Best be Done: Through your ability to keep alertness and time-consciousness. If you are awake, you may not allow others to sleep. This is the simple rule to achieve success in life.

8. The Best Way is to Maintain Punctuality and Regularity as a Part of your Personality Development: Inculcate this habit from the beginning of your career which afterwards might become a part of your habit. That's a good habit.

Questions

1. Discuss the relevance of time management.
2. What are the common actions needed in regard to time management?